Visual Intelligence

Visual
Intelligence

. . .

Sharpen Your Perception, Change Your Life

AMY E. HERMAN

An Eamon Dolan Book
Mariner Books
Houghton Mifflin Harcourt
BOSTON   NEW YORK

First Mariner Books edition 2017

Copyright © 2016 by Amy E. Herman

www.hmhco.com

Library of Congress Cataloging-in-Publication Data
Names: Herman, Amy, author.
Title: Visual intelligence: sharpen your perception, change your life /
Amy E. Herman.
Description: Boston : Houghton Mifflin Harcourt, [2016]
"An Eamon Dolan Book." | Includes bibliographical references and index.
Identifiers: LCCN 2015037245 | ISBN 9780544381056 (hardcover)
ISBN 9780544381063 (ebook) | ISBN 978054494712-2 (pbk.)
ISBN 9780544882003 (pbk. (international edition))
Subjects: LCSH: Visual perception. | Visual literacy.
Classification: LCC BF241 .H436 2016 | DDC 152.14 — dc23
LC record available at http://lccn.loc.gov/2015037245

Book design by Chrissy Kurpeski
Typeset in Bulmer & Avenir

Printed in the United States of America
DOC 10 9 8 7 6 5 4
4500690327

To Ian. Everything. Always.

The world is full of magic things,
patiently waiting for our senses to grow sharper.

— AUTHOR UNKNOWN

Contents

Author's Note xi

Introduction xiii

PART I: ASSESS

1. Leonardo da Vinci and
Losing Your Mind 3
The Importance of Seeing What Matters

2. Elementary Skills 23
Mastering the Fine Art of Observation

3. The Platypus and the
Gentleman Thief 37
Why No Two People See Things the Same Way

4. Delta Employees Do It on the Fly 60
The Who, What, When, and Where of Objective Surveillance

5. What's Hiding in Plain Sight? 83
Seeing the Forest and the Trees

PART II: ANALYZE

6. Keep Your Head on a Swivel 115
Analyzing from Every Angle

7. Seeing What's Missing 144
How to Prioritize Like an Undercover Agent

PART III: ARTICULATE

8. Making Your Unknown Known 175
How to Avoid Communication Breakdowns

9. Big (Naked, Obese) Sue and the High School Principal 211
How to See and Share Hard Truths

PART IV: ADAPT

10. Nothing Is Black-and-White 239
Overcoming Our Inherent Biases

11. What to Do When You Run Out of Gurneys 258
How to Navigate Uncertainty

Conclusion: Master Work 273
Acknowledgments 278
Notes 282
Illustration Credits 304
Index 308

Author's Note

It has been my great privilege to teach The Art of Perception for fourteen years. In doing so, I have spoken with and written to thousands of people from around the world about their experiences with art, observation, perception, and communication. Since some of these conversations took place years before this book was even an idea, since my wonderful program participants didn't plan on being part of this book when they signed up for my class, and since many of my interviewees have extremely sensitive jobs, I have changed the names and identifying details of most of the people whose stories appear in this book to protect their privacy. Any resulting resemblances to persons living or dead are entirely coincidental and unintentional. *Visual Intelligence* is a work of nonfiction. All stories are recounted as they happened or were told to me, subject to the limitations of memory. I couldn't fact-check all of the personal stories people told me, but I included only those I believed to be true.

Introduction

AS I STOOD in the hallway outside the apartment, everything took on a hazy, slow-motion quality. Shouting echoed behind the door. Dust particles floated in the fluorescent light. A cat mewed from somewhere to my left. The officer in front of me raised his fist to knock, while his partner — tense, armed, ready for action — covered him. As the domestic dispute blared beyond the door, the black hole of the second officer's gun barrel gaped like a silent scream. How had I gotten here?

Since I was little, I had seen the art in everything: in the beautiful asymmetry of sunlight streaming through the trees and the unique patterns of stones and shells left behind when the tide washed out. I was never a particularly creative person myself, but that didn't stop me from studying art history. Following college, though, my upbringing by my scientist father and ultra-practical mother and a desire to serve led me to law school. And this particularly intense police ride-along.

To detach myself from the worry bubbling in my gut, I studied my surroundings as I would a painting, analyzing each nuance, taking stock of both foreground and back, trying to find meaning in small, seemingly incongruent details. I knew this was an unusual way to think — I'd been told so often enough — but I always found my art background useful in the practice of law, where the need to be an objective observer is critical.

And then I had a terrible thought: what if the officers I was with didn't have these skills? What the first officer saw when the door opened—be it a crying baby, a confused elderly woman, or a gun-wielding madman—and how he conveyed it to his partner in that split second would affect the outcome for every one of us. My life was in the hands of a virtual stranger and his ability to see and accurately convey what he saw.

Thankfully the police were able to defuse the situation and my experience didn't end in disaster, but as generally happens when we're nose-to-nose with a deadly weapon for the first time or forced to face our own mortality, it haunted me for years after. How many times do our lives depend upon someone else's observation skills? For most of us, it's too many to count: whenever we get on an airplane or a train, into a taxicab, or onto an operating table. It's not always life-or-death; sometimes it's just life-altering. Other people's attention to detail and follow-through can also affect our job, our reputation, our safety, and our success. And we can affect theirs. It's a responsibility we shouldn't take lightly, as it can mean the difference between a promotion and a demotion, between a triumph and a tragedy, between a normal Tuesday in September and 9/11.

Seeing clearly and communicating effectively are not rocket science; they're straightforward skills. We're born hardwired for both. But more often than we'd care to admit, we fail to use these skills. We show up at the wrong airport gate and try to board the wrong plane, we send an email to the wrong recipient saying something we never should have said, we miss a key piece of evidence that was staring us right in the face. Why? Because we're hardwired for those errors as well.

Our brains can see only so much, and can process even less. I knew this from years of practicing law and witnessing firsthand the unreliability of eyewitnesses and the fallibility of first-person accounts, but it wasn't until I followed my heart back to the art world that I began to actively investigate the mysteries of perception. As the head of education of The Frick Collection in New York City, I helped bring a course created by a dermatology professor at Yale to NYC medical schools, teaching students to analyze works of art in order to improve their patient observation skills. It was very successful — a clinical study found that the students who took the course had diagnostic skills that were 56 percent better than peers who didn't — and I wanted to understand the science behind it. I wanted to know more about the mechanics of how we see and how simply looking at art could improve.

I became a neuroscience fanatic, reading all the research I could find and interviewing the researchers who'd conducted it. I even signed up for an online community neuroscience "video game." And I discovered that while my own perceptions about how we see were wrong on many levels — apparently the retina is part of the brain, not the eye — they were spot-on in the most important ways: while we might not fully understand the human brain, we can change it. We can train our brains to see more, and to observe more accurately.

And as I often do when I learn something fantastic, I wanted to share it with everyone, not just medical students. I was out to dinner with friends sharing some of what I learned one night soon after 9/11, when the city was still reeling from the terrorist attacks and resulting stories of heroism and heartbreak. One of my friends asked if I had considered training first responders. I hadn't, but as I thought back to my fear in the hallway on that law student ride-along, not knowing how the officers I was with would see or react to what they saw, it made perfect sense. I fell in love with the idea of pairing cops with Rembrandt; I just had to convince the law enforcement community. The following Monday I cold-called the NYPD.

"I'd like to bring your cops to our museum to look at art," I told the bewildered deputy commissioner. I half expected him to hang up on me, but to his credit, he agreed to give it a try. Within a few weeks, we had weapons in the Frick for the first time ever, and The Art of Perception® was born.

I've been teaching the class for fourteen years now, training officers from thirteen divisions of the NYPD, as well as the police departments in Washington, DC, Chicago, and Philadelphia, the Virginia State Police, and the Ohio Association of Chiefs of Police. Word of the program's effectiveness spread quickly, and my client list grew to include the FBI, the Department of Homeland Security, Scotland Yard, the US Army, Navy, National Guard, Secret Service, and Marshal Service, the Federal Reserve, the Department of Justice, the State Department, and the National Park Service.

The *Wall Street Journal* soon profiled my class and its positive effects on the law enforcement, legal, and military sectors in a story about an undercover FBI agent who credited my training with helping him sharpen his observation skills. After taking The Art of Perception, the agent was able to collect incriminating evidence against a Mob-controlled garbage collection syndicate that resulted in thirty-four convictions and the government seizure of $60 to $100 million in assets. Almost immediately, I started getting calls from private companies, educational institutions, and even workers' unions. Because in reality, all of us — parents, teachers, flight attendants, investment bankers, even doormen — are first responders on some level.

The Art of Perception's unique pedagogy has been called "invaluable" by the Department of Defense and credited with "stimulating the innovative thinking necessary to generate viable future war-fighting concepts" by the chief of naval operations. After attending my seminar at an FBI National Academy program, Inspector Benjamin Naish arranged for me to present to the Philadelphia Police Department, stating, "I felt like I had my eyes opened wider [in this course, and I knew it was] the most unusual training they're ever going to have a chance to see."

What's so unusual about it? I show pictures of naked women with breasts sagging on their stomachs and sculptures made from urinals to teach the fine art of accurate observation and effective communication.

And it works.

I've helped thousands of people from dozens of walks of life — law firms, libraries, auction houses, hospitals, universities, Fortune 500 companies, entertainment companies, banks, unions, and even churches — strengthen and sharpen their visual analysis and critical-thinking skills. And I can teach you.

Because medical and law enforcement professionals aren't the only ones who need to know how to identify pertinent information, prioritize it, draw conclusions from it, and communicate it. We all do. A single missed detail or miscommunicated word can just as easily botch a cappuccino order, a million-dollar contract, or a murder investigation. I know because every week I stand in front of the best and the brightest and watch as they miss critical information . . . over and over again. No one is immune to this failure to see, not presidents or postal workers, not babysitters or brain surgeons.

And then I watch them get better. Whether I'm teaching customer service or information technology agents, artists or archivists, students or surveillance experts, people who are already very good at their jobs *invariably* get even better. I watch the transformation every single session, and I'm delighted to have the opportunity to help you transform as well.

JR, Women Are Heroes, Kenya:
Self-Portrait in a Woman's Eye, Kenya, 2009.

This photograph is a self-portrait of the artist JR — or at least one perspective of him in someone else's eye. JR had a problem in that he was becoming increasingly famous for his photographic portraits that were blown up to billboard size and attached to the tops and sides of buildings all over the world — to "put a human face to the most impoverished areas of the world"—but since he never got permits for them, warrants for his arrest had been issued in several countries. He was asked to create a self-portrait but was hesitant to show his facial attributes out of fear it might facilitate his arrest. His solution: *Self-Portrait in a Woman's Eye*. I love this photograph because it encapsulates exactly what The Art of Perception is all about: shifting our perspective and our expectations further than we ever thought possible.

Think of this book as your new self-portrait. You can use it to step back and see yourself through new eyes. What do you look like to the world? How well do you communicate? How well do you observe? What's behind you and around you and inside you?

From this book, you'll learn how to sharpen your own inherent intelligence gathering, strategic and critical thinking, decision making, and formulation of inquiry skills using the amazing computer between your ears. Unlike other books by psychologists or reporters, though, this one will not just *tell* you what your brain can do or how people are using theirs to the limit, it will show you.

We'll use the same interactive training I use to engage leaders around the globe. We'll practice reconciling larger concepts with more specific details, articulating visual and sensory information, and conveying it in an objective and precise manner with the help of water lilies, women in corsets, and a nude or two.

Take a look at the photograph on the next page. It hasn't been retouched or digitally altered; what you see actually existed this way. What do you think is going on in the photograph, and where was it taken?

The most common answer I get is flowers in an old abandoned building for some kind of art installation. And that's partially correct. It is an old building, those are real flowers, and they were put there intentionally by an artist. What kind of building do you think it is? We see a hallway with many doors, and a window at the end of that hallway. People guess it's an office building or some kind of school, but it's not. It's something most people never consider: a psychiatric hospital.

Anna Schuleit Haber, *Bloom: A Site-specific Installation*, 2003.

When the Massachusetts Mental Health Center was slated for de-molition after ninety years in service to make way for more modern facilities, artist Anna Schuleit Haber commemorated its closing by filling it with what it had always lacked. (Sadly, she was inspired by her observation that patients in psychiatric hospitals rarely receive flowers, as there are no wishes for a speedy recovery.) Her result-ing installation, *Bloom,* turns our thinking about mental health care upside down. We do not associate vibrant color with a deteriorating building or expect to see life oozing from the halls of a psychiatric fa-cility. In the same way, this book will alter the way you observe the world. You will see color and light and detail and opportunity where you swore there were none. You will see life and possibility and truth in the emptiest spaces. You will see order and find answers in the most chaotic and messiest places. You will never see the same way again.

All of my requests for The Art of Perception live presentation come from enthusiastic referrals because once people's eyes are opened, they can't shut their mouths about it. They want everyone to experience the same revelation and reward. Past participants flood my email in-box with stories of how the training gave them more confidence in their jobs, helped them win promotions, improved their customer service, saved their companies hundreds of thousands of dollars, doubled and tripled their fund-raising outcomes, raised their standardized test scores, and even kept their children out of unnecessary special education classes.

Learning to see what matters can change your world as well. I invite you to open your eyes and see how. I bet you'll discover you didn't even know they were closed.

PART I

. . .

Assess

We find only the world we look for.

— HENRY DAVID THOREAU

1

Leonardo da Vinci and Losing Your Mind

The Importance of Seeing What Matters

WHEN DERRECK KAYONGO stepped into the shower in his Philadelphia hotel room, he noticed something that millions of business travelers and families on holiday before him had seen and not paid any particular attention to: the tiny bar of soap on the corner shelf. It was different. Instead of the smooth green oval he had used the evening before, a small cardboard box sat in its place. Inside was a brand-new bar of soap.

The Ugandan native, who as a child had left everything behind when he and his family fled Idi Amin's murderous dictatorship, was a recent American college graduate, and on a tight budget. He turned off the water, dressed, and took the unused soap down to the concierge desk.

"I want to make sure I am not charged for this," he told the employee. "I have not used it, and do not need it."

"Oh, don't worry, it's complimentary," the concierge answered.

"Thank you, but I already got one yesterday when I arrived," Kayongo explained. "Where is that one?"

"We replace the soap every day for every guest," the concierge assured him. "No charge."

Kayongo was shocked. Every room, every day? In every hotel? Throughout America?

"What do you do with the old bars?" he asked. Unlike the slivers of soap used in the African refugee camps he had grown up in, the bar from his shower was fairly substantial; it seemed almost brand-new even after he had used it.

"Housekeeping throws them away," the concierge said, and shrugged.

"Where?"

"Just the regular trash."

"I'm not a great mathematician," Kayongo tells me, "but I quickly realized that if only half of the hotels did this, it was an incredible amount of soap — hundreds of millions of bars just being dumped into landfills. I couldn't get it out of my head."

Kayongo called his father, a former soap maker, back in Africa and told him the news. "You won't believe it. In America, they throw away soap after they have used it only once!"

"People there can afford to waste soap," his father told him.

But in Kayongo's mind it was a waste no one could afford, not when he knew more than two million people, most of them toddlers, still died every year from diarrheal disease, a malady easily prevented by the simple act of washing one's hands with soap. Soap was a luxury item many in Africa could not afford, yet in America it was simply thrown away. Kayongo decided to try to do something with his new country's trash to help his old country.

Back home in Atlanta, he drove around to local hotels and asked if he could have their used soap.

"At first they thought I was crazy," he remembers, a smile spilling through his voice over the phone. "Why do you want those? They are dirty. Yes, that was a problem, but we can clean them. We can clean soap!"

Kayongo found a recycling facility to scrape, melt, and disinfect the bars of soap he collected, and the charity Global Soap Project was born. He has since recycled one hundred tons of soap and distributed repurposed, life-saving bars along with a hygiene education program to people in thirty-two countries on four continents. In 2011, Kayongo was deservedly named one of CNN's "Heroes."

Unlike the heroes of old movies and swashbuckling fables, we don't have to be the strongest, fastest, smartest, richest, handsomest, or luckiest to get ahead or make a difference in the world. The most successful people in modern times — people such as Bill Gates, Richard Branson, Oprah Winfrey, and Derreck Kayongo — prove that it doesn't matter what physical attributes we have or don't, our level of education, our profession, our station in life, or where we live.

We can survive and thrive today if we know how to see.

To see what's there that others don't. To see what's not there that should be. To see the opportunity, the solution, the warning signs, the quickest way, the way out, the win. To see what matters.

Even if we don't long for front-page accolades, acute and accurate observation yields rewards big and small across all aspects of life. When a housekeeper at a Minneapolis hotel noticed a young girl alone in a room who wouldn't make eye contact, wasn't dressed for the cold weather, and had no luggage, she reported it, and helped uncover an international sex trafficking ring. When an astute waiter at a crowded Israeli coffeehouse noticed that the schoolboy who asked for a glass of water was sweating profusely while wearing a heavy overcoat on a mild day, he looked more intently and saw a small wire sticking out of the boy's large black duffel bag. His observation kept the boy from detonating a large explosive that the local police chief said would have caused "a major disaster."

The ability to see, to pay attention to what is often readily available right in front of us, is not only a means to avert disaster but also the precursor and prerequisite to great discovery.

While millions of people have enjoyed using a new bar of hotel soap each day, only Kayongo saw the potential for a life-saving recycling program. What made him see exactly the same thing that others had, but see it in a different way? The same thing that allowed Swiss hiker George de Mestral to look down at his burr-covered socks and see a new type of adhesion; Mestral's discovery of what he christened Velcro revolutionized the way astronauts and skiers suited up, saved an entire generation of kids from learning how to tie their shoes, and still posts $260 million a year in sales. The same thing that made Houston mom Betsy Ravreby Kaufman see plastic Easter eggs as a way to cook hard-boiled eggs without their shells. Tired of wasting food and time when the process of peeling eggs left behind a mess, Kaufman envisioned boiling eggs in an egg-shaped container from the start, thereby eliminating the need for shells altogether. Her invention, Eggies, plastic egg-size cups with lids, sold more than five million units in 2012 alone. The same thing that helped propel Apple icon Steve Jobs to the top of the technological heap: an ability to see. Jobs reported, "When you ask creative people how they did something, they feel a little guilty because they didn't really do it, they just saw something."

Leonardo da Vinci attributed all of his scientific and artistic accomplishments to the same concept, which he called *saper vedere* ("sah-PEAR veh-DARE-ay") — "knowing how to see." We might also call his gift "visual intelligence."

It sounds easy, doesn't it? You just have to see. We're born with the inherent ability; in fact, our body does it involuntarily. If your eyes are open, you are seeing. But there's more to the neurobiological process than just keeping your eyelids propped up.

A BRIEF BIOLOGY OF SIGHT

I'm not a scientist, but I was raised by one — my father is a parasitologist — so I knew that the best way to investigate why we see the way we do was not to just read the cutting-edge studies on human vision and perception but to go out and meet the people who conducted them. My first stop: Dr. Sebastian Seung.

Thanks to his captivating TED talk and EyeWire, the visionary retina-mapping project he heads, Dr. Seung is something of a rock star in neuroscience. As I pull open the front doors of his lab at the new Princeton Neuroscience Institute, a labyrinthine complex of glass and aluminum, I can feel my blood pressure rise. The building is intimidating from the first step. There is no receptionist or directory listing, just an unmarked, open elevator. I step inside and quickly determine that I might not be smart enough for the building. I can't get the elevator to move; push and hold as I might, the buttons won't stay lit. There is no signage, no slot for a key card.

Help arrives in the form of an affable young student wearing a LINEAR ALGEBRA IS MY HOMEBOY T-shirt. He presses his ID against a small glass panel, and we rise. I tell him whom I'm here to see.

"Good luck," he says with a smile. I hope I won't need it.

Returning to Princeton is something of a full-circle moment for me, as I moved to the town for my first job out of law school and lived just off Nassau Street for five years. To keep my sanity, on the weekends I volunteered as a docent at the Princeton University Art Museum.

When I meet Dr. Seung and see that he's wearing a Mickey Mouse T-shirt, I instantly relax. Seung exudes an easy charm and has a gift for making the extraordinarily complex seem not so. As he explains, seeing doesn't have as much to do with our eyes as I once thought.

While our sense of sight is most often associated with the spherical organs that occupy the orbits of the skull, the brain is really the workhorse of the visual processing system. Not only does processing what we see engage a full 25 percent of our brain and over 65 percent of all our brain pathways — more than any of our other senses — it begins in a part of the eye that is really the brain.

The process starts when light passes through the pupil of our eye and is converted into electrical patterns by neural cells on a membrane at the back called the retina. When I tell Seung I remember learning in high school that the retina is like the film in a camera, he shakes his head at this common misconception.

"It's definitely not film," he says. "The retina's such a complicated structure that it's not even a camera. It's more like a computer."

The retina isn't a passive pathway but a part of the brain itself formed in utero from neural tissue.

"Studying the retina is our easiest way into the brain," Seung explains, "because it is the brain."

3D printout of a neuron.

To thank him for introducing me to the beauty and complexity of the retina, and for referring me to scores of other scientists, I have brought him a gift: one of the first-ever 3D-printed neurons.

I had downloaded the printable file, a J cell named IFLS mapped for EyeWire by citizen scientists, from the National Institutes of Health (NIH) 3D Print Exchange, and then visited my local MakerBot store, which had the technology to print out a vastly enlarged replica of the neuron. The delicate sculpture resembled a lumpy seed, reminiscent of a tiny brain itself, sprouting a serpentine system of slender branches, the dendrites that conduct the electrical messages between cells.

I have seen the network of retinal neurons laced together — referred to as "the jungle" by Seung — in the EyeWire computer program he runs, each neuron a different neon color to make its paths more apparent, but as I hold it in my hand, the importance of each connection is magnified. With 100 million retinal receptors, the retina not only does the bulk of image preprocessing, it must also spatially encode or compress an image before it is sent along the 1.2 million axons in the optic nerve traveling to the brain.

"Some of the first steps of perception are actually happening inside the retina itself, even before the information reaches the brain," Seung asserts.

This explains why it is easier to transplant or artificially create other organs than working prosthetic eyes, since they are so intricately interwoven with our brains.

What this all boils down to is that we don't "see" with our eyes; we see with our brain.

USE IT OR LOSE IT

Our ability to see, make sense of what we see, and act upon that information relies on the brain's incredible processing power, a power that is entirely dependent upon our neural connections. Assuming all of our physical wiring is healthy and intact, turning visual inputs into meaningful images takes time, time that increases with age or lack of use.

Scientists have discovered that as we slow down or stop flexing our mental muscles, the speed of neural transmission dramatically slows, which in turn leads to a decrease in visual processing speed, the ability to detect change and movement, and the ability to conduct a visual search. Since our brain controls every function of our body, any lag in neural processing will likewise cause a delay in other systems, including what we see and how we react to it. Slower reflexes and remembrance times aren't caused only by physical aging. It might be that we just haven't exercised our brains enough or in the right way.

Fortunately for all of us, throughout our lives, our brain is continually making new connections and reinforcing old ones based on learning experiences . . . as long as we are learning. Researchers have found that stimulating environmental input—like studying something new, reading about a concept that makes you think, or playing any kind of "brain games"—will increase cortical growth at *every* age, even among the very oldest humans. Just as cognitive conditioning can be used to stave off dementia, it can also be used to sharpen our ability to observe, perceive, and communicate. If we can keep our senses and our wits quick, our reactions will follow, making us better employees, better drivers, and more capable of caring for ourselves and others longer in life.

To stimulate our senses and set our neurons ablaze we'll employ the same techniques I use with the FBI, intelligence analysts, and Fortune 500 companies every day in my class: we'll study art.

Jan Steen, *As the Old Sing, So Pipe the Young*, 1668–1670.

Carel Fabritius, *The Goldfinch*, 1654.

Looking at old paintings and sculptures is definitely not the first thing most people think of when I tell them we're going to get their neurons firing and increase their brain-processing speed. They picture engaging in cutting-edge 3D computerized training or at least wearing Google glasses while walking down a busy street, not strolling through a museum viewing objects that have sat still for hundreds of years. But that's exactly the point: art doesn't walk away. If you want to study human behavior, you can park yourself somewhere public and people watch: guess at who they are, why they're dressed that way, where they're going . . . until they leave. And you'll never know if you're right or not. Or you could analyze works of art that we have the answers to: the who, what, where, when, and why. Art historian David Joselit describes art as "exorbitant stockpiles of experience and information." It contains everything we need to hone our observation, perception, and communication expertise.

If you can talk about what is happening in a work of art, you can talk about scenes of everyday life; you can talk about boardrooms and classrooms, crime scenes, and factory floors. The Department of the Army retained me to work with officers before they were deployed to the Middle East. Why? Because when they go overseas, they encounter the unexpected and the unknown. The army teaches them cultural differences and etiquette, but I teach them how to be effective communicators in unfamiliar situations. Describing what you see in a painting of a woman wearing a foot-long, four-layered starched collar uses the same skill set as describing what you see in a foreign market or international airport. I teach the same techniques to hiring managers so they can better describe the candidates they are interviewing, and to elementary school principals so they have more effective tools for evaluating their teaching staff.

Art gives us myriad opportunities to analyze complex situations as well as seemingly more straightforward ones. Ironically, it is often the simple, the everyday, and the familiar that we have trouble describing because we have ceased to notice what makes them interesting or unusual. By adulthood, we become so inured to the complexity of the world that only the new, the innovative, and the exigent capture our attention and dominate our field of vision. We rely on experience and intuition rather than seeking out nuances and details that can make a difference in our success. Yet it is the things that we see and negotiate on a regular basis to which we must be especially attuned.

To be a hero to our bosses, our families, and ourselves, we need to shake up our worldview and shift our perspective. Art enables us to do that because we see it in so many places, because it manifests themes of human nature in all their complexity, and because it often makes us uncomfortable. And surprisingly, discomfort and uncertainty bring out the best in our brains.

When we're forced to use our personal and professional skills in an unfamiliar venue — which art analysis is for most people — we engage an entirely new thought process. In 1908, Harvard psychologists discovered that the brain is most effective at learning new material when stress hormones are slightly elevated by a novel experience, a theory verified by modern brain imaging. Therefore, the best way to rethink something we've been doing for years — the way we do our jobs, the way we interact with others, the way we see the world — is to step outside of ourselves, and outside of our comfort zone.

Art transports us away from our everyday life to rethink how we see and perceive and communicate. Art inspires conversations, especially when it makes us squirm. There are women with noses where their eyes should be, men in curlers with manicures, clocks dripping from trees, spider-legged elephants, and lots of people screaming.

Part of the beauty of art, especially the more unsettling pieces, is that anyone can discuss it. You don't have to be an art historian to talk about what you see; in fact, I prefer that most of my participants have little or no art training because it's completely unnecessary to strengthening our observation and communication skills and it might color their ability to view works of art objectively. We're not studying brushstrokes or palettes or historical periods. We're simply using art as confirmable visual data, talking about what we see — or what we think we see.

Gerrit van Honthorst, *Smiling Girl, a Courtesan,*
Holding an Obscene Image, 1625.

Throughout the book, we'll use images of painting, sculpture, and photography — some you may have seen and some you might not be able to imagine are real — as tools to reconsider the way we've previously looked at the world. Take this portrait of a young woman. You don't have to know who painted it or from what art-historical era it hails to investigate and discuss it. How would you describe her? Handsome or homely? As we'll learn, both descriptions are subjective, grounded in the eye of the beholder, so neither is useful in a professional context where the objective is everything. What about the term "Caucasian"? Is that objective? Yes, but is it accurate? "Caucasian" can broadly refer to people with a white skin tone or more specifically to those who come from the area of the Caucasus mountain range between Europe and Asia. Where does that leave a light-skinned person from Australia or a dark-skinned person from Turkey? Did you notice the enormous feather on her head, the dimple on her left cheek, the ring on her finger, or that she's holding a painting of someone's naked backside? What about her own exposed cleavage? Is that an objective or even appropriate detail to talk about?

You'll know the answers and many more once we've mastered the core of the Art of Perception program—I call them "the four As" —how to assess, analyze, articulate, and adapt. We'll start with how to *assess* a new situation by studying the mechanics of sight and our built-in blindness, and I'll give you an orderly process for efficient, objective surveillance. Once we've figured out how to gather all of the information, we'll learn what to do with it: how to *analyze* what we have uncovered, including prioritizing, recognizing patterns, and the important difference between perception and inference. Finding what we find and knowing what we know are no good if we don't tell someone else, though, so next we'll work on how to *articulate* our discoveries to ourselves and others. And finally, we will look at ways to *adapt* our behavior based on the first three elements.

But before we begin, I have one more, very important *A* for you: *autopilot*. Turn it off.

AUTOPILOT

Alexander Graham Bell was sixty-seven years old when he took the stage at the Sidwell Friends School in Washington, DC, to deliver the graduation address to the class of 1914. Sporting a snowy beard that swooped up at the end, the communications pioneer was now a grandfather and nearing the end of his illustrious career. Although he was best known for inventing the telephone, he held thirty patents and had foreseen modern advances such as air conditioning, the iron lung, metal detectors, and the use of solar panels to heat a house. So it surprised the crowd when he confessed to being inattentive.

As he told the audience, he had recently taken a walk around his family's long-held property in Nova Scotia, land he believed he was intimately familiar with. He was shocked to discover a moss-covered valley that led to the sea.

"We are all too much inclined," he said, "to walk through life with our eyes shut. There are things all round us and right at our very feet that we have never seen, because we have never really looked."

Habit, boredom, laziness, overstimulation — there are many reasons we tune out. And in doing so, we miss out. We might brush off something as simple as how a burr attaches to a sock and miss an opportunity for riches. We might overlook something as commonplace as a travel-size bar of soap and miss a chance to better the world. What amazing innovation did Bell miss by not always being attuned? What have we ourselves missed?

Zoning out leads to more than just missed opportunities. The tendency to "shut down" or get lost "in the fog" when doing things we've done a million times before, like driving, or when we're in busy, crowded environments, like a train station, can put us in physical danger.

I was in a Metro station in Washington, DC, recently, studying the people surrounding me as I now know to do. I saw businesspeople and friends chatting, children holding their parents' hands, students lugging heavy backpacks. And then I noticed a man sitting on the steps; he had a wiry, dirty beard, wore threadbare, soiled clothes, and scowled while he chipped away at the wall with something sharp. No one nearby paid any attention to him. When the train rolled in, he stood up, shoved the shank into his pocket, and stumbled onto a car with dozens of other people. How many of them would have chosen a different car had they seen him five minutes before? Being oblivious to their surroundings put them in a closed car with a disturbed man concealing a sharp object in his pocket. How does an entire person escape the view of so many others? Because not only do we fail to look, we are often also wearing electronic blinders in the form of earbuds and smartphones.

When we walk through the world on autopilot, our eyes might seem to take everything in, but in reality we are seeing less than we could if we were paying closer attention. As we'll learn in later chapters, attention is a finite resource that our brains must delegate. We do ourselves and our attention spans a great disservice when we are not fully engaged.

THE AGE OF DISTRACTION

Thanks to a wireless web with a constant flow of information available to us anytime, anywhere, there are more things competing for our attention than ever before. Today more people have access to cell phones than to working toilets, and the average person checks his phone *110 times a day* and nearly once every 6 seconds in the evening. Our perpetual, byte-size interactions are not only a detriment to our concentration, focus, productivity, and personal safety, but they're also hurting our intelligence. A 2005 study at King's College at London University found that when distracted, workers suffered a ten- to fifteen-point IQ loss — a greater dumbing down than experienced when smoking marijuana. A fifteen-point deficiency is significant, as it brings an adult male down to the same IQ level as an eight-year-old child.

Our brain's prefrontal cortex is responsible for analyzing tasks, prioritizing them, and assigning our mental resources to them. When we inundate it with too much information or make it switch focus too quickly, it simply slows down. How much? The *Journal of Experimental Psychology* reported that students who were distracted while working on complicated math problems took 40 percent longer to solve them.

Ironically, compounding the problem is our need for speed. The immediacy of information delivery in today's world has also created a culture that places a premium on speed, spontaneity, and efficiency, but those ideals come at a cost. In the hospitality industry, the desire for a quicker room turnaround negatively affected both employee safety and customer satisfaction. As the daily room-cleaning quota for hotel housekeepers rose from fourteen rooms per shift in 1999 to twenty rooms in 2010, so did the injury risk rate, rising from 47 percent to 71 percent. While the changes meant that the management companies saved money on staffing, healthcare costs for the injured workers rose, and the properties' cleanliness — the number one reason guests don't return to a hotel — was compromised. In 2012, scientists found that the level of colony-forming units of bacteria on surfaces in hotel rooms was twenty-four times higher than what hospitals deem the "highest limit acceptable."

Similarly, in the managed-healthcare world, where monetary rewards are given for seeing as many patients as quickly as possible, medical professionals can be tempted to sacrifice quality care for quantity care and go straight for the patient's chart in an effort to expedite the visit, relying on what the caregiver before them has written before personally evaluating a patient and making observations of their own.

Thankfully, there is a natural and easy buffer against letting the stress of speed and the steady stream of distraction overwhelm us: simply slowing down. In a commencement speech at Sarah Lawrence College, industrial designer and "Mythbuster" Adam Savage reminded the 2012 graduates that they didn't have to be in a constant hurry, that they in fact had plenty of time: "You have time to fail. You have time to mess up. You have time to try again, and when you mess that up, you still have time." Savage also reminds us of the ironic pitfall of impatience: "Rushing leads to mistakes, and mistakes slow you down far more than slowing down does."

In 2013, researchers at Princeton University and the University of California, Los Angeles, found that students who handwrote lecture notes rather than typing them out retained more of the information precisely because they were slowed down. A quick keyboard transcription doesn't require critical thinking. The slower process of handwriting means not everything will be captured verbatim; instead the brain is forced to exert more effort to capture the essence of what's important, thus committing the information more effectively to memory.

Slowing down doesn't mean being slow, it just means taking a few minutes to absorb what we are seeing. Details, patterns, and relationships take time to register. Nuances and new information can be missed if we rush past them.

In July 2013, Beyoncé stopped her concert in Duluth, Georgia, to remind a fan that he was missing the opportunity of a lifetime. In her self-professed favorite part of the concert, she offered her microphone to a select few people from the audience to allow them to sing the song "Irreplaceable" with her. One lucky gentleman she picked, though, couldn't stop recording her with his camera phone long enough to get the words right.

"You can't even sing 'cause you're too busy taping," she scolded. "I'm right in your face, baby. You gotta seize this moment. Put the damn camera down!"

Portable technology is not just a sensory distraction; we allow it to be a sensory substitution. I'm always confounded when I see people taking pictures of iconic paintings in museums, especially when they jostle for space, snap the shot, and then walk away. The resulting image, mediated through a camera lens, is not the same as a close, careful observation of the work. It is akin to reading the wall label next to a work of art and then failing to examine the object it describes. Writer Daphne Merkin voiced the same sentiment recently, recalling her inability to enjoy Vermeer masterpieces in Amsterdam's Rijksmuseum because they were "blocked by a throng of phones." She wrote, "I wonder what part of the experience gets lost in the hubbub. Instead of your own lens being enough, everything gets distilled through a second LCD screen. You end up living life removed, dissociated from your own sensations, perceptions, and feelings."

One of the first things I encourage participants in my class to do is put their phones away. I'd rather they not record the information electronically or take pictures for one simple reason: I want them to trust themselves. I don't want them to rely on anything else except what's within them: their inherent sense of observation, their intuition, and their ability to comprehend and retain information.

Everyone is generally very nervous at first, especially if they work in jobs that are report-driven. But I assure them, as I do you, that if you simply engage all of your senses, they will deliver everything you need and more. Your brain is more powerful than any gadget. Just turn it back on.

Dr. Sebastian Seung turned his retina research into a crowd-science project because computers couldn't handle it. When he and his team tried to map images of the retinal neurons taken with an electron microscope by applying artificial-intelligence algorithms, they discovered that it couldn't be done without human help. Believe it or not, computers can't recognize patterns or transform 2D images into 3D objects as effectively as the human brain can. Essentially Seung needed neurons to map neurons.

Similarly, the first iterations of the Art of Perception program evolved at medical schools because instructors such as Dr. Glenn McDonald noticed that their new students were relying too much on advanced technology and not enough on their own powers of observation. McDonald says, "Students need to realize that no matter how helpful technology has become, it is no match [for] a good set of eyes and a brain."

To get our own brains and eyes engaged and focused, we're going to look at a well-known work of art, one you may have seen before. But we're going to observe it more slowly than most people ever would. If you can, plant yourself in an area where you won't be distracted or disturbed. If you can get out of your normal surroundings, even better. Now look at the painting on the next page. There is no specific assignment here; I just want you to look. What do you see? List everything, in your mind or on paper.

Look at it for as long as you like. The average museum visitor spends seventeen seconds viewing each work of art, which I think is far too short. Harvard art history professor Jennifer L. Roberts requires her students to sit before a painting for three full hours, an exercise that she says is "explicitly designed to seem excessive" so that they might truly take the time to excavate the wealth of information proffered. Find a time somewhere in between seventeen seconds and three hours that feels comfortable but also allows you to really take in what you see.

To kick-start your observational skills, ask yourself the follow-

ing questions while you look at the painting: What do you think is going on in the painting? What relationships do you see — between people and objects? What questions does the painting elicit for you?

The point of this exercise is to get comfortable slowing down and truly studying works of art. With a quick glance we can see that there are two people in the painting, one standing and one sitting. It takes longer to discover details and realize relationships.

In the amount of time you looked at the painting, did you notice the orange sash in the seated woman's lap? That she was holding a quill pen in her right hand? That the blue tablecloth was bunched up on the far left of the scene?

Give yourself another full minute or two to really absorb details.

Did you look long enough? Perhaps, if you took note of the white ribbon tying the seated woman's pearls together at the nape of her neck or that writing covers the top half of the paper on the table. If you didn't, look longer.

Can you say with certainty from which direction the light is coming? If not, look again.

If you've seen that the light enters from the left as evidenced by the shadow across the seated woman's legs, you've most likely also observed the painting's primary colors — the yellow of the seated woman's fur-lined mantle, the bright blue of the standing woman's apron — but what about textures? Did you see the deep gathers at the top of the seated woman's left sleeve? The swooping amber folds in the background? The reflection of windows in the inkwell and glass?

Now that we've assessed the scene, what can we make of the information we have gathered? What relationships can we detect or dismiss? Is the standing woman a servant, friend, or mother? Her smooth complexion, similar to the seated woman's, suggests that they are close enough in age not to be mother and daughter. Analyzing the standing woman's plain, untrimmed clothing, lack of jewelry, and that her hair is pulled straight back from her face rather than curled in decoration further supports the notion that they are not in the same relational or social circle. If you look even more closely, you will see a line below the standing woman's right wrist that distinguishes her red working hands from the lighter skin of her more often protected forearm. Such a distinction is conspicuously absent on the seated woman's uniformly pale arm. From the former's posture and open mouth, it appears that she is delivering a letter to the seated woman, whose own gestures suggest that she is receiving rather than having just handed it over. Based on the facts presented, we can determine that the women are most likely not twins or sisters, mother and daughter, or strangers. Our best guess is servant and mistress, a supposition confirmed by the title of the painting: *Mistress and Maid.*

Studying this Vermeer painting shows us in practice that the longer and more attentively we look, the more we will discover. George de Mestral, Betsy Kaufman, Steve Jobs, and Leonardo da Vinci all believed that invention is less about creation than it is about discovery. And discovery is made possible by simply opening our eyes, turning on our brains, tuning in, and paying attention. Sir Isaac Newton agreed, stating, "If I have ever made any valuable discoveries, it has been owing more to patient attention than to any other talent."

We all have the talent to observe and make discoveries that will lead to greater things in any number of fields, but we must first be prepared to see.

When Derreck Kayongo returned from the concierge to his room with the knowledge that American hotels routinely discarded barely used bars of soap every day, he knelt down on his bed and cried. He had been the child who helped his father make soap, the child who lived in a squalid refugee camp without soap, and he was now living in a country where soap was simply thrown away. He didn't know what to do with that information but was determined not to let it go until he found a way to, as he says, "connect the dots." That connection came back to the bar of soap in his hotel shower, the bar he knew he could find a way to share with the world.

By preparing our minds to observe and absorb everything, and to discover the possibilities around and inside us, we open ourselves up to success in our own lives. We've already started by recognizing that observation is not just passively watching something but an actively engaging mental process. Before we can truly master it, though, we need to know our own blind spots.

2

Elementary Skills

Mastering the Fine Art of Observation

René Magritte, *The Portrait*, 1935.

IN 1877, AN EIGHTEEN-YEAR-OLD student slid into one of the two hundred seats arranged in a steep semicircle in the dark wood-paneled Anatomy Lecture Theatre, a new state-of-the-art classroom at the University of Edinburgh's Medical School. The occupants of the room tittered with anticipation for the arrival of the appointed speaker, a local legend as well known for his deep knowledge of a wide range of subjects as for his dynamic delivery of it. He was going to teach the young students what he called "the Method," a disciplined approach to diagnosis that relied on keen observation skills above all.

With a flourish, the man — tall and lean with an aquiline nose and piercing eyes — bounded into the lecture hall, tore off his cloaked coat and deerstalker cap, and called for the first subject to be sent in. A line of outpatients the man had never set eyes on before waited in the hallway to be presented live to his pupils.

An elderly woman dressed in black entered.

"Where is your cutty pipe?" he inquired.

The woman started. How could he know she had one? Shocked, she pulled a small clay pipe from her purse.

"I knew she had a cutty pipe not because I saw it, but because I observed her," he told his rapt audience. "I noted the small ulcer on her lower lip and glossy scar on her cheek, sure signs of habitual use of a short-stemmed pipe that lay close to the cheek when smoking."

Another patient limped in. The teacher called on one of his students.

"What is the matter with this man, sir?" he asked. "Come down, sir, and look at him! No! You mustn't touch him. Use your eyes, sir! Use your ears, use your brain, your bump of perception, and use your powers of deduction."

The nervous student answered with a guess he hoped seemed confident: "Hip-joint disease, sir!"

"Hip-nothing!" the instructor cried out. Without a backward glance, he announced, "The man's limp is not from his hip, but from his foot, or rather from his feet. Were you to observe closely, you would see that there are slits, cut by a knife, in those parts of the shoes where the pressure of the shoe is greatest against the foot. The man is a sufferer from corns, gentlemen, and has no hip trouble at all."

The speaker continued to divine with ever-increasing alacrity the profession, off-duty vices, and world travels of people whom he had never met.

"Gentlemen, we have here a man who is either a cork-cutter or a slater. If you will only use your eyes a moment you will be able to define a slight hardening—a regular callous, gentlemen—on one side of his forefinger, and a thickening on the outside of his thumb, a sure sign that he follows the one occupation or the other. The shade of tan on his face shows him to be a coast-sailor, and not a deep-sea sailor —a sailor who makes foreign lands. His tan is that produced by one climate, a 'local tan,' so to speak."

When another student got a diagnosis incorrect, the teacher admonished, "The gentleman has ears and he hears not, eyes and he sees not!" In his view nothing was more important to discovery—in medicine, criminal law, or life in general—than finely tuned observation skills. He let no fact, however small, escape his notice, frequently pointing out what others had failed to observe: tattoos, accents, skin marking, scars, clothing, even the color of soil on someone's shoes.

"Glance at a man and you find his nationality written on his face," he instructed, "his means of livelihood on his hands and the rest of his story in his gait, mannerisms, watch-chain ornaments and the lint adhering to his clothes."

If the speaker's sharp senses and rapid-fire delivery of his deductions sound like Sherlock Holmes, it is for good reason: he was the real-life inspiration for the fictional detective. Dr. Joseph Bell, a professor of surgery, prolific writer, and a relative of Alexander Graham Bell, enthralled his young student Arthur Conan Doyle with his uncanny and uncommon yet in his words "elementary" talents. According to Bell, who often chanted, "Use your eyes, use your eyes" in his classes, the most important skill was a simple differentiation between passive sight and active assessment.

Bell's Sherlockian summation: "Most people see but do not observe."

What's the difference? Doyle had Sherlock Holmes himself explain it in one of his first published short stories, "A Scandal in Bohemia," when Dr. Watson claimed to have eyes just as good as Holmes's.

Holmes countered, "You see, but you do not observe. The distinction is clear. For example, you have frequently seen the steps which lead up from the hall to this room."

"Frequently."

"How often?"

"Well, some hundreds of times."

"Then how many are there?"

"How many? I don't know."

"Quite so! You have not observed. And yet you have seen. That is just my point. Now, I know that there are seventeen steps, because I have both seen and observed."

Although we frequently use the terms interchangeably, seeing can be thought of as the automatic, involuntary recording of images. Observing is seeing, but consciously, carefully, and thoughtfully.

WHAT DO YOU SEE?

To help everyone take a personal inventory during every Art of Perception class, I show the photograph opposite of a young woman walking outdoors and ask the simple question: what do you see? In just one sentence, tell me what you see.

Go ahead and test yourself right now. What single sentence would you use to completely and accurately describe this scene?

I've been doing this for over a decade now with professionals from every walk of life. People tell me about the young woman; the most astute note what she's wearing, where she's looking, that she appears to be holding something, and which leg she is leading with. People tell me about the large tree on the left and its lack of leaves; some go so far as to estimate its height based on the comparison of the woman, but true to Holmes's assertion, no one ever tells me the number of branches. I hear about the bushes along the fence and the fence itself, the bench, the fallen leaves and shadows in the foreground. But perhaps most shockingly, about half of the people who view this photograph don't mention the giant letter *C* in the background.

Do you see it? Did you see it originally? Did you include it in your

descriptive sentence? It's not an illusion or a postprocessing photography trick. The *C* really exists. Is it an important part of the photograph? Is it worth mentioning? It is, for many reasons. It places the photograph in a unique location, as a bit of research would uncover that the *C* is painted on a one-hundred-foot-high rock wall on the Bronx side of the Harlem River in New York City across from Columbia University. It helps establish the time frame in which the photograph was taken, since the *C* first appeared in all white in 1955 and was repainted to feature pale blue outlined in white in 1986. And since the *C* is an impressive 60 feet tall by 60 feet wide — possibly New York City's largest graffiti — noticing such a sizable object that takes up much of the photograph is a testament to elementary observation skills.

Those who fail to see this *C* are normal people with normal vision who just haven't sharpened their observation skills. What if the 50 percent who didn't see it included the detective assigned to your robbery, or your surgeon, your boss, your boyfriend, or your child's bus driver? What if you didn't see the *C*? Missing such a large detail might not seem critical right now while you're reading a book, but what about when you're babysitting, behind the wheel, or just crossing the street?

Before we can really hone our observation skills, however, we need to understand the built-in biological mechanisms that render all of us at one time or another "blind" to objects, even when they're massive, moving, or should otherwise be memorable. And we can do that with a little help from an orangutan named Kevin.

THE GORILLA IN THE ROOM

The first thing you need to know is that Kevin isn't conscious. I'd say he isn't "real," but his owner, Dr. Michael Graziano, would argue those semantics, since Kevin does exist, albeit in acrylic fiber form. Kevin is a puppet.

Dr. Michael Graziano.

Dr. Graziano, another neuroscientist at Princeton and author of *Consciousness and the Social Brain,* uses Kevin in his lectures as a unique ventriloquist demonstration of the power of perception. While his students giggle nervously at first when Graziano, a tall man with a salt-and-pepper beard and twinkling eyes, puts Kevin on his hand, only a few minutes later they find themselves unwittingly assigning a personality to the pretend primate.

To watch the performance with eyes wide open, as it were, knowing full well that it's a social illusion, is a fascinating experience. As much as I prepared myself skeptically — an ape puppet in the Ivy League? Really? — I found myself drawn in anyway. Kevin makes crude jokes, claims to be Darth Vader, and looks around the room seemingly independently of his master. I couldn't help but smile as Kevin squealed in agony when Graziano finally pulled his hand free. Even though I knew it was a puppet, Kevin did seem at times to have a mind of "his" own.

Graziano attributes this phenomenon to what he calls "attention schema theory." As we sit in his office — delightfully dominated by a colorful painted mural of a dinosaur named Science eating a scientist, who he gleefully confesses is him — he explains the basics. Since humans are bombarded with stimuli, both externally in the form of sights, sounds, and other sensory information and internally in the form of thoughts, emotions, and memories, the brain cannot process every bit of information it encounters. Instead, it must focus on some things at the expense of others. How the neurons in the human brain decide what to deal with is called attention.

"We don't magically become aware of something," Graziano says. "It's an act of the brain processing data."

By walking us through the experience of attributing a social awareness to an orangutan puppet, Graziano allows us to feel the otherwise automatic process.

He is quick to point out that attention, while hard to capture, is also finite. We do not have an unlimited capacity for decoding every single stimulus, both external and internal, that we encounter.

"It's partly a source-parsing problem," he says. "In many ways, your attention focuses you. You attend to one thing, and effectively your brain suppresses or filters out everything else."

It's hard to believe what the brain sometimes filters out, as evidenced by another simian experiment, this one involving a woman dressed as a gorilla.

In 1999, Harvard psychologists Daniel Simons and Christopher Chabris set out to prove that even though our eyes may be open and looking right at something in our field of view, we don't always see it — an anomaly known as "inattentional blindness." They re-created a famous 1970s video experiment in which a woman with an umbrella walks through a scene of students passing basketballs; test subjects were asked to count how many passes were completed, and in doing so, many missed the woman and her parasol entirely. Simons and

Chabris's new version made the unexpected intrusion even more dramatic by taking away the woman's umbrella and putting her inside a gorilla costume. Just as in my Columbia University letter *C* experiment, half of the participants of their study failed to notice the gorilla even when she was on screen twice as long as the woman with the parasol, looked directly at the camera, and thumped her chest instead of just walking straight through the crowd.

Fifteen years later, inattentional blindness experiments continue to prove that conscious perception requires attention, and that attention is selective. If our attention is absorbed by anything, even a task as mundane as counting, we can miss something else huge (and hairy) right in front of us.

Inattentional blindness can affect the best professionals in all fields, even those whose job entails looking for details. Attention researchers at Harvard Medical School did their own version of the "invisible gorilla" experiment by superimposing a two-inch gorilla on slides of lungs and asking radiologists to review them for cancerous nodules. *Eighty-three percent* of the radiologists never mentioned the gorilla shaking its fist at them from inside the slide.

Sometimes inattentional blindness has deadly effects. Boston police officer Kenneth Conley was pursuing a shooting suspect on foot when he ran right past a group of fellow police officers beating a man so viciously that the victim was left with severe head and kidney damage. When federal authorities investigated the assault, no officer would admit to taking part in or even seeing the incident. Conley was called to testify and admitted that he had been right there but had not seen the beating. Investigators did not believe it was possible to miss such an event, and Conley was convicted of obstruction of justice and perjury, removed from the police force, and sentenced to three years in prison.

While Conley could only attribute his inability to see the fight he ran right past to some kind of "tunnel vision," a claim even the Supreme Court did not buy, psychologists Simons and Chabris of the woman-in-the-gorilla-suit experiment believed the officer was suffering from inattentional blindness. To prove it was possible, they recreated the situation with volunteers, asking them to jog after a man and count how many times he touched his hat. The joggers were led right past a staged fight scene; 67 percent of them failed to see it. Simons and Chabris published the results in a paper titled "You Do Not Talk About Fight Club If You Do Not Notice Fight Club."

We are all so susceptible to inattentional blindness that we often miss important information. We can work to overcome this inborn tendency, however, by teaching our brains to have better attention and observation skills. Samuel Renshaw, an American psychologist whose research on vision helped the armed forces quickly recognize enemy aircraft during World War II, believed that "proper seeing is a skill which needs to be learned, like playing the piano, speaking French or playing good golf." He claimed that just like a pianist's fingers, the eyes could be trained to perform better. Likewise, multiple studies published in the *Journal of Vision* have confirmed that we can increase our attention capacity dramatically with challenging visual attention tasks. Studying provocative, intricate, multidimensional, and even off-putting art affords us exactly that opportunity.

OBSERVING ART

The success of using art to enhance observation skills among medical students was proven in 2001 by researchers at Yale. A two-year study published in the *Journal of the American Medical Association* found that those who studied artwork improved their diagnostic skills considerably but that their actual observational skills, specifically "their detection of details," also increased by 10 percent. Dr. Irwin Braverman, professor of dermatology at Yale School of Medicine, called the 10 percent improvement "statistically significant" because it showed that "you can train someone visually to be a better observer."

Allison West is living proof. When I first met her, she was a medical student at New York University, fresh from a small town in Georgia. One of West's favorite pastimes was strolling through art museums, and Manhattan had them to spare. She wasn't an art major, though, so she didn't have a practiced way of looking at paintings; she just enjoyed them each for a few moments before moving on to the next. So she was excited to find out that her medical school offered the Art of Perception course, and she signed up.

"I had no idea how much I was missing," she remembers. "I like to think of myself as a very observant person, and I didn't see the Columbia University *C* staring me right in the face! I felt like I had been walking around with smudged lenses coloring everything, and I didn't even know I was wearing them!"

After learning how to observe rather than just see, West noticed that the way she encountered and documented her patients changed dramatically.

"In a typical report, I used to write something like: 'Middle-aged white male reclining in a bed. He has tired eyes, pale skin, a somber expression, and is wearing a hospital gown. His surroundings are plain: bare walls, white sheets with a bloodstain on the right side of the bed.' Descriptive, but very clinical," she tells me. "After the class, I started writing down, 'He has a crossword puzzle in his hand, a local newspaper written in Spanish at his side, card on the bulletin board reads 'Get Well Soon, Grandpa.' Where I used to just see flowers in a room as a sign of an ill patient, I now pay attention to what kind they are and if they're wilting, who sent them, and when."

West also now notes what stuffed animals may be lying on the windowsill, what TV show the patient is watching, and what books are on the bedside table.

"These new details that I'd never noticed before might not tell me a diagnosis," she explains, "but they give me something just as important: information about what motivates the patient to live, how he can live best with his illness, and what sort of alternative treatments he might consider to palliate his suffering."

Like a modern-day Dr. Bell, West uses what she initially observes to uncover even more. Seeing the Spanish newspaper at one patient's side prompts her to investigate his diet at home: Is it rich in Hispanic foods that might worsen his condition? What does he do for a living? Can he return to a job that will engage his mind and help his overall healing? What are his favorite pastimes and hobbies? Will he be able to take them up again during his recovery?

"Knowing that he likes to build model trains might seem like an insignificant detail for a doctor to know," she says, "but quality of life is key to recovery, and knowing that he can return to an activity he loves can mean all the difference for a patient."

It's made all the difference for West as well. She is now a doctor specializing in internal medicine at the University of Chicago Medical Center and was profiled in *New York* magazine's 2012 "Best Doctors" issue.

Like any other skill, observation can be mastered with practice. In his 1950 book *The Art of Scientific Investigation,* Cambridge scientist William Ian Beardmore Beveridge gives the following instructions: "Powers of observation can be developed by cultivating the habit of watching things with an active, enquiring mind. Training in observation follows the same principles as training in any activity. At first one must do things consciously and laboriously, but with practice the activities gradually become automatic and unconscious and a habit is established." Practice also makes permanent, as neuroscientists believe that practicing new skills rearranges the brain's internal connections. So technically, biologically, we can wire our brains to see better.

We can do this with exercises that improve our attention and memory, as both are integral to observation skills. And we'll start with art.

Without looking back, try to recall the painting at the beginning of this chapter on page 23. Can you visualize it? I'll give you a hint: it's a still life spread out on what appears to be a table.

If you can't quite remember the painting, you're in good company. In my class I show the same picture quickly as I introduce myself, and many people don't pay attention. If you have no idea what I'm talking about — *a painting? What painting?* — because you flipped right past it, don't worry, you're still in good company. A lot of us have learned to skim or skip over the beginnings of things to get to "the meat," but when we do that we're quite possibly skipping over vital, valuable information. We're going to learn, starting right now, how not to do that.

Turn back to the painting on page 23. I love this particular, peculiar work because you don't have to know anything about art or who painted it, when, or why to appreciate the striking visual scene:

a seemingly ordinary place setting starring an open, unblinking eye in the oddest of places. Study the picture for a few minutes, and then come back.

◉

Welcome back! So, what did you see? Let's start with the basics: How many objects were on the table, and what were they? Try to remember as many as you can.

If you can recall that there were five — a glass, a bottle, a knife, a fork, and a plate with a slice of something on it with an eye in the middle of it — then good for you! If you can tell me that the glass was empty, the bottle full, that they were above the plate and utensils, that the fork was to the right of the plate and the green-handled knife to the right of the fork, and the eye was a blue-gray, even better!

What food was on the plate? I've heard "a pancake" quite often, but if you look closely, you can see thin white marbles of fat throughout, growing thicker at the edges; it's really a piece of ham. Bonus points if you noticed the dark red staining on the glass.

Now let's really observe. Go back and look at the painting again but even more closely, more slowly this time. Savor the stain on the side of the glass. Puzzle over whether or not everything is really on a table. Notice the light reflecting off the surface of the bottle, glass, and silverware. Calculate which direction the objects' shadows are pointing. What could be causing the reflection and shadows, and where would we look for such an object? Appreciate how an image that might seem simple at first glance is really a complex series of relationships — why is the bottle full if the glass is already stained? The fact that we keep uncovering more questions and more details the longer we look is how we know we're not just seeing but observing.

Now, without turning back, draw the painting yourself, capturing as many details as you can. When you're finished, go back and compare it with the original, noting anything you might have missed. Add those details to your drawing.

To further enhance your retention abilities, wait an hour and then draw the painting again. Again, go back and correct it by adding any missing information.

You can also practice on a single everyday object: your watch, your handbag, or a water bottle. Select something with a lot of detail, and really study it for one full minute. Then put it away or cover it up, and write down as many details — shapes, colors, textures, words, measurements — as you can. Retrieve the object, but instead of subtracting time, add it. Observe the same object for three times as long, or three minutes, and see how much more you can find. Do this with a different item every day for a week, and you will notice by the end how the practice has increased your ability to focus and remember what you've seen.

The more you exercise your memory skills, the better you will become at them not only in these specific tasks but in your general observation of life as well. One of my students told me she used to walk around her neighborhood every day for exercise, listening to music, not noticing anything, just trying to log her thirty minutes. After taking my class, she decided to reengage her senses on the exact same route, and the differences were startling. She noticed cracks in the sidewalk, handprints in cement she'd never seen, a secret bike path. She said it was as if she were "seeing with new eyes."

Similarly, the more you consciously observe your environment, the more natural the process will become. To engage your sense of awareness, go outside at lunchtime, plant yourself in one spot, and practice observing every single thing that crosses your visual path. Doing so will help train your eyes to look beyond what's right in front of you or what you are used to seeing.

Arthur Conan Doyle's real-life inspiration, Dr. Joseph Bell, didn't have ESP or X ray vision. He wasn't able to see more because he was born with a superhuman power. He just practiced using his powers of observation on a daily basis. We all have the same abilities; we just don't always know it.

In the early 1980s, Philadelphia physician Arthur Lintgen received international attention when he demonstrated his uncanny ability to "read" vinyl records on a television show. Dubbed the "man who sees what others hear," Lintgen could look at a phonograph record with the label completely obscured and quickly and correctly detect which classical piece it played by simply studying the grooves. Expert after expert tested the veracity of his claim, and all came to the same conclusion: Lintgen's ability was legitimate.

Lintgen was able not only to identify the recordings' titles and composers but also to relay how many movements were in each piece, how long each movement was, the volume and percussiveness of each movement, and sometimes even which orchestra had recorded it. He did so not by reading the music on the record but by examining the smallest physical details on them. He looked at the spacing, coloring, and contour of the grooves and then correlated that with his knowledge of the patterns in classical music; for instance, he knew that a Beethoven symphony has a longer first movement in relation to its second, and could recognize that pattern.

Lintgen didn't have special eyes; in fact he was extremely nearsighted and wore thick glasses. He simply looked at a record closely and consciously and practiced looking until the process of identifying the piece become quicker and more natural to him. We can all do the same.

That's not to say we all see things the same way. The way our brains choose to sort through the millions of bits of information available is unique to us and entirely dependent upon our own perceptual filters. To see like Sherlock Holmes, we need to be familiar with them because, whether we realize it or not, they are altering our observations.

3

The Platypus and the Gentleman Thief

Why No Two People See Things the Same Way

FOR ALMOST A DECADE the Rubin Museum of Art in New York has hosted a unique series of events called Brainwave. The program pairs performing artists, writers, and musicians with neuroscientists to explain to a lay audience what is happening in the brain when they experience something. I was fortunate enough to attend a session with Dr. Marisa Carrasco, a cognitive scientist from New York University, and deception specialist Apollo Robbins, a short man with an earring in his left ear and a small soul patch.

During the presentation the following photograph was shown on the screen. "What do you see?" Robbins asked the audience.

I didn't really see anything, so at first I thought the image was not a photograph. I figured it was some sort of Rorschach inkblot test to reveal a secret about our psyche.

Aside from being a professional speaker, Robbins is a charming theatrical larcenist who calls himself "the Gentleman Thief." He could take the bracelet off my wrist and the glasses off my head without my ever knowing. Before the show, while posing as an usher, he had done exactly that to many guests, shaking people's hands and robbing them blind. (He returns everything.) After picking the pockets of former president Jimmy Carter's Secret Service detail, Robbins became a security advisor and now trains law enforcement on sensory awareness.

Now Robbins assured us that we were indeed viewing a genuine unaltered photograph. He even threw in a hint: "It's a four-legged mammal."

Still, I saw nothing.

The person sitting next to me recognized a definitive animal almost immediately. She settled back in her seat, satisfied. I continued to look. Harder. I looked upside down. I squinted.

The woman next to me whispered, "I can't believe you don't see this."

I do this for a living! How could I not see it? Finally, I had to guess. It was a platypus, I decided. Before you look at the photo below, take another look at the one on the previous page. What do you see?

It's a photo of a cow. Do you see it now?

Renshaw's Cow with face outlined.

Without the outline, I would never have seen the cow. A cat maybe. A platypus, sure. But not a cow.

While Robbins's lesson was on "illusion confusion" and how our brains can play tricks on us, I use the same photograph in my class for a different purpose: to prove that no two people see things, even facts, the same way.

I've shown the cow photograph to thousands of people through the years and have gotten just as many different answers as to what it is—from a dragon to the *Hindenburg* to a woman shopping for bras. While most people can see, not everyone sees the same things. This premise gets more complicated when we're looking at things that aren't as black-and-white as a black-and-white photograph and could be subject to so many interpretations.

Eve Oosterman.

For instance, Toronto mother Ruth Oosterman posted this picture of her two-year-old daughter and her latest creation and posed the same simple question to her online readers: what do you see? The responses that poured in from around the world were as varied as the people sending them: rabbit ears, wildflowers on a seashore, a willow tree, a bucking Shetland pony, a robot dance party.

"Almost every single person saw something different in the shapes and lines," Ruth recalls.

Ruth's own ability to interpret her toddler's drawings led to a mother-daughter collaboration years before she thought such a joint effort would be possible. Ruth, a professional artist, would strap baby Eve into a carrier on her chest and paint furiously in her studio.

As Eve's coordination grew, the toddler took up residence next to her mother, playing with paint at first just to enjoy the texture but then eventually painting on her own canvases. Ruth couldn't wait for Eve to be old enough to collaborate with her ... until she realized that she already was.

"She would frequently 'add' to my pieces, and one day I looked at one of her drawings," Ruth says, "and in the scribbles, I saw two people standing by the shore."

Ruth used watercolors to fill in Eve's vision, and their first painting, *The Red Boat*, came to life. The pair has become an international sensation celebrated from Austria to South Korea for their whimsical portraits. Eve begins each sketch on her own, usually with an ink pen, and her mother fills in the details and color based on the little girl's stories, songs, and daily activities.

Eve's drawing, and the collaborative result:
The Red Boat by Ruth and Eve Oosterman.

Each of us brings a similar and unique set of brushes to fill in what we see. If someone else tried to complete Eve's drawings, the results would certainly differ from her mother's. Ruth is partial to and proficient in watercolors, and that determines how she interprets the sketches. Someone like me, who has no artistic ability, would most likely use other materials — I don't even own watercolors — and produce another sort of image entirely.

It seems obvious that we all see things differently. Yet we constantly forget, and act as if there is only one true way to see. However, knowing now that we are *all* susceptible to inattentional blindness and other perceptual errors, we cannot assume that anyone else sees what we see, that we see what they see, or that either of us accurately sees what's really there.

OUR PERCEPTUAL FILTERS

No two people will see anything the exact same way. Everything from our inherited biology to our learned biases influences the way we take in the world. Not only do we as individuals observe, notice, and gather information differently, we also perceive what we've gathered differently.

Perception is how we interpret the information we gather during observation; think of it as an internal filter. It can color, cloud, or change what really exists into what we think we are seeing.

Much like seeing, the process of perceiving is subtle, automatic, and hard to recognize if we're not consciously aware of it. Want to feel it right now? Look back at the black-and-white photograph on page 37. Now try *not* to see the cow. It's impossible. You can unfocus your eyes or turn the page around, but you will not be able to not see the cow now. Why? The power of your new knowledge — that it is a cow — has effectively erased your previous perceptions.

This is indicative of the experience we have every time we see, don't see, and can't un-see something. Being aware of how easily our perceptions can change, and refuse to un-change, can help us to be attuned to them.

Our perceptive filter is shaped by our own unique experiences in the world. Everyone's is different from everyone else's, sometimes wildly so.

Claire, a lawyer in the Trial Division of the Manhattan District Attorney's Office, lived just two blocks from the World Trade Center with her husband, Matt, and their three children. On the morning of 9/11 they evacuated together, grabbing what few possessions they could and hopping onto a van to New Jersey, where they lived for the next several weeks. A few months later, her husband's uncle, an author, talked to her and her husband separately about their experiences on that day and wrote up their two accounts.

Claire was shocked when she read them. Even though she and her husband were together the entire time, in the same place, before, during, and after the attack, and left New York at the same moment, you would never have believed from reading the narrative that they lived through the same experience. They didn't recall the same things, and the things they did both recall, they didn't see the same way. While Claire remembered looking through their ash-splattered apartment window and seeing people getting trampled in the street and struck by falling objects, Matt recalled that the window was blacked out completely and that he didn't look and didn't want to look outside. When they decided to move outside into the hallway, Claire talked about her children needing snacks and sweaters, while Matt focused on the elderly residents who needed chairs. Matt thought the falling towers might crush them; Claire was sure the smoke would kill them.

It wasn't just their recounting of the events that was different, their emotional responses were too. Claire called colleagues nearby and begged, pleaded, and cried for help. Matt was "dead calm." Matt spoke to his uncle on the phone but doesn't remember their conversation; Claire can still recall every word of the good-bye call she placed to her father in Oregon.

The published account of their "reflections on terror and loss" still resonates with her as a firsthand example of how your own perceptions of a situation are just that — your own — and of the fact that you can never assume other people experience anything the same way you do, even if you are right there with them.

If two parents who are the same age, and came from the same race, socioeconomic class, and physical location, don't see things the same way, think of how differently disparate people do: employers and employees, defenders and prosecutors, Republicans and Democrats, teachers and students, doctors and patients, caregivers and children. What we see might be completely different from what the person right next to us, let alone the person across the room, on the other end of the telephone, or the other side of the world sees. What might be apparent to us someone else might overlook entirely.

When I'm in Washington, DC, there's a work in the Smithsonian American Art Museum that I often use with my classes. It's a 9-foot-by-6-foot painting of a black girl sitting on the floor at the top of a set of stairs near a bookcase. Over the girl's head are two translucent cloud shapes with the same set of three letters in each: "SOB . . ."

While many people's first assumption is that *SOB* is a cry of despair or sadness, the girl's mouth is set, her eyes dry. I challenge my class: could *SOB* mean something else? We don't have a definitive answer. The title of the work by Kerry James Marshall is simply *SOB, SOB*.

Each person brings along his or her own unique experience, history, education, background, and viewpoint. Medical professionals have told me *SOB* means "shortness of breath," while maintenance crews claim it's "son of the boss." For Texan law enforcement agents, *SOB* stands for "south of the border." To Long Islanders, *SOB* is New York State Route 135, the Seaford–Oyster Bay Expressway. My favorite is the mother of a teenage texter who said that while *SOB* was an acronym for "son of a bitch" when she was younger and referred mostly to males, today's kids use it exclusively for girls and mean it as "self-obsessed bitch."

For success with anything — a case, a collaboration, or a new client — you cannot rely on someone else seeing or interpreting things the way you do. If you stop inquiring with your own interpretation of what you see, you could be missing untold information. If when viewing the black-and-white image presented by Apollo Robbins I got up and left right after I concluded that I saw a platypus, I might never have learned that the photograph really showed a cow. And if I relayed my experience to others as fact — "and then Apollo Robbins showed us a photo of a platypus"—I would be spreading incorrect information. To get the most accurate picture of anything, we need to see others' perceptions and recognize others' points of view.

How do we find out what other people see or think they see? We don't have to look any further than public art, especially contemporary sculptures and installations, and the very public reaction to it.

When South African artist Jane Alexander's exhibit *Surveys (from the Cape of Good Hope)* was on view at the Cathedral Church of Saint John the Divine in New York in April 2013, I was excited to go and see it for myself. Half human, half beast, mostly naked statues were installed in front of altars, in the nave, in courtyards, and on windowsills. There was a young boy with the face of an ape, a dog-headed man, a long-beaked bird without wings, and a feline-faced female wearing a white gown and a gold tiara whose arms ended in stumps. Some creatures sat on ammunition boxes; others were blindfolded, bound, and dragging machetes and toy trucks on the end of ropes.

While my experience of meeting these strange sculptures in a place normally reserved for prayer and spiritual repose was definitely extraordinary, the observations I've listed are objective. Not everyone's were, however. The exhibit was met by equal parts delight and disgust. While the *New York Times* praised the show as "wonderful" and "uncannily beautiful" and believed "the cathedral setting couldn't be more perfect," other critics found the exhibit "subversive," "disturbing," and "off-putting considering it was in a house of worship."

Jane Alexander's installation *Infantry with beast,* at the Cathedral Church of Saint John the Divine, 2008–2010.

Of course not everyone is going to like the same things—we are all subjective beings—but what's important to note is that our subjectivity can color the "truth" of what we see. While every visitor looked at the same setup, they all saw different things. A rusted sickle was seen by some as a sign of fertility and by others as one of destruction. Which was right? Neither. Unless the curved blade was marked as one or the other, and it wasn't, neither can be proven. The only objective and accurate answer is that the rusted sickle is a rusted sickle. To call it anything different is to alter the facts.

Look at the photograph of Alexander's work on page 44. What do you see? What stands out to you?

Now think about how various people's answers might differ based on their experience, priorities, or even profession. A frequent churchgoer might focus on the ornate relief in the background, while a retailer might zero in on the statues' footwear. A student of anthropology would look at it differently from someone with a fear of dogs. Perception is also shaped by a person's values, upbringing, and culture. Our natural inclination to either notice the canine-headed, human-bodied forms' nudity or avert our gaze from it could affect whether or not we see that the creatures' arms are unnaturally long. What would a medical professional have to say about the statues' ribs? Or an organizational consultant about the straightness of the group's lines? More important, would they notice each other's focus—would the physician notice the lines and the consultant see the ribs?

Since we live and work with all different types of people, we need to be attuned to how others might see something. To test our awareness of others' perceptions, let's look at a photo of another sculpture installation, on page 46. How would you describe this statue's expression? How do you think a probation officer would describe it? Since most probation and parole violations often involve drugs, he might see the sculpture's closed eyes, slack mouth, and lazily tilted-back head as an indication of being under the influence. What about a victim of sexual assault? She might see the sculpture's head as deliberately cocked back rather than tilted, eyes momentarily closed and mouth opened as a prelude to a threatening situation.

Tony Matelli, *Sleepwalker*, 2014.

Tony Matelli's February 2014 installation of a realistic-looking man in his underwear on the Wellesley College campus elicited a divisive uproar that was covered everywhere from *Time* magazine to the *International Business Times* in India. Reactions ranged from a parody Twitter account to protests and petitions against it. While some viewers found the statue comical and were openly amused, dressing it in hats and costumes, others found it so frightening that they demanded its removal. Some saw the statue as a lost, sympathetic figure, others as a threatening attacker.

This artwork is a not a performance piece. It is an inanimate structure made of painted bronze. In its still facial expression, some see melancholy, others menace.

The artist himself is an unwitting example of how even though we know that everyone sees things differently, we still don't always believe it. While Matelli concedes, "Each person comes to an artwork with their own history, their own politics, their own hopes and fears and all that stuff," he goes on to surmise, "I think people might be seeing things in that work that just aren't there."

The artist might not have intentionally infused his work with emotion, politics, or innuendo, but people still see what they see. We will never all see the same way, but the challenges that come with that are mitigated when we acknowledge our visual disparity instead of insisting it doesn't exist.

Simply knowing how many things shape perception and that perception shapes what we see can help alleviate miscommunication and misunderstanding, preventing us from getting upset with others when they don't see things the way we do. The fact is, they don't. They can't. No one can see things like you do except you.

SEEING THROUGH OUR SUBCONSCIOUS FILTERS

Since we all see reality through powerful but almost imperceptible perceptual filters, we must compensate for them to get a more accurate picture of the facts of life. We can do so the same way we can improve our active observation skills: with practice.

Just as our ability to consciously process what we see and think is entirely dependent upon our brain's neural connections, the same is true for things that dwell in our subconscious. Every bit of information, whether we sense it or not, is passed along our neural pathways, pathways that can be strengthened or rewired. These connections are so powerful and yet so malleable, just thinking about something like motion can promote actual physical change.

Experimenters at the Cleveland Clinic in Cleveland, Ohio, conducted a study in which people increased the strength in their fingers by 35 percent solely by mental training — imagining exercising their finger fifteen minutes a day for twelve weeks — and not any real physical movement. The muscle gain without moving was possible because the mental rehearsal of movements activates the same cortical areas of the brain as physical movement. Similarly, mental practice can influence processes controlled subconsciously because they share the same neural circuits. Scientists at the University of Oslo found that although people cannot adjust the size of their eyes' pupils voluntarily, their pupils would constrict by as much as 87 percent when they thought about an imaginary light.

We can work on avoiding our own subconscious pitfalls — such as perceptual filters — by bringing them into our consciousness, which happens as soon as we pay attention to them. The moment we become aware of a normally subconscious process, it crosses into our consciousness. Once these filters are exposed to our awareness, we can address them, sort through them, and overcome them if necessary. After we have perfected this new skill, it will itself become a subconscious process; we will be able to observe things *through* our perceptive filters and find the salient facts automatically. We know this is true because we all once learned to tie our shoes. At first the process required active thought and concentration, but after some practice it became an action we could perform without thinking, indeed even with our eyes closed.

Let's begin sorting through our own personal perceptual filters by examining them more closely. Take a few moments to think about what might unintentionally be coloring the things you see. For instance, analyze your own reaction to the Matelli sculpture. How does it make you feel? Amused? Offended? Ambivalent? There's no right or wrong answer; we all feel how we feel. How would you feel if you saw someone defacing it with spray paint? If you saw someone crying next to it?

How we innately feel about something is informed by our personal experiences, which in turn contribute to our perceptual filters — filters that distort or enhance the way we see. To uncover yours, as you imagine each scenario ask yourself the following questions about *Sleepwalker,* and if the answer is yes for any of them, note what the specifics might be.

Am I being influenced by . . .

- my own experiences or the experiences of those close to me?
- my geographic history, affinity, or present location?
- my values, morals, culture, or religious beliefs?
- my upbringing or education?
- my professional desires, ambitions, or failures?
- my personal desires, ambitions, or failures?
- my inherent likes and dislikes?
- my financial experience or outlook?

- my political beliefs?
- my physical state (illness, height, weight, et cetera)?
- my current mood?
- groups I identify with and organizations I belong to?
- media that I've consumed: books, television, websites?
- information or impressions passed on to me by a friend or colleague?

To help get you started, I've shared my own answers to the exercise below:

How does the Matelli sculpture make me feel?
Slightly uncomfortable because it is so realistic-looking. I'm not threatened by it personally, but I can understand how some people might be.

How would I feel if I saw someone defacing it with spray paint?
I would be upset because I consider it vandalism to deface a work of art and I don't think it is an acceptable way to express your difference of opinion.

How would I feel if I saw someone crying next to it?
Concerned, although I would find it hard to believe that the person crying was upset because of the sculpture.

Am I being influenced by . . .
. . . my own experiences or the experiences of those close to me?
YES—I'm thinking about a close friend of mine from high school who after being dropped off by her boyfriend after a date stumbled upon a strange man waiting for her in her garage. He tried to rape her, but she was able to escape him by biting off the tip of his finger. Now I'm thinking of another friend from high school whose older sister was not so lucky and was unable to fend off a rapist who attacked her at her job in the back of a Christian bookstore. Now I'm thinking of a college professor who was raped on a bicycle ride in the French countryside, and the daughter of

a dear friend who was attacked walking home to her dorm in college. That I can recall so many instances of sexual violence against women so quickly is profoundly disturbing to me and makes me understand the questions about the appropriateness of placing this sculpture on a women's college campus. I might not agree, but I understand why the issues were raised.

... my geographic history, affinity, or present location?

YES — I'm in my office, safe and sound, far away from the sculpture. That's probably why it's easy to think it isn't threatening to me, because I'm not in front of it. If I were, and saw that it was life-size, perhaps even taller than me, it might change my perception of it.

... my values, morals, culture, or religious beliefs?
NO

... my upbringing or education?

YES — I have an art history degree and have worked in and around art for many years, so I'm probably more familiar with sculpture than the average person. This might make me less emotional about the sculpture than someone without a similar background.

... my professional desires, ambitions, or failures?
NO

... my personal desires, ambitions, or failures?
NO

... my inherent likes and dislikes?

YES — I hate to admit it, but I'm just not a huge fan of bald men. It might just be a matter of personal taste and aesthetics, but I'm admitting it so I can consider how it might affect my perception of this sculpture.

... my financial experience or outlook?
NO

... my political beliefs?
NO

... my physical state (illness, height, weight, et cetera)?
YES — I am an average-size female, and the sculpture is a life-size, average-size male. I might have a very different reaction to the piece if I were a male.

... my current mood?
NO

... groups I identify with and organizations I belong to?
NO

... media that I've consumed: books, television, websites?
YES — I've read quite a few articles about the Matelli sculpture outcry, including the original petition from some of the students.

... information or impressions passed on to me by a friend or
   colleague?
YES — I had a friend tell me she thought the statue was "creepy," a word I probably wouldn't have used to describe it.

* * *

The more familiar we are with what might alter our observations, the more astute and accurate they will be. When you're asked to report objectively on something, ask yourself if you are reporting raw observational data or assumptions about observational data drawn after running it through the filter of your own personal experience.

Observation is a study of facts. We know that we have perceptual filters that can color or cloud what we see, and we know that others have their own filters, but what we want to cull are facts. Sometimes our perceptual filters disguise opinions as facts, such as with Matelli's half-naked man sculpture. A viewer who had experienced trauma might see the statue's raised hands as aggressive. A *Walking Dead* fan might describe the statue as a zombie. Neither is a fact. A correct description: the statue's hands are raised, arms outstretched. Is the statue lost or lustful? Neither. It is a bald man in his briefs. Saying you find him creepy is subjective. Explaining the objective reasons *why* you find him creepy could reveal facts that are useful to someone who thought the statue was merely funny.

When searching for facts, we need to separate subjective discoveries from objective ones, and we'll study the concept of the subjective versus the objective more thoroughly in the next chapter. Here I want to emphasize that subjective filters and their subjective findings aren't necessarily useless. We don't need to toss them out automatically. Instead, use the way other people look at things to lead you to new facts you might have missed otherwise. If coaxed, perhaps I would reveal that I was disturbed by the length of the statue's fingernails. Another observer could use my revelation to examine a part of the sculpture she might have missed. Someone who owns a gym might point out the statue's distended belly, while a podiatrist or someone with foot pain might point out the statue's odd posture. A six-year-old would focus on different aspects of the statue than the owners of the Hanes company. To mine the most information possible, don't close your eyes to anything, even someone else's subjectivity.

MOST COMMON PERCEPTUAL FILTERS

While we are all prone to subjectivity in our initial inspection of anything, we are especially vulnerable when we need to glean specific information to fulfill our personal or professional desires. Whether you look for a living or you're just studying a single occurrence, make sure you're not seeing something just because you want to see it or because it's your job to find it.

Seeing What We Want to See

This very common filter goes by many different names, including cognitive bias, confirmation bias, myside bias, wishful seeing, and tunnel vision. It puts us at risk of gathering information selectively, subconsciously seeking data that support our expectations and ignoring those that don't. It's a common trap in many fields. You can see it when police officers engage in racial profiling, when journalists only interview experts who support their initial opinion about a topic, when academics construct case studies to support their hypotheses, and when managers conducting employee evaluations only focus on performance events that uphold their preexisting opinion of an employee. Parents do the same thing, struggling to accurately assess their child's aberrant behavior.

We find personal proof that wishful seeing shapes our perceptual experience in "frequency illusion," which occurs when we first learn about something and then suddenly see it everywhere — for instance, when you buy a new car and then see that same car everywhere. More of that particular vehicle didn't just flood the roads, you just didn't notice them before. By the end of this book, the same thing is likely to occur with art. After being asked to pay close attention to works of art, you might start to see images of art everywhere: in cereal advertisements, on umbrellas and laptop covers. The frequency of your encounters with artworks won't have mysteriously increased; those images were always there. You only start to notice them because they align with your new observation-skills enhancement, and you've stopped blocking them out.

While confirmation bias is relatively easy to comprehend from the wide angle of wish fulfillment — she desperately wanted it to be true, so she saw things that way — it is less well known that our preferences can also change the way we see the minute, material qualities of things, especially in relation to size, length, or distance. In experiments around the world, researchers have found that our desires make things seem physically larger or closer than they really are. In the Netherlands, subjects were asked to guess the size of a chocolate muffin; dieters estimated that the muffin was much bigger than nondieters did because it was something the calorie counters were craving. In New York, subjects were shown a water bottle and asked how close it was to them; thirsty participants reported that the beverage was closer than others did.

While the tendency to see what we believe is largely unconscious, we can reduce its effect simply by knowing that expecting a certain outcome predisposes us to look harder for evidence that supports that expectation. Confirmation bias is especially prevalent with data that give us a sense of self-verification or self-enhancement. To make sure you aren't mistaking your desires for facts, ask yourself two questions: "Is this information consistent with what I initially thought?" and "Does this information benefit me personally or professionally?" Your findings may still be factual even if you answer yes to either question, but by addressing your expectations up front, you can add more transparency to your information-gathering process.

Seeing What We're Told to See

Sometimes other people can add perceptual filters to our own observations. The integrity of our search for facts can be compromised when we look for what we think we need to find. If before I had shown you the photograph, I had told you that Jane Alexander's exhibit at Saint John the Divine was being censured for obscenity, you probably would have noticed the canine-human statues' nudity much more quickly than if I hadn't. If I had told you a story about a man who smuggled illegal jewels in his underwear before I showed you the photograph of Tony Matelli's sculpture, you would have focused on his attire and any bulges therein more readily than if I hadn't. Even if we don't realize it, we often see what we're told to see.

To offset this, pay special attention to any outside suggestions or restrictions that might be placed on your observation skills. I had a student at the University of Virginia School of Nursing come up to me following a presentation and confess that she found the common medical practice of "charting by exception" unduly constraining. Meant to streamline medical record keeping and make it easier to quickly review trends, charting by exception instructs personnel to document only unusual findings or exceptions to the norm. As a result, doctors and nurses are tempted to limit what they look for, especially if the chart is already filled with WDLs ("within defined limits") from previous shift workers.

Don't go right to the chart; go right to the patient. How does the patient look? What is the patient's reaction to *you?* Apply the same principle to any form or evaluation or standardized report in any field. Be careful not to let it box you in. Your initial observation should be as unbiased and unlimited as possible. If a manager is fixated on following a form for evaluating an employee's punctuality or profitability, she might miss other telling benchmarks such as the employee's attire, demeanor, or body language. Look beyond the list. Focusing all of our attention on benchmarks and checking off boxes will inhibit a complete and accurate analysis from the start.

This is one reason why I don't allow participants in my class to read the labels next to works of art when we're in a museum and why I don't mention the name of the artist or work in this book right away: because labels shape opinions and create prejudice. If I had immediately told you that the black-and-white photograph on page 37 was called *Renshaw's Cow,* you would have missed the experience of looking at the image unfettered and the lesson you learned from the difficulty of identifying the cow. If you'd known Tony Matelli's sculpture was entitled *Sleepwalker,* you might have had trouble imagining the man as an active intruder or understanding how someone else might see him that way.

In a group of government agents I took to the Smithsonian American Art Museum, while standing beside a sculpture of smooth, round balls stacked in a pyramid and cracked half open with faces inside, one person reported seeing new life coming out of eggs, another saw death masks inside cannonballs, while someone else said the spheres reminded him of buckeye candy, spoonfuls of peanut butter half dipped in chocolate. Had they known ahead of time that the piece was titled *In Memoriam,* every observation would have been slanted in the direction of loss and war. Instead we got a more honest range of input and learned that the third observer hailed from Ohio and felt hungry. Is this sort of information relevant or useful? It certainly could be. It opened a door of personal experience in an otherwise impersonal setting, allowing this man's coworkers to view him in a way they never had before — as a small boy in his mother's midwestern kitchen.

To get a complete and accurate picture of anything, we need to aggregate all possible information and as many perspectives as possible so we can then sort through, prioritize, and make sense of it. Labels and prewritten accounts and existing information can then be included in our collection, but only after we have looked on our own first. So here's the order:

We're basically looking at things twice: first without any external influence, and then with a view informed by new data. You first experienced the photo at the beginning of this chapter for yourself, with no outside influence. Now that you have more information — that it's called *Renshaw's Cow* — go back to page 37 and look at it again. Does the name mean anything to you or sound familiar in any way? Renshaw is in fact the same Samuel Renshaw mentioned in the previous chapter, the vision expert whose system for recognizing aircraft at a glance was used to train 285,000 preflight cadets during World War II.

Renshaw used to spring the poorly developed bovine print on visitors to his Ohio State University lab and ask them to guess what it was. Nearly every adult got it wrong. One reporter investigating Renshaw's contribution to the war effort was confident it was a map of Europe, thus exposing his confirmation bias. In contrast, every small child Renshaw ever showed it to identified it immediately as a cow. Why? With fewer years of experience and a natural penchant for not listening, children don't have as many perceptive filters obstructing their view.

Not Seeing Change

The final entry in our triad of prevailing perceptual filters is change blindness, the failure to notice fluctuations in our visual field. Both the psychologist behind the "invisible gorilla" experiment and our friend the Gentleman Thief have staged dramatic, public displays of how easily we can fall prey to this perceptual malady.

Daniel Simons and his colleagues staged an experiment during which someone would approach pedestrians at a university and ask for directions. While they were talking, two men carrying an opaque door crossed in between them, at which time the person asking directions was replaced with someone new. Only 50 percent of the people giving instructions noticed the switch. Apollo Robbins appears on and consults for the National Geographic television show *Brain Games,* which demonstrated change blindness through an episode set in a Las Vegas hotel. As guests talk with a hotel employee, he drops his pen, bends down behind the desk to pick it up, and is replaced by someone new. Fewer than half of the guests recognized the appearance of a new person.

Considering that our brain encounters an estimated eleven million bits of information each second and knowing the finite nature of what we can process and pay attention to, change blindness isn't that surprising. One way of combating it is to recognize that everything changes constantly, even if those changes are too small for us to observe in real time. Think of a tree. You can't see it grow, but it still does, maybe as slowly as an inch a year. You could pass by the same tree every day and think it looks the same, but what happens if you take a closer look?

Mark Hirsch, *That Tree, March 14, 2012.*

Mark Hirsch, *That Tree, Day 320: February 6.*

Mark Hirsch, *That Tree, Day 51: May 13.*

Mark Hirsch did. He drove by the same tree in Platteville, Wisconsin, every day for nineteen years. Although a photographer by trade, he'd never considered snapping a shot of the tree until he got a new iPhone. One January evening as he passed by the tree, shrouded in blowing snow, he pulled over and decided to christen his new phone's tiny digital camera. He was so taken with the photograph of the towering bur oak rising from the edge of a cornfield that he documented the same tree every single day for a year.

Even though he lived just a mile away and had viewed it thousands of times, after taking the time to really look Hirsch discovered that the tree and its familiar valley were a "foreign land full of strange and wonderful discoveries."

When we go into any situation thinking it's going to be the same thing we've seen or done before, we're putting up our own perceptual filter that will make any change even harder to find. The resulting blinders can cause us to miss important details, to go into autopilot, or worse, to become presumptuous about our expertise, abilities, or safety. And that's when things can get dangerous. One of the detectives who attended my class admitted that he often thought, "I know exactly what this crime scene is going to look like," before he even arrived to an investigation. It's a natural inclination after years on the job, and we're all tempted to do it. But we can't. When doctors or police officers or teachers say, "I've seen this before," they're wrong. They may have seen or handled similar things or cases or people but not the new one in front of them; that one has never existed before. Think of Hirsch's tree photographs: it might be the same tree, but the weather, the humidity, and the light won't ever be exactly the same. The ladybug climbing up its bark has never gone exactly the same way with exactly the same steps at exactly the same time ever before.

No two jobs, classrooms, crime scenes, customers, students, patients, people, or problems are the same. There is no such thing as the same pneumonia, the same second-grader, or the same business deal. Every person and situation is unique. To treat them otherwise is to deceive them and ourselves.

THE ART OF ILLUSION

Illusionists and magicians take advantage of perceptual filters such as change blindness and confirmation bias to entertain us. Con artists and crooks do the same in order to fleece us. According to Apollo Robbins, the best defense against the latter is "the knowledge that you're always vulnerable to a thief with the right skills."

The same can be said of the tricks our brain can play on us; we are all vulnerable to our unconscious and ever-evolving filters. If we fail to acknowledge and examine them, they can hurt us. To arm ourselves against them, we must know them. Once we're aware of our personal perceptual lenses, we can see past them.

4

Delta Employees Do It on the Fly

The Who, What, When, and Where
of Objective Surveillance

AS IT WAS MOST Saturday afternoons, the upscale mall was packed with shoppers. Students, mothers with their babies, businesspeople, couples, people of all ages and ethnicities strolled through the gleaming, five-story retail paradise. In the center of the mall, bright, auburn escalators crisscrossed the sunny, domed atrium where customers could sample yogurt, see a movie, or seek out the latest fashions. With a supermarket, bank, casino, cinema, and more than eighty stores in the 350,000-square-foot complex, there was a lot to see and do. Perhaps too much.

On September 21, 2013, four men walked toward the main pedestrian entrance of the mall and started throwing grenades. Once inside, they were joined by an indeterminate number of others and started firing automatic weapons at anyone and everyone. For four days the small terrorist group — perhaps as few as eight — held the Westgate Mall in Nairobi, Kenya, under siege, killing 68 people, injuring 175 more, and blowing up much of the building in the process.

How did a handful of people manage to keep hundreds of others captive inside a sprawling modern mall for so long? Because of a complete observation and communication breakdown among locals, visitors, shopkeepers, shoppers, and law enforcement agents.

After receiving texts from friends trapped inside the mall, local citizens arrived to help and found no SWAT team, no command center, and no coordinated government response. The mall security force had run away. The armed guards from the in-mall bank were cowering in a corner. Hours after the attack started, there was still no perimeter set up, causing many to suspect that some of the first assailants had simply walked away.

When police and soldiers did finally show up, they couldn't communicate with one another because their radios were set on different frequencies, they didn't have night vision goggles so they were limited in what they could do after dark, and no one could find a blueprint of the building. The only map they could produce was a printout from Westgate's own website — until that crashed as the rest of the world flooded it, looking for information.

Throughout the siege, one of the biggest challenges facing victims and authorities was that it was hard to tell who the good guys were. People with guns on the scene included not just the attackers but off-duty policemen, a local gun club, a neighborhood watch, a British Special Air Service officer, and regular armed civilians. And their uniforms were as varied as their languages. Midway through the attack, the terrorists changed clothes. When word got out that their captors were sparing Muslim hostages, shoppers began sharing *their* clothes to disguise their nationality. Outside, local Kenyan police mistook one of their own undercover cops for an attacker and killed him. The deadly confusion delayed them from entering the building for days.

While the rescuers waited and argued among themselves, the terrorists restocked their weapon supply with ammunition previously stashed in the mall and spent four days hunting down, interrogating, torturing, and mutilating shoppers who had managed to find hiding places.

What if you were inside? What if your loved one was? The Westgate attack is an extreme case of public violence, but it is not as unusual as it might seem. From 2005 to 2012, there were sixteen mall shootings around the world, twelve of them in the United States; and in 2015, Somali terror group al-Shabaab urged followers to deploy an attack like the one in Kenya at the Mall of America in Minnesota.

Missing or mismanaging important data isn't just a matter of personal safety; it also affects our and our companies' professional reputations and profitability. A mishandled event from the mailroom to the boardroom can erode multiple facets of a company's value, from stock and financial to job and customer trust. In our current digital age, the news of company crises spreads internationally in an instant, and according to a global study done by Freshfields Bruckhaus Deringer, 53 percent of companies still don't see their share prices return to pre-crisis levels a year afterward.

While crises are crucibles that quickly bring organizational failings to light, they aren't the only situations where we need to accurately catalog and communicate what we see. We must be able to objectively survey the scene in which we find ourselves, sort fact from fiction, prioritize information, and disseminate it efficiently in all manner of instances — whether it's our life or our livelihood that hangs in the balance. Let's investigate how to do that step by step so we're better prepared.

FACT VERSUS FICTION

The perceptual filters we learned about in the last chapter can sometimes cause our brains to treat assumptions as facts. We'll practice sorting through the difference the same way we do throughout the book—by analyzing works of art. To start, take a look at these two paintings:

Each features a seated white woman with short hair and exposed legs looking down. Do the pictures look similar? They might because they were painted by the same artist, Edward Hopper. But be careful not to jump to any conclusions based on that information.

Take a look at these two women:

Is it the same woman? Indeed it is: Maud Dale, the wife of a wealthy patron of the arts who had two different artists paint her portrait. Is it the same artist? No. The one on the left was painted by the French artist Fernand Léger, the one on the right by American George Bellows, sixteen years earlier.

To gather data successfully from what we observe, we cannot assume anything—including who someone is—based on a feeling, a look, or what we might have experienced in the past. Likewise, moving too quickly or too early in many situations—implementing a solution to a business problem, reprimanding an employee, or walking away from a relationship—without confirmation of the facts can be detrimental and in some situations fatal.

During the Westgate Mall siege in Nairobi, captive shoppers who incorrectly guessed the identity of the armed men they encountered paid dearly. Police, helpful citizens, and the attackers were all armed and dressed similarly, since terrorists often don official-looking uniforms, and many undercover officers were wearing casual clothes. Survivors who hid inside the Nakumatt supermarket recounted how after several hours a group of men with guns arrived at their location, proclaimed they were rescuers, and urged shoppers to come out of hiding. Those who did emerge, grateful, arms raised, were shot down by the untruthful terrorists.

Just because someone says something is a fact doesn't make it so. People lie, and as we've just learned, we can't even rely on our own eyes to always tell us the truth. To make sure a fact is a fact, you need to verify it every time.

I travel around the world by myself giving lectures, and I think I'm fairly good at protecting my personal safety, but apparently I'm not good enough, according to some law enforcement professionals. Once when I arrived at the train station in Harrisburg, Pennsylvania, to speak at an FBI training event, I received a text from the driver they had arranged for me that my ride would be waiting outside: a gray Toyota pickup truck. I easily found the vehicle, happily handed my luggage to the nice driver, and got inside. When the doors were closed and we started to pull away, the driver surprised me.

"I expected more from you," he said.

More from me? For what?

"You didn't ask me for identification," he continued. "I could have been anyone."

"But I got a text about the make and model of your car," I protested weakly.

"This unmarked gray truck?" he said. "How many other gray trucks were parked out there at the train station?"

I didn't know. "But you texted me," I began again.

"How do you know it was me?" he asked. "Your phone number is easier to find than you think. If someone wanted to kidnap you, you sure made it easy for them."

He was right, of course, and I learned my lesson. We need to be more watchful. We can't let our guard down, because criminals — or our competitors — won't.

We also must remember that appearances can be deceiving. Just because a man shows an outstretched hand and a ready smile doesn't make him a good guy, or the guy you were supposed to meet. Working with behavior-detection officers at the Transportation Security Administration (TSA), I've learned that a well-dressed man at the airport terminal may not be wealthy; he may instead be a drug smuggler disguised to dispel assumptions based on appearances. Likewise, the modestly dressed old woman may have tremendous wealth. The facts of an elderly woman's clothing might include "threadbare sweater, scuffed canvas shoes, small gold ring on left ring finger" but not "middle-class" or even "widow." The gold ring does not automatically indicate that its wearer is married.

JUST THE FACTS (MA'AM)

To find only the proven in the haystacks of information that often lie before us, we must set as our first goal in assessing a new scene or environment the collection of *all* the facts. By definition, a fact is "a truth known by actual experience or observation." Always use an open mind, and look past the obvious, but focus only on what you can observe to be true, not what you assume to be.

When looking at anything — a painting, a patient's room, our peers at a party, a public square, or a line of people at the airport —

we must study it using the same basic model of information gathering employed by journalists, law enforcement agents, and scientific researchers: who, what, when, and where. Who is involved in this scene? What happened? When did it happen? And where did the action take place? (The why will come later, in chapter 7, when we look at content.)

Let's begin by studying the Edward Hopper painting back on page 60 and seeing how many facts we can gather. Remember, we are using the piece not as an objet d'art but rather as a collection of data points. You may find the level of analysis of this Hopper painting on the following pages ridiculously detailed, but that's the point. Don't skim over any of it. Take your time and really absorb the process.

WHO?

Who is the subject of this scene? A lone woman. Are you sure? Look again. Is there anyone else in the room? In the reflection of the window? No, she appears to be alone.

What else do we know about the person? Is she married or single? We can't tell. Do we know her name? No. How can we definitively describe her? She appears to be white and in her twenties or thirties, although not too young to be alone. She doesn't have any wrinkles on her face, so that would put her age anywhere from late teens to early forties. We don't have an actual age as a fact, but we have eliminated other possibilities: she is not ten, nor is she sixty.

How about her height? Can you tell how tall she is? Yes, since according to the proportions in the room, she is sitting at what appears to be a regular-size table on a regular-size chair. We could do some calculations with a stand-in person seated at a standard-size table or even measure our woman in relation to the door handles on the left and come up with a fairly close approximation of her height.

What about her weight? She is wearing a bulky coat that hides her midsection, but we can see a slender neck, thin fingers, slim legs, and a rather flat chest. We can conclude that she is of average weight or slightly under but not overweight.

What is she wearing? A coat and a hat. Be more specific. If you had to describe her to someone else, differentiate her from another woman in a coat and hat, how would you do it? She's wearing a long-sleeved green coat trimmed with a brown fur collar and cuffs. The coat reaches her knees when she's sitting, which means that it's longer when she's standing up.

What else can we observe about her attire? She's wearing a yellow hat with a tiny cluster of artificial cherries on the right. The hat has a drooping brim that shadows her face. Knowing what kind of hat she chose to put on can tell us a lot about her. So what kind is it? Unless you're a milliner, which I'm not, we're going to have to look this one up. We can easily find out by researching it on the Internet, but we'll need a good, factual description of it to get good results. When I searched Google for "women's hats" I got sixty-nine million results. When I searched for "women's hat tight fitting turned down brim," the results narrowed to three million, and the first three sites listed all gave me the answer right away: it's a cloche. After another quick search I discovered that the cloche is a fitted, bell-shaped hat invented in 1908 that was very popular in the 1920s.

We cannot see her shoes, but did you notice she's only wearing one glove? Where's the other one? We can't see it. At this point, you might be saying, "So what? Who cares?" But the secrets of life are often revealed through small details. Small details can solve crimes. Small details can lead to significant diagnoses. Small details reveal big things.

That she's only wearing one glove, on her left hand, is important to note. It might be the most important fact, especially if the right-hand glove turns up somewhere. The discovery of a single glove at the crime scene became the crux of the O. J. Simpson murder trial.

That our subject is wearing only one glove might indicate her state of mind. Is she distracted? In a hurry? That she's sitting with a cup and saucer in front of an empty plate would suggest that she's been sitting at this table for some time. Is she wearing the glove to conceal something on her left hand? A deformity? A stain? A wedding ring? We don't have the answers to those questions, but cataloging the facts will get us to ask the right questions.

What about jewelry? Is that a red earring on her left ear, or a curl of her hair? It looks like it could be an earring, but if we study where her ear should be in relation to the bottom of her nose, the red circle proves to be too high for an earring.

There is a glint on her right ring finger that could be a ring, or perhaps her fourth and fifth fingers are just slightly apart, allowing the white table to peek through. A closer examination of the placement of her hand reveals that if her fingers were separated, the dark brown cuff of her coat, and not the tabletop, would show through at that particular spot.

We can't tell if she's wearing any bracelets, but she doesn't appear to be wearing a necklace.

What about her body language? Her lips are pursed, and she's not engaged with anyone. She's still wearing her coat. And she's looking down into the cup she holds in her right, ungloved hand.

What's in the cup? Coffee? How can you be sure? The presence of a cup instead of a glass suggests a hot drink, not cold. The most likely choices of hot drink are coffee, tea, and hot chocolate. There's no discernible whipped topping or brown residue that typically comes from drinking hot chocolate. There's no tea bag or spoon that would typically accompany hot tea. So coffee is a good guess but not a fact.

Employing a similar investigative method of objectively assessing a person's attire, behavior, and interactions with objects can help us uncover the identity or intentions of unknown people in any situation, from a traveler in the airport who might be a potential terrorist to a driver waiting curbside who might be a potential kidnapper. Noting whether people's shoes matched their official uniforms, what kind of guns they were carrying, and how they walked might have told those hidden inside the Kenyan mall volumes about who might rescue them and who might murder them.

WHAT?

The second question in our investigative model is *what* happened or what's happening. What is the main action? In the Hopper painting there's not much action: a single woman sitting at a table holding a cup. There's no one else in the picture, or even a hint of another person. The woman is looking down, her mouth closed. There is an empty plate in front of her, aside from the cup and saucer, that indicates she's been at the table long enough to finish eating something.

Such simplicity is not always the case, however. Many paintings, like many scenes in life, are complex. Let's take a closer look at a painting we passed by in chapter 1 on page 10. What's going on here?

Jan Steen, *As the Old Sing, So Pipe the Young*, 1668–1670.

Three women and a bearded man are seated around a small food-laden table; one of the women holds a paper, one holds a baby, and the other a drinking glass in her outstretched hand. A man with long hair stands over the table pouring liquid into the seated woman's glass. Another man, possibly seated, possibly just short in stature, is to his immediate left holding a long pipe to a young boy's mouth. Another boy looks on. Behind him, against the wall, a man holding an instrument resembling a bagpipe, reed in his mouth, looks directly at the viewer — the only person in the painting to do so. The group is surrounded by animals. A tropical bird with long tail feathers, possibly a parrot, gazes down at them from a tall perch in the corner of the room next to two smaller birds in a cage mounted high on the wall. A spotted dog, nose and tail up, looks out of the frame at something we cannot see.

What is the group doing? We cannot conclude definitely, but we can gather facts that will help eliminate incorrect assumptions. Are they eating dinner? Not likely, since the table they sit around is small and doesn't contain place settings. Most people in the painting are smiling, some have no expression, and the piper might be pensive, but there seems to be an absence of tension or conflict. Are those in the group related to one another? We have no facts that prove either for or against, so we cannot assume. They could be neighbors or guests at an inn.

We might not have a full picture of what is going on, but we have discovered many facts that can point us toward what is and is not happening. The group has food and drink, music and companionship. They are fully dressed and seated on and around carved furniture. Children are present. The animals pictured are calm. From this we can tell what is not happening. There is not a storm raging outside. The people are not starving. Aside from the possibly pensive pipe player, the body language of the group is relaxed and suggests they all know one another.

Taking the time to analyze what is happening matters. In the firestorm of the Nairobi mall, many people failed to realize what was going on in their immediate surroundings, and suffered for it. Some shoppers first thought the gunshots were a gas heater exploding or a bank robbery. Those who fled without first assessing what was happening ran right into the gunmen's line of fire. Those who waited, evaluated, and figured out that it was a terrorist attack found safe hiding places. Even though it may seem obvious and not worth investigating, especially when things are calm, resist the urge to rush past the *what,* or you'll leave behind valuable facts you might not otherwise have recovered.

WHEN?

Now let's investigate *when* the action is taking place. What facts can we find about when this scene in the Hopper painting back on page 63 occurred?

What time of year is it? The woman's fur-trimmed clothes would usually put us in late autumn or winter, yet her yellow, cherry-adorned hat doesn't seem to match those seasons. Could it be early spring and unseasonably cold? In either case, we might eliminate the dead of winter, as her hat seems a bit flimsy, and the height of summer, as her coat seems too substantial for warm weather.

What time of day is it? It is after dark, but when? Since days are shorter in the early spring and late fall, it could be fully dark by 5 p.m. in many places, and stay dark until 7 a.m., so we have a fourteen-hour window. We can shorten that time span, though, by noting that the scene outside the window lacks any artificial light as well. The bright, clean interior suggests that the location might not be in a dicey or isolated part of town, so there should be other activity outside the window: streetlights or car headlights. That there isn't suggests either an odd, late hour, when most people are not out and about, or simply an aesthetic choice to create a mood of isolation and solitude. Either should be taken into account as observations.

What about the year or time period? Researching the woman's hat put us in the 1920s. Further research on the evolution of the cloche shows that by 1928 the brims were either gone or upturned, so we are most likely before that year, since our subject's hat has a downturned brim.

Finally, we need to assess *where*. Where is the scene from the Hopper painting taking place? Without a logo on the window or a written word anywhere, we must do a little more in the way of observation.

Based on the walls, doors, windows, and electric lights, we can see that the scene is indoors. The place is clean, well kept, and well lit. The golden radiator and door handles don't show any signs of scuff or wear.

We can see one white-topped, round table with two dark brown chairs. In the lower right corner is the back of another chair that suggests there is at least one more set of table and chairs. Did you miss that chair corner? Is it important?

Noting the facts of your location — what's around you or the subject of any scene you are studying — can be critical or even life-saving if something unexpected happens. Knowing where the emergency exits are in a darkened theater, which are the exit rows on a plane, or where the storm shelter or strongest doorway is in the event of a natural disaster can make all the difference. Situational awareness is imperative for decision making in many situations from air traffic control and emergency services to driving a car or maneuvering a bicycle along a busy street.

As I've mentioned, I travel frequently for my job and often find myself alone in hotel rooms — a possibly unsafe situation for anyone, since hotels can be cavernous, convoluted spaces with a crowded, transient clientele conditioned to ignore the noises in adjoining rooms. Therefore, I will not take a room on the first floor, as those are too easily accessed from the outside. In case there is an unexpected emergency, I take time to locate the nearest elevator and stairs. Carefully noting where I am, who is around me, and the nearest means of egress is critical for my personal safety, and an assessment I make before I enter an elevator or a stairwell or get on a subway or bus.

Westgate Mall survivor Elaine Dang did the same thing, and it saved her life. The twenty-six-year-old from San Diego who works in Kenya was attending a children's cooking competition when the first grenades exploded. She told CNN that one of the contest presenters told everyone to run to the parking lot. She followed at first but then changed her mind, deciding that the crowd was vulnerable. She instead turned back to the competition area knowing there was a large, silver kitchen counter she could hide behind. She did, and she lived. Many others ran blindly toward the parking lot and did not.

Let's go back and look more closely at the location in the Hopper painting to see what else we can discover. On the table is an empty plate, and the woman holds a cup that has its own saucer. What kind of place would serve a hot drink and food, and have multiple tables and chairs? A restaurant, diner, or coffee shop? There is also nothing else on the table that you would typically see in a restaurant or diner; there are no napkins, no condiments, no salt and pepper, no menu. We cannot see a hostess stand or welcome sign or cashier.

What can we see? On the windowsill behind the woman is another nod to food: a bowl of shiny red, orange, and yellow fruit. On the right side we can see the top of a rail for a staircase that leads down. The front of the establishment is dominated by a large window. All we can see in it is two rows of electric lights stretching back into the building.

So what location in the mid-1920s would be clean, well kept, offer food and drink, be open at night, and be safe for a woman by herself? With that information, you could search the Internet and find the answer: an Automat. Automats were "restaurants" without waiters. Self-service vending machines lined the walls; patrons could choose whatever food they wanted for a combination of nickels. Horn & Hardart opened the first Automat in 1902; at one point it was the world's largest restaurant chain, serving 800,000 people a day. Automats typically had round tables with white Carrara glass tops, as we see in the Hopper painting. And they were well known for the best coffee in town.

Since we're using works of art to hone our observational skills, knowing anything about the background of this painting, the style in which it was painted, or the painter is neither essential nor required. However, since we do have some information about the painting, we can use it to confirm our success or failure as observers.

The title of this piece is *Automat,* and it was first exhibited in 1927. The woman in the painting is modeled after Hopper's wife when she was younger, but we do not know who she is meant to be, where she came from or is going, or how she feels. We will never have all of the answers — not many people do — but the more observant we can be, the more facts we can collect, catalog, and process, the more we will know.

If more people in the Kenyan Westgate Mall had observed and organized what facts they knew and didn't know, more of them might have been saved. For instance, people hiding in the back room of the mobile phone store Safaricom heard noises in the air vents and considered climbing into them to escape when they realized they didn't know if the noises were from other hostages or from wandering terrorists. Without the facts, they stayed put, and lived.

When an injured Kenyan was being evacuated with other shoppers, someone noticed a machine gun magazine falling out of his pocket. If they hadn't, would this terrorist have gone free? Instead, he was detained.

How many details weren't noticed or reported by anyone for the months leading up to the attack? The BBC reported that the terrorists had been renting a store inside the Westgate Mall for months, smuggling and storing a massive stockpile of weapons. How did their activities and the transfer of arms go unnoticed? The same way we all miss pertinent facts when we're busy or distracted or just not looking. A week after the Kenyan mall attack, riders on a crowded San Francisco commuter train failed to see Nikhom Thephakaysone raise a .45-caliber pistol several times, wipe his nose with it, and aim it at the young student across the aisle from him. According to the *San*

Francisco Chronicle, dozens of passengers were standing and sitting just a few feet away, "their eyes focused on smartphones and tablets," and didn't lift their eyes until twenty-year-old Justin Valdez was shot dead.

Good objective observation skills aren't necessary only in life-threatening instances; they're imperative for so many facets of our personal and professional lives. I regularly teach people who interact with children as part of their jobs — medical personnel, educators, family service investigators — who remind me of the gravity of reporting objectively. One woman, a caseworker from Maryland, showed me the importance of bruises.

There is a significant difference between reporting that a child is "covered in bruises" and "has three dime-size, round, yellow and purple bruises just under the kneecap, one on the left leg and two on the right." The latter could probably be said for the majority of active kids because of how often they bang their shins. Other places, such as the face, head, neck, and buttocks, are not normal bruising sites. The color and shape of bruises can be just as telling as their location. Round bruises typically result from bumping into something. Long, rectangular, or hand-shaped bruises do not. Bruises may have red in them until they are fully healed, but yellow bruises typically indicate that at least eighteen hours have passed since the initial impact. And since bruises fade, it's crucial to describe them in clear, objective detail as soon as you observe them.

The importance of objective description applies equally to seemingly inconsequential things in life such as a cappuccino order. Getting it right requires an accurate and descriptive order that starts with the customer, continues with the cashier, and ends with the barista. Any laziness in observation or communication can cost time, money, and frustration for all parties. Is a botched cup of coffee really a big deal? It is if you can't face the day without your morning cup, or if you're in the business of selling coffee. Small errors add up. If just one incorrectly prepared drink a day is thrown away in each of its twenty thousand stores, Starbucks loses about $8.5 million a year; two faulty orders doubles that to over $17 million — all preventable loss.

Occasionally a skeptical participant in my class will protest that cataloging facts in a painting is nothing like her daily job. I disagree. Almost every job, especially those on the "front lines" of a business, such as doormen, greeters, receptionists, and executive assistants, requires objective surveillance. We're just not always aware of how much we or those around us are doing it. Take a flight attendant. Not only are flight attendants ambassadors for the airline, hosts and waiters, safety experts, administrative and inventory specialists, schedulers, porters, and sometime concierges, they are also emergency services coordinators and, in essence, first responders. Even during the seemingly mundane ritual of greeting and seating passengers, the cabin crew are also on the lookout for what the International Civil Aviation Organization calls ABPs, or "able-bodied passengers"— people they can count on to assist in an emergency. There must be three ABPs per exit. The size and shape, age, and seat location of ABPs changes on every flight. There is no sign-up list or predetermined ABP indicator. As new passengers board, the flight attendants must quickly find them through astute and discreet assessment; most ABPs don't even know they've been mentally marked.

An ABP must be over fifteen years of age; have sufficient mobility, strength, and dexterity in both arms, hands, and legs; be able to read, understand, and communicate in English; not require a seat belt extension; and not be traveling with anyone else, since people are more likely to help their family members before assisting strangers. Flight attendants are trained to not only spot ABPs with the correct physical, cognitive, and mental abilities, they need to identify passengers who can understand and take direction while remaining calm under pressure.

All of this is determined through objective observation. Serving thousands of people a year, flight attendants know better than most that you can't assume anything from appearance. Just because someone looks a certain way doesn't mean he doesn't speak English or have a strong stomach or isn't related to the pretty girl he's splitting his snack with. The flight attendants must reach their conclusions by looking, listening, and piecing together the clues they're presented. The six-foot-plus guy who asked the flight attendant about turbulence? He's out. The woman who shuffles in with a cane? No. The gentleman who graciously helps the person in front of him store her bag overhead? A good candidate.

When we are fact gathering, we must be careful that our observations are objective, though, and not subjective. The distinction can be small, but it's critically important; it's literally the difference between fact and fiction. An objective observation is based on empirical or mathematical facts. A subjective observation is based on assumptions, opinions, feelings, or values. *The bruise is nasty* is subjective; *the bruise is round, approximately one inch in diameter, and purple* is objective.

HOW TO AVOID THE SUBJECTIVE

One way to ensure that our observations remain objective is to quantify them by counting, estimating, or using measuring tools. "Small" might mean different things to different people: a ladybug is small compared with a dog, but a dog is small compared with an elephant. Adding numbers will help remove interpretation and doubt. "Small" is subjective; "one inch across" is not. Measure whenever you can, estimate when you can't, but always use numerical values. Instead of saying there are "many" lights on the ceiling above the woman in Edward Hopper's *Automat,* note that there are "two rows of seven lights." Rather than stating that "there are a few chairs" in the scene, be specific: "there are three dark, wooden, armless chairs visible."

Even phenomena that can't be counted or measured can be quantified. Instead of saying that the dog is "smelly," quantify it: "On a scale of one to five, five being the worst, the smell emanating from the dog was a four."

Finally, replace descriptive adjectives with comparative nouns. "Smelly" is subjective. So is "smells bad." What smells bad to some — cut grass, gasoline — smells wonderful to others. Instead, find a concrete noun to compare with the smell you're describing: "The dog smelled like dead fish."

Striving for the objective doesn't end with observation, however; we must ensure that when we draw conclusions, we are also using only facts, not opinions. Suppose you hadn't seen the Hopper painting at all but were presented with two different summaries of it. Which one is objective and which one is subjective?

- A forlorn woman sits alone in a coffee shop at a round, white, marble table.
- A woman with a closed mouth and downcast eyes holds a cup and saucer while sitting alone at a round, white-topped table.

Both describe the scene, both convey that the woman is not dancing and laughing but sitting quietly, looking down. However, the first sentence reaches the conclusion that the woman is forlorn, an adjective that means lonely or sad. This is a subjective interpretation of the woman's expression, not a statement of fact. The second sentence describes the woman's face and countenance based on objective facts —she's looking down, her mouth is closed—without adding any assumptions about her mood.

The first sentence also concludes that the woman is sitting in a coffee shop. The second instead factually states that the woman is holding a cup, without guessing what type of place she is in or what —if anything—is in her cup. What's the big deal with "coffee shop" versus "holds a cup and saucer"? A lot. Where she is hasn't been proven or disproven. To state something as important as location as a fact, even casually, especially to someone unfamiliar with the scene or someone down the chain of information, can lead to more untrue assumptions that turn into "facts."

For instance, location was at the crux of the argument against Matelli's *Sleepwalker* statue, as some of the protesters asserted that by installing it at an all-women's college the school's administration was neglecting to provide a "safe" environment for its students—a serious allegation. The debate was not over "a schlumpy guy in underpants," as a Wellesley College English professor described him, but over where he was: a school with an all-female student body. By subjectively reporting the statue as being in a "prominent" place on campus, the *Boston Globe* ignited a controversy rather than objective examination. "Prominent" is subjective; it is an opinion of importance.

Yet citing that as the statue's location without any factual or logistical information fanned the flames of reports that students were "freaked out" by it or could not avoid it.

If you were a reporter, a parent of a Wellesley student, or a member of the board of trustees, it would be in your best interest to gather all of the facts regarding the statue's placement. And a "prominent" place is not a complete, factual location assessment. The statue was not placed thoughtlessly; it was set right across from the on-campus Davis Museum, specifically situated so that it could be seen from the windows on the first and fifth floor that contained *the rest of Matelli's exhibit,* which included other realistic human sculptures. As Davis Museum director Lisa Fischman explained, *Sleepwalker* was put there to "connect the exhibition — within the museum — to the campus world beyond"; she saw it as "art escaping the museum." School officials also noted that the work was not put in an area that might invade personal privacy such as outside a dormitory; indeed, it was purposefully put on a grass enclosure that contained no sidewalks so students would not be forced to interact with it.

Unearthing all objective observations about the location of *Sleepwalker* is critical to determining whether Wellesley meant to confront or assault its students with art. Similarly, we have a responsibility to glean as many objective observations as possible — not stopping at a first look, cursory glance, or checked-off box — so that we are sure conclusions reached are based on facts and not assumptions.

THE RISK OF ASSUMPTIONS

While researching this book, I was reading with my son and came across a wonderful description of the downsides of assumptions in *The Austere Academy* by Lemony Snicket:

> Assumptions are dangerous things to make, and like all dangerous things to make — bombs, for instance, or strawberry shortcake — if you make even the tiniest mistake you can find yourself in terrible trouble. Making assumptions simply means believing

things are a certain way with little or no evidence that shows you are correct, and you can see at once how this can lead to terrible trouble. For instance, one morning you might wake up and make the assumption that your bed was in the same place that it always was, even though you would have no real evidence that this was so. But when you got out of your bed, you might discover that it had floated out to sea, and now you would be in terrible trouble all because of the incorrect assumption that you'd made. You can see that it is better not to make too many assumptions, particularly in the morning.

Even subtle differences between subjective and objective conclusions can be crucial. In describing the Hopper painting, while "a round, white, marble table" and "a round, white-topped table" are just one word off, it's an important word. That the table is made of marble has not been proven; it's not a fact. It could just as easily be painted wood or Carrara glass; popular craftsman Oscar Bach made tabletops out of white onyx in the 1920s. The first description also states that the table is "white" and "marble" but doesn't signify how much or where. There is a marked difference between a table that is all white and one that is just white-topped, as well as one that is made entirely out of marble or just topped with it.

Does it matter what a table is made of? It could matter a great deal. Noticing the composition of an object saved the life of Goran Tomasevic and the policemen he followed into the Westgate Mall in Nairobi. The chief photographer for Reuters in East Africa, Tomasevic was hiding behind a large column with the police during a gun battle with the terrorists. When he noticed that the pillar wasn't attached to the building and knocked on it, he discovered that it was hollow. He told his companions to knock on it as well, and they did, answering, "So what?" Tomasevic explained that the thin material wouldn't stop bullets or offer the protection they were seeking. They quickly moved to a better-fortified location and lived.

Assumptions can be harmful whether they are formed about subjective things or formed from facts. We already mentioned how an elderly woman in line at the airport wearing a ring on the fourth finger of her left hand is not necessarily married or engaged or widowed. She might have been single her entire life. Turn back to the painting on page 13 of the white woman, feather on her head, holding a painting of someone's naked backside. We noted in chapter 1 that she was wearing a ring, and it's still true, visible on the fourth finger of her left hand. To assume that this means she is either married or engaged or widowed would not necessarily be correct. She is, in fact, a prostitute. Similarly, we cannot assume the people around the table in the painting on page 69 are related, or that the woman in Hopper's *Automat* is waiting for someone.

Subjective inferences are not always easy to spot or dismiss, since they are informed by observations and grounded in perceptions. Even the best organizations fail to weed out assumptions.

In 2005 the Iraq Intelligence Commission, formed to determine how the American intelligence community had misjudged Iraq's weapons of mass destruction (WMD) program, presented a 601-page report on its findings to the president of the United States. The commission concluded, "Its principal causes were the Intelligence Community's inability to collect good information about Iraq's WMD programs, serious errors in analyzing what information it could gather, and a failure to make clear just how much of its analysis was based on assumptions, rather than good evidence." It went on to state that "analysts were too wedded to their assumptions" and "much of their conclusions rested on inferences and assumptions."

How many other public or private companies could withstand the same kind of scrutiny brought by an outside investigation with access to all of its communications? Could yours? We all make assumptions more often than we think, and like a snowball, even the smallest ones get bigger as they go downhill.

The earlier the assumption is made, the more dangerous it is because it skews subsequent observations. Accuracy in the first stages of the observation process is critical. If you're the eyewitness or the first person to get the news or the one filing the initial report, you have a heightened responsibility to be objective and detailed in your observations.

Now that we have a firm grasp of the building blocks of effective observation—the who, what, when, and where—we're ready to look beyond what lies in plain sight in search of the subtleties that can reveal key information.

5

What's Hiding in Plain Sight?

Seeing the Forest and the Trees

John Singleton Copley, *Mrs. John Winthrop*, 1773.

MEET *MRS. JOHN WINTHROP*. You can visit her "in person" at the Metropolitan Museum of Art in New York City. Mrs. Winthrop's portrait was painted by John Singleton Copley in 1773 when she was married to her second husband, a professor at Harvard. The painting is notable for its realism and a perfect opportunity to practice objective surveillance. Take a few minutes to observe as much as you can about the who, what, where, and when of this scene.

Did you note the vibrant blue of her dress; the double white lace cuffs; the blue, black, and white striped bow on her chest; the red, black, and white striped bow on her cap; her brown hair with slight widow's peak; the six strands of pearls wound around her neck; her multiple chins and her dimples; the red upholstery of the chair; her short, clean fingernails; the garnet and diamond ring on her left ring finger; and the nectarines she holds in her hands, one still attached to its branch?

Although this painting depicts a lone figure against a plain, dark backdrop, similar to the scene out the window in Hopper's *Automat*, the detail here is exquisite, and it gives the attentive observer much more information about its subject than Hopper does. We can see varying textures in her bodice, the folds of skin at her wrist, and many glorious wrinkles on her face.

When cataloging what they see, many people miss one feature that is among the most compelling attributes of the painting: the mahogany table at which she is sitting. Did you see it at all? If you did, did you really study it? This prop is actually the painting's tour de force and a testament to the artist's technical skill. In it, the artist has painted a perfect reflection of Mrs. Winthrop's skin, her fingers, the intricate lace patterns of her sleeves, even traces of the nectarine.

The table dominates almost the bottom third of the painting. It seems impossible that we could miss something so large, yet most of us do. In countless situations big and small, we overlook the "mahogany table," and in doing so miss a crucial piece of information that is hiding in plain sight. The phenomenon is so common it has its own idiom — "If it were a snake, it would have bitten you" — and has been facetiously referred to as "refrigerator blindness" by the *Canadian Medical Association Journal* for where it frequently occurs. (I can't count the number of times I've been looking right at the mayonnaise jar but didn't see it.)

A couple of years ago I had to take my sister to the hospital for pain in her back. In the cubicle next to us lay a ninety-year-old man attached to a heart machine and an oxygen mask. Near him sat his wife; she and I started chatting as my sister faded into Valium happiness.

As we talked, two emergency room residents who looked to be in their mid-thirties came in and wheeled a very fancy machine up to the elderly man. Without saying a word or acknowledging our presence, they stuck patches on his chest, peered at images on the screen, and then talked very loudly to each other: "I wonder what caused this?" "I wonder how long the lungs have been functioning at this level." "I would love to know the pulmonary history on this one."

The patient's wife politely interrupted them and said, "I can answer all of your questions."

"Who are you?" they asked, startled, as if they'd just noticed her.

She answered, "I am his wife. This is our sixth time in the ER in as many months, and I can give you the whole history of his condition."

One of the residents replied, "Oh, I didn't see you when we came in. Tell us what you know." The residents were so fixated on their machinery that they missed the patient's entire case history, which sat before them — in plain sight.

When we miss things in plain sight — a patient's wife, a mahogany table, a mayonnaise jar — it isn't always as harmless as overlooking a condiment or a piece of furniture. In many instances, the thing we miss is obscuring other, key information we need to solve a problem, to make a diagnosis, or to crack a case.

On October 30, 2007, Linda Stein, a famous rock music manager and a real estate broker to the stars who counted Sting, Billy Joel, and Andy Warhol as longtime clients and friends, was found dead inside her Manhattan penthouse. The discovery rocked New York City not just because Stein's death was ruled a homicide but because she lived in one of the city's most secure buildings.

Stein's eighteenth-floor apartment was accessible only by a private elevator hand-operated by an attendant, and every visitor had to be checked in and announced at a front desk where surveillance cameras recorded every arrival and departure. A stranger would not have had access to Stein in her own home.

Detectives found no sign of a break-in, and other than the pool of blood in which her body lay facedown, Stein's apartment was clean. An autopsy determined that she had been bludgeoned between twenty-four and eighty times with a heavy stick, but no weapon was found at the scene. Stein hadn't been molested, no significant property had been stolen, and she hadn't sustained injuries consistent with a struggle. It appeared that Stein was killed by someone she knew, but who?

Records revealed that Stein had never left her building on the day she was murdered and had had just one visitor before her daughter discovered her body late that evening: her personal assistant, Natavia Lowery. Lowery had entered the building at 11:56 a.m. with only an envelope in her left hand, and had exited at 1:19 p.m. with a large red shopping bag hooked over her left elbow and an oversize green purse — Stein's — slung over her left shoulder. Lowery admitted that she left with Stein's wallet and cell phone, and after leaving the building alone, she answered Stein's phone and told Stein's ex-husband that her boss was "out running" in Central Park — odd, since Stein was suffering from breast cancer and a brain tumor that left her so weak she couldn't lift her hair dryer on her own. Detectives discovered that Lowery had been stealing from her employer and had a criminal past. But stealing and lying don't automatically make someone a murderer. Law enforcement needed something to confirm their suspicions, a fact that would prove Lowery's guilt beyond any doubt.

Investigators thought the answer could be found in the raw surveillance footage of Lowery arriving at and leaving Stein's building, but after hours of studying it frame by frame, they found nothing out of the ordinary. Yes, Lowery left with a bag and Stein's personal effects, but personal assistants often do in the course of running errands and caring for their employer's needs. What was inside the bags: dirty laundry or a bloody weapon? No one could see. Lowery's exit was quick but unremarkable.

Late in the investigation, after the videotape had been seen countless times by those involved in the case, someone made the connection that Lowery's pants had been turned inside out, thus no blood was evident when she exited the building. It seemed impossible, since so many people had examined the tape thoroughly, that they could have all missed such a crucial detail. Yet there it was: Lowery's pants were totally different when she walked into the building than when she walked out. And the change wasn't so subtle: Lowery was wearing cargo pants. The baggy pocket on her left thigh, visible when the pants were worn correctly, was missing on her exit. In its place darkly stitched seams stretched vertically along both legs.

It was possibly the break they'd been looking for. Lowery could lie about the contents of the bags she was carrying that were never recovered, but the fact remained: she had consciously turned her pants inside out when she left Linda Stein. There was no common or casual reason for it. Detectives surmised that Lowery had done it to hide bloodstains.

Stills from the video camera proving Lowery had turned her pants inside out were submitted during the trial as crucial evidence. The jury was convinced. Juror Kelly Newton said, "The pants were huge. It solidified the arguments." Lowery was convicted and sentenced to twenty-seven years to life in prison.

How could investigators initially miss this essential detail? The same way we miss the mahogany table and the mayonnaise: because we're wired to.

BIOLOGICALLY "BLIND"

While the names psychologists have for our ability to not see something we are looking at are many — inattentional blindness, attentional blindness, perceptual blindness, familiarity blindness, change blindness, et cetera — they share a commonality: blindness. For no physiological reason, sometimes we fail to see something that's in our direct line of sight. We overlook things when they are unexpected or too familiar, when they blend in, and when they are too aberrant or abhorrent to imagine. However, our cognitive blind spots are not breakdowns in our visual processing system but rather a critical adaptive skill and a testament to our brain's remarkable efficiency.

While the world is filled with limitless information and stimulation, our brain cannot, and should not, process everything we see. If it did, we would be overwhelmed with data. Imagine standing in Times Square. If our eyes are wide open, they are encountering thousands of physical things all at once—dozens of flashing billboards, garishly lit buildings, flagpoles, taxis, shops, street performers, and some of the 330,000 people who pass through the same spot daily—but we do not "see" it all. Our brain automatically filters our surroundings and allows only a small percentage of information to pass through to protect us from an information overload that might otherwise paralyze us.

Consider what the modern brain manages as we walk down a street talking on the phone. Our body is navigating the pavement and potential obstacles; we are headed in a certain direction; we are noticing people and landmarks as we pass them, possibly interacting with them or making a mental note of something; we are carrying on a conversation with the person on the other end of the phone, talking, listening, responding; and we do it all effortlessly. We are only able because our brain has filtered out the unnecessary: the ants on the sidewalk, the breeze in the branches, the crumbs on the mustache of the man who just passed us. If we paid attention to every piece of information in our path, we wouldn't get far past our front door.

Dr. Barbara Tversky, professor of psychology and education at Columbia University and professor emerita at Stanford University, explains, "The world is terribly confusing; there's too much happening at the same time—visually, auditorily, everything—and the way we cope is by categorizing. We process the minimum we need in order to behave properly."

The process of sorting out the pertinent or important from the inordinate amount of information received by our senses is quick, involuntary, and, scientists believe, somewhat unconscious. The brain scans information received from our environment until something captures its attention; only then is it uploaded into our consciousness. Since our capacity for attention is finite, only a relatively small amount of input is "realized." Information that is not categorized passes through the brain unassimilated; it exists, but we don't perceive it. Of course our failure to register something doesn't mean it doesn't exist. The cowboy playing a guitar in his underwear in Times Square is there whether we "saw" him or not, just as the elderly patient's wife was in the room and Natavia Lowery's pants were inside out whether anyone saw them or not.

FILLING IN THE _____

This innate ability to filter also allows us to focus on the finite in the midst of multiple sensory inputs. Without it, we might not have thrived as a species. If a prehistoric hunter had to hide in tall grass waiting for a gazelle to wander by and he was fixated on every swaying blade in direct view, dinner might never be served. Being able to hone in on just a select amount of information in our chaotic world is why we can carry on a conversation in a crowded restaurant, drive a car while helping our children recite their multiplication facts, or play a sport in front of a screaming crowd. In the course of our daily lives we routinely perceive only what's critical to our current situation, and we do it so expeditiously that we hardly notice the process.

"We need to quickly get to abstractions," Tversky says, "to know what's happening, to recognize the setting, major objects, actions, and activities of what we are seeing in order to act ourselves." To do that, our brains "form fast, general categorizations of our surroundings."

This instant organization of data, even with what we now know is incomplete information, is only possible because our brains are built to automatically fill in gaps for us. That we cna stlil reda wrods wtih jumbeld lettres and whn vwls r mssng without missing a beat proves this. This skill accounts for more than just why texting has replaced talking as the most common form of daily communication, though; historically, it has contributed to our survival.

Our friend the hunter might be ignoring the grass and focusing on a small gazelle that just wandered into his line of sight, but that doesn't mean his brain wouldn't receive and perceive a heavy rustling sound nearby. The sound alone could cause him to run without thinking, without confirming the presence of a predator, and save his life. The knowledge that rustling might mean a lion is filled in automatically by the brain, which doesn't wait for permission before sending flight instructions.

In terms of self-preservation, our brain's ability to bridge the gaps is quite useful, but in the modern world it can be a detriment when we're not facing a life-or-death decision but just trying to employ first-class observation and communication skills. For instance, read the following sentence just once, counting all of the *F*s as you go:

ARTIST FABIO FABBI PAINTED DO-
ZENS OF DEPICTIONS OF ORIENTAL
LIFE ALTHOUGH HE WAS OF ITA-
LIAN HERITAGE HIMSELF.

How many did you get? Four? Six? There are seven *F*s in the sentence.

While some of us might have gotten it correct, the majority of us would not, since our quick-thinking brains filled in a *V* for the *F* in words like *of*, because that's the sound the letter is making.

A similar version of this exercise (in which I'll admit I initially saw two fewer letters than were there) made the rounds online several years ago labeled as either a "genius test" or an early Alzheimer's indicator. It's a far cry from either, but it is a good example of how our brains can trip us up even when we know what we're looking for and we're not hampered by any distractions. No matter how good we think our observation and perception skills are, the reality is that because of how we've evolved to cope in a complex world, we don't see everything and we don't perceive everything. While missing the *F*s in a sentence might not seem like a crucial problem, in many cases what we fail to see is.

THE IMPORTANCE OF (NOT MISSING) DETAILS

Small details make a big difference. There is a huge difference between EST and PST when scheduling an important conference call, between picking up a child after soccer practice at 6:30 p.m. instead of 5:30, between 1 teaspoon of salt and 1 tablespoon. Missing the important details in business can erode trust. Missing the important details in life can cause catastrophe.

The opposite is also true, however: finding and focusing on the details doesn't just help avoid disaster, it can lead to success or the solution. Think of the billion-dollar companies built on their attention to detail. Apple didn't come by its reputation for aesthetic perfection by accident. The company consciously sweats every detail from examining each pixel on a screen with a photographer's loupe to employing a team of packaging designers who spend months perfecting the box-opening experience. Pioneering a new form of robotic animation, the trademarked Audio-Animatronics, wasn't enough for Walt Disney. Even though his engineers told him it would be extremely difficult, he insisted that the tropical birds in the Enchanted Tiki Room and the presidents in the Hall of Presidents breathe and fidget and shuffle realistically even when not in the spotlight. "People can feel perfection," Disney reasoned. It's not a coincidence that the same airline ranked number one in customer satisfaction by the Institute of Customer Service, Virgin Atlantic, prides itself on small touches: complimentary amenity kits, kids' entertainment backpacks, and even in-flight massages. The company even advertises its focus on its website: "We get all the details just right."

Mastering the details will give you a competitive edge. Thoroughness and thoughtfulness are not core values for everyone, and if you make them a priority, they can help you stand out from the crowd of people who just don't bother.

Once you hone your ability to tune in to telling details, you'll also find that they are critical for good problem solving — whether you're diagnosing a faulty catalytic converter on a car or trying to determine the correct answers on the SAT. The solution is often in the details we are programmed to overlook. Zeroing in on the things that others don't see can be the difference between success and failure in all fields.

Marcus Sloan wasn't as worried about the SAT as most high school math teachers might be. It was the New York State Regents Exam that had him up at night. Passing the mathematics portion is one of the requirements for a high school diploma, and the small, inner-city public school where he worked had a heartbreaking drop in its graduation rate in just one year, from 76 percent to 53.6 percent. He knew that if his students were going to break the cycle of poverty —the school classified 99 percent of its students as "economically disadvantaged"—they needed to graduate.

Walking through the Bronx school's metal detectors every morning, Sloan knew he had his work cut out for him. An external audit found that students were disengaged and disrespectful—when they showed up. The school suffered from chronic absenteeism; average attendance was just 72 percent, compared with 90.5 percent for the city's other similarly sized schools. Even worse: their scores on the Regents exam. While 77 percent of all the students in the state met the passing requirements for the mathematics portion of the exam, in Sloan's school only 39 percent did.

The students in Sloan's own classroom reflected this. "They had limited attention spans and trouble catching on to new concepts," he recalls. But after completing his first year, Sloan concluded that the students' poor grades weren't due to their lack of intelligence. Instead he realized their problem-solving deficiencies came from their difficulty focusing on an extended task and attending to details, both necessities when solving multiple-step mathematical problems.

He explains, "On standardized tests, after eliminating one or two choices, these students would have difficulty identifying the necessary information provided in the question, or necessary inferences from that information, in order to select the correct answer. They would overlook the key pieces of information in the problem statements or try to use all of the information in the problem rather than selecting only the relevant details needed."

He cites an example from the New York State Regents Exam administered on June 15, 2006. "One of the questions stated the angle of depression as measured from the top of a wall to a point on the ground at a given distance from the base of the wall. When I was grading their tests, I saw that many of my students had mistakenly used the angle of elevation instead of the given angle of depression," he says. His classes had been practicing problems from previous Regents exams, many of them involving solving for angles of elevation. Missing the single word change from *elevation* to *depression* in their live exam resulted in an incorrect answer, regardless of the amount of work they showed or their mathematical ability to solve for either angle.

Sloan realized this simple but critical mistake—missing key details—was jeopardizing his students' futures, and he was determined to fix it. He knew he'd need something out of the ordinary to reach his disenchanted charges.

"I wanted a creative means of engaging them in the kind of thinking that would enable them to succeed in mathematical learning," he says.

He'd heard about my training for medical students at The Frick Collection in Manhattan and wanted to know if Vermeer might be able to help his struggling students.

"I thought if it could improve medical students' diagnostic abilities, it might work for my high school students as well," he recalls. "A keen sense of attention to detail is important to medicine, but it's just as important in many other fields, including math."

I wholeheartedly agreed, and visited Sloan's school to introduce his students to the concepts of objective observation and searching for pertinent details with a slide show of selected pieces of art. A week later Sloan brought a group of his ninth- and tenth-graders to the Frick for a walk-through of the galleries. The students discussed the observational process and completed written exercises about the artworks they'd seen. We split the students into groups to study the art, then asked them to present their subgroup observations to the entire group to practice articulating their global and detailed observations.

The results were remarkable. They listened attentively, participated enthusiastically, and provided thoughtful responses to questions. Sloan marveled at the difference.

"I barely recognized some of them: they were alert, eager, even energetic," he recalls. "It was exciting to see students who usually struggled with and often obstructed their own learning really get into the experience."

Back in the classroom, Sloan noted that the students who took part in the museum training could more easily see connections in math problems than the students who had not.

We continued the program with two groups of math students from the high school, each visiting the museum on two different occasions. In written surveys following the course, the overwhelming majority of the students indicated that they had enjoyed closely observing the artwork and asked for more opportunities to do so. Almost two-thirds of the students taking the surveys wrote about the importance of looking for and focusing on details: exactly what Sloan wanted to instill in them. Even better: the percentage of students who met the mathematics standard on the Regents exam that year increased to 44 percent and climbed to 59 percent the following year.

Sloan had set out to solve a big problem: how to raise underperforming students' scores on standardized tests. Every other teacher had tried the same approach — making students take practice tests — and it hadn't worked. Those educators had missed the key detail that was hiding in plain sight: their students' faces, unfocused and uninterested. Sloan saw this and knew that before he could throw more problem sets at them, he first needed to address their poor attitude and chronic inability to focus. The solution to the problem wasn't in mathematics; it was in their mind-sets. Once they were engaged by the novel activity of looking at art, their eyes were opened to more of the details they were missing in their everyday lives.

DETAIL-ORIENTED

Knowing what we now know about how the brain processes and filters and misses and forgets and transforms, how can we become more detail-oriented? The first step is the easiest because we've already accomplished it: recognition.

We can't fix something if we don't know it's broken. Dr. Marc Green, a psychologist and professor of ophthalmology at West Virginia Medical School, asserts, "Most people falsely believe that they seldom experience inattentional blindness because they are unaware of being unaware." Now that we're aware of our inbred blindness, we can work on consciously overcoming it.

Every automobile has a blind spot, the space we cannot see when we're sitting behind the steering wheel. To make the seemingly invisible visible, we must first be aware of the issue, and then physically do a shoulder turn or mirror adjustment to compensate for it. The State Farm insurance company counsels new drivers that the only way to truly understand and then learn how to drive safely with blind spots is to spend time behind the wheel. The same concept applies to our other visual blind spots.

Perception requires attention, so we need to actively seek out the details. The more we observe art specifically for the details, the more we will see them. To help us learn to see the mahogany table hiding in plain sight, let's go back and look at it. Turn to page 83 and study the mahogany table at which Mrs. Winthrop is sitting. What details on and around it can you find that you might not have noticed before?

Do you see the highlight along the beveled edge at the bottom left corner of the table? The wood grain running diagonally from northwest to southeast? What about the reflection of Mrs. Winthrop? We see the blue of her dress and the white of her lace sleeve, but we can also see the scalloped flounce of the shaped edge of the lace. The stem of the nectarine branch she holds is reflected on the tabletop; in fact it appears that she is holding it just millimeters above. Her arm is visible in the reflection, as are just her eight fingers. We cannot see her thumbs.

Look closely at Mrs. Winthrop's hands. She was married to a prominent Harvard professor and one of America's first notable astronomers. We can see her garnet and diamond wedding ring on her left ring finger; however, close examination of that hand in the mahogany table shows that the ring is missing.

If we had missed the mahogany table the first time around, we would have missed the vanishing wedding ring as well. And it's a telling detail not to be missed, since the artist Copley, so diligent in his re-creation of the reflection in the mahogany table, would likely not leave out such an item accidentally. There are no records of why Copley omitted the ring in the table's reflection. It could be a comment on the state of Mrs. Winthrop's marriage, or it could simply be the artist playing a visual game with the viewer. We don't need to know the significance of the missing ring to catalog its absence, but we must acknowledge it. If we don't, we could be omitting crucial information we'll need later. You never know when that one small detail will crack the case or provide the elusive answer.

Missing key details means missing the other important details they might lead to. When we see the mahogany table, we can then see the missing ring. When we see the patient's wife at the end of his bed, we can then see a more thorough case history. When we see the inside-out pants, we can then see a conscious cover-up. The more we see, the better the odds that we, or someone else working with us, will uncover the solution previously eluding all of us.

DETAILS IN NONVERBAL COMMUNICATION

Another place important information often hides in plain sight is in the physical cues that other people give us: body language. Nonverbal communication is so telling that police officers in high-crime neighborhoods are trained to not put their hands in their pockets because it sends a signal of authority or boredom, and officers should remain ready and alert.

Look at the way Mrs. Winthrop is holding the nectarine stem. It's peculiarly arranged in her fingers, almost as if it were a writing instrument. Did the artist do this on purpose to leave us a clue about Mrs. Winthrop? If we did further investigation in this vein, we would find that Mrs. Winthrop was a prolific and expressive writer during the Revolutionary War; her letters, almanacs, and journals are archived at Harvard University for their importance as first-person sources.

When searching for details, be attuned to how someone is holding a nectarine stem. Note facial expression, posture, tone of voice, and eye contact. The way someone is standing, if she bites her bottom lip — these are facts that anyone can collect. I'm not a body language expert, but I have learned — by consciously looking for it — to have a heightened awareness of others' nonverbal cues. I can tell if someone doesn't want to talk to me—there is a conspicuous lack of eye contact, and the person might speak quickly to make his point and move on or away. A person who doesn't want to engage in prolonged conversation tends to stand farther away from me. You don't need to know the normal blink rate to note that someone can't hold your gaze, but you'll never see it if you never look a person in the eyes.

Bonnie Schultz, an insurance investigator for the State of New York, told me that after ten years on the job she can tell if someone is lying simply by observing body language.

"It's the subtle things, but you can see them," she said. "They'll shift their eyes or won't make eye contact at all. They'll turn away slightly, or their shoulders will stiffen."

I went to a spa recently to redeem a massage certificate I had gotten as a birthday gift. I had just walked into the darkly lit treatment room, and before I could say a word the therapist asked me if I was cold and whether my neck hurt. In those first few seconds while I was surveying my unfamiliar surroundings, the therapist had been surveying me. She had seen me glancing at the heater standing in the corner and nervously rubbing my neck—two tiny, unconscious actions. She delivered world-class customer service just by collecting details from my body language.

Marcus Sloan's students didn't hold up flash cards saying, "We're bored." And I didn't voice my discomfort at the spa. Sloan and the massage therapist had to read those messages in our posture and our gaze. Not everyone is comfortable saying what they want or what they mean out loud, but if you tune in to the other ways people express it, you will win their business, their loyalty, and their trust.

STRATEGIES FOR SEEING

Aside from being aware and attentive, we can use a few other specific strategies to combat our unintentional visual lapses. Since some of my clients use code names for their work, I've decided to do the same to help us remember the steps. I call it COBRA, not just because it sounds cool but also because the king of snakes has excellent eyesight. Cobras have built-in night vision, can see prey from 330 feet away, and have a nasty habit of spitting venom exceedingly accurately right into their opponents' eyes.

For our purposes, COBRA—which stands for **C**amouflaged, **O**ne, **B**reak, **R**ealign, **A**sk—will help us uncover hidden details by reminding us to concentrate on the *camouflaged,* work on *one* thing at a time, take a *break, realign* our expectations, and *ask* someone else to look with us.

Concentrate on the Camouflaged

Inconspicuous objects, such as the mahogany table, are harder for us to see because we have a natural, survival-based instinct to look for what stands out or is out of place. We have trouble noticing things that fade into the background or into the crowd or are naturally camouflaged, physically small, or subtle. While survivalists, soldiers, and criminals take advantage of this to blend in, the rest of us must work extra hard to spot what doesn't automatically stand out.

Investigators didn't see Natavia Lowery's inside-out pants because at first glance they weren't out of the ordinary. They expected her to be wearing pants, and the pants appeared clean, so perhaps they didn't feel the need to look at her pants any longer. If Lowery had walked out of the building in just her underwear, that would have been unusual—it would have stood out, and most likely caused the investigators to spot it right away. If the elderly patient's wife had electric-purple hair, the residents might have noticed her right away because the unusual hair would have caught their eye. Instead, the woman blended in with all the other people in the hospital.

We are drawn instinctually to the new, the innovative, and the exciting. To see the things that are truly hiding in plain sight because they appear ordinary, we must consciously look for the details our eyes might have skipped over on the first glance. To do this, we need to look again. We need to look at the entire scene, all the way to the edges and back again. Then, if possible, we must try to change the item or scene by repositioning it. Finally, we should reposition ourselves. Get closer, then step back. Walk around to change our perspective. An unusual angle can help uncover a not-so-unusual detail.

One Thing at a Time

To improve our chances of finding "hidden" details, we need to keep our focus sharp and single-minded, paying attention solely to this task. In our multitasking world where juggling multiple things at once is the norm, concentrating on just one thing can seem counterintuitive, but in reality multitasking leads to less effective and efficient work, since our brains cannot keep track of or focus on a million things at once. How many can we manage? A new study puts the limit of our working memory at a less-than-impressive four things.

Stanford professor Clifford Nass takes it one step further and argues that "multitaskers are terrible at every aspect of multitasking." After using fMRIs (functional magnetic resonance imaging) to study the brain while it was in juggling mode, he found that people who regularly multitasked were "terrible at ignoring irrelevant information, terrible at keeping information in their head nicely and neatly organized, and terrible at switching from one task to another."

Charles Folk, PhD, director of Villanova University's Cognitive Science Program, explains why: "Any time you do a task—whether it's visual, auditory or otherwise—it draws on a specific set of cognitive operations. The more tasks you perform, the more you draw from that limited pool of resources."

When the brain is taxed with a heavy cognitive load, it lets more unfiltered information slip by than normal. So if investigators were filling out reports on a different crime and talking on the phone while looking at the surveillance footage of Linda Stein's building, they would have dramatically decreased their chances of seeing the important details.

To avoid this multitasking brain drain, concentrate instead on just the task at hand. Called "mono-tasking" or "single-tasking," the idea is now taking off in the business world. Set aside other distractions, close your computer, ignore your telephone, and just observe. It can be difficult in a world that demands multiple things from us at once —it's been reported that average workers have thirty to one hundred projects on their agenda, are interrupted seven times an hour and distracted up to 2.1 hours a day — but *Forbes* magazine insists that "focus is a mental muscle that you have to develop, especially if yours has been weakened by years of multitasking." This is one of the reasons I don't allow phones in my class and enjoy taking people out of their offices. Without constant distractions hovering about, people can really focus on what they're observing, and as a result, they see so much more.

Take a Break

Be sure when flexing your mono-tasking muscle that you don't overdo it. The human brain was not designed to focus on one thing for hours at a time. To avoid overstimulation, our brains quickly become habituated to whatever's in front of us. This is why we stop feeling the chair we're sitting on or the clothes we're wearing. This built-in filter also helps explain why we still don't see "the mahogany table" — or our car keys or lost receipt or the way our budget could be balanced — that we know is there after staring and staring.

Psychologists believe that we can keep our cognitive control system from losing vigilance and help retain long-term focus by simply taking breaks. The formula recommended by experts is twofold. First, take a brief mental break every twenty minutes: just a momentary deactivation from your singular focus. The key is to pick an activity completely different from what you were doing. If you've been reading a report, don't switch to reading emails, switch to something that uses a different set of skills, like talking to someone face-to-face. Second, relax for ten minutes for every ninety minutes worked. Take a walk, outside if possible; exercise, even if that means only doing at-your-desk yoga; do something that gives you pleasure; or take a power nap.

Excessive noise and sensory overload can also add to our brain's stress and make it work less effectively. If the scene is noisy or crowded, consider returning later. Get yourself to a quiet location. (I highly recommend any nearby museum!)

Many famous people have found their famous solutions while taking a break. Sir Isaac Newton solved his obsession with gravity while watching an apple fall at his family's home, where he retreated when the University of Cambridge shut down during an outbreak of the plague. In 1901, after weeks of struggling in vain, French mathematician Henri Poincaré found success for his mathematical proofs only after he left his worktable for a geological field trip and a day at the seashore. Analyzing his own success, he wrote, "Often when one works at a hard question, nothing good is accomplished at the first attack. Then one takes a rest, longer or shorter, and sits down anew to the work . . . It might be said that the conscious work has been more fruitful because it has been interrupted and the rest has given back to the mind its force and freshness."

When I take homicide detectives into museums, they are forced to step away from the challenges they face to gather sufficient evidence against suspects, to focus on something entirely outside the world of law enforcement, and ultimately, to think differently about what they do. Seeing things anew refreshes their perspective and often leads to the break that had previously eluded them. The same is true for anyone for whom studying art is a new and unusual activity. Unless your job is to stare at the exact paintings in this book all day every day, analyzing the art presented here will help "recharge" your brain as well.

Realign Your Expectations

We often miss the unexpected because we're too focused on what we think should be there. Investigators were convinced that when Natavia Lowery left Linda Stein's building carrying a large bag it contained the murder weapon. They studied the shape of it, the way it bulged at the bottom, how heavy it looked. During the trial, the lead prosecutor spoke of the footage showing Lowery leaving carrying a bag "heavily laden with something in it." So much of the attention was on the bag, but it was the pants, in plain view, that appeared to convince the jury unequivocally of the suspect's guilt. They were looking for a smoking gun (well, literally a bludgeoning instrument) instead of just looking.

This inherent expectation adds extra filters to our cognitive processing and can make us miss information our brains perceive to be irrelevant. Since we don't "know" what our brain is filtering, we need to remind ourselves to let go of our preconceived notions and just look. And in some cases, we just might need to let someone else look.

Ask Someone Else to Look with You

Finally, since every person perceives the world differently, you might want to enlist help in your search. Bring someone in to look with fresh eyes, preferably someone with a different perspective, background, and opinions from yours.

I've found that people who don't ask for assistance are often afraid doing so will make them seem incompetent, but I think the opposite is true. Someone else might see the answer to the problem that we articulated, and by seeking another set of eyes, we are proving that we are dedicated to the pursuit of a solution.

* * *

Dave Bliss knew the answer was in front of him, he just couldn't see it. A sales manager for a commercial cleaning company, he had a huge new client on the hook, but one thing was standing in his way: the client's current contract with a competitor.

The potential client was a medical services facility with forty buildings, a monster deal for Bliss's company, and he was determined to close the deal. When Bliss had shown how switching to his company's service would save $137,000 a year, the client was willing to sign up immediately. There was just one catch: the client was locked in a five-year agreement with another company and still had three years left.

"If you can find a way to get us out of this, I'll sign," the facilities manager told Bliss.

Bliss knew there had to be a loophole in the contract, but after staring at the tiny legal print for hours, he still hadn't found it. The terms were pretty cut-and-dried; in fact, he'd highlighted the dates: "This agreement is effective as of the date of execution for a term of 60 months from date of installation." The contract was signed on April 4, 2013, the services had begun a week later, and by all accounts they were acceptable.

Having recently taken my class, Bliss decided to try COBRA. He remembered the first step: camouflage. The answer could be right in front of him but hidden. He had spent the majority of his time trying to work out the dates and find a way out of the contract, but maybe that wasn't the answer. Maybe he should concentrate on a different part of the document.

One thing at a time. Bliss turned his phone to voicemail so he wouldn't be distracted, closed his laptop, and just looked.

Break. After twenty minutes, Bliss still hadn't found anything, and the words were starting to swim on the page. He decided to get up and take a walk to the break room. He felt better when he returned to his office, buoyed by the change of scenery and leftover birthday cake he'd discovered.

Realign your expectations. What am I expecting to find? Bliss asked himself. A way out of the contract. Perhaps that's the wrong expectation. Should I look for the opposite? he wondered. A way for the client to stay *in* the contract? Could the client somehow hire his company and still honor his current contract with the other?

Ask someone else to look with you. He called a friend who was an attorney.

"Is there any way for a company to honor their old contract and still use our services as well?" he asked.

"Sure," the attorney replied. "Just figure out what the minimum requirements on the other contract are."

Minimum requirements? Bliss's company didn't have minimum order requirements, he thought, but perhaps it should. A quick scan revealed the following under Article 12: "Minimum charge: $50 per service."

There it was. The phrase that would win Bliss an $832,000 annual contract. To honor its commitment, the medical facility only had to use its current cleaning company for a minimum charge of $50 per service. Scaling its service back to cleaning one building one day a week would cost the company just $2,600 for the year and allow it to sign with Bliss for an annual savings of over $134,000. Bliss got the deal.

While it's in our biology to miss things, we can use our cognitive powers to make sure the important details aren't slipping through our filters unnoticed. Training our brains to be more effective at objective observation and perception will help us not only to see more but also to miss less.

THE IMPORTANCE OF THE BIG PICTURE

As you master your ability to capture key details, be careful not to let the hunt for meaningful minutiae override other important information.

At 11:32 p.m. on a clear December night in 1972, as the pilots of Eastern Air Lines flight 401 were preparing to land the Lockheed Tristar jet at their home airport of Miami International after a smooth ride from JFK, the first officer noticed the landing-gear indicator light in the cockpit was dark. The captain, a thirty-two-year veteran who had logged more than 29,000 flight hours, radioed the control tower: "It looks like we're gonna have to circle; we don't have a light on yet."

At a safe cruising altitude of 2,000 feet, the captain engaged the plane's autopilot and set about determining why the square-shaped "down and locked" button beneath the gear handle wasn't glowing green. Had it burned out, or was the landing gear really not locked into place? For the next seven minutes the cabin crew obsessed over the little light. They wiggled it, tried to remove it, cursed at it, worried about breaking it even more with a pair of pliers, cushioned it with a handkerchief, wondered if the button had worked during a previous test, twisted it, pushed on it, discussed how the light lens might have been assembled incorrectly, and tried everything they could to get it to light. And in the meantime, according to cockpit voice-recorder transcripts, they missed everything else.

At some point the captain leaned against the control column, the *W*-shaped "steering wheel" of the plane, possibly while turning to talk to someone behind him, switching the autopilot into hold-the-last-position mode. He didn't notice that leaning against the yoke was sending the plane down. The jet went into a gentle descent over the Everglades. No one in the cockpit noticed. After the plane had lost 250 feet, an altitude warning sounded in the cockpit and also went unnoticed. The men were so engrossed with a $12 light bulb that they failed to notice until ten seconds before impact that they had steered the aircraft right into the ground.

After examining the wreckage, the National Transportation Safety Board determined that the landing gear had been down and locked into place, and that the bulb in the landing-gear indicator button had indeed burned out. The pilots could have known this if they had correctly accessed the small viewing window under the flight deck that provides visual confirmation of the landing gear's status; and even if the wheels were up, they could have been manually lowered. The flight could have landed safely if the pilots hadn't been distracted by a button. Instead, 101 of the 176 passengers, including everyone in the cockpit, lost their lives in the crash.

We may be tempted to judge the pilots, but inattentional blindness happens to all of us. The cure for tunnel vision is the same as the strategies we should employ to combat our other unintentional visual lapses: Look in a different direction, look to the edges, take a break from your current activity, and step back to make sure you're seeing the whole picture.

Educators believe that the students who best see the big picture — in both simple and complex systems — are visual learners. Likewise, studying art, a visual medium, forces us to use and sharpen our visual-spatial intelligence capabilities and ultimately can help us, too, to see the big picture more clearly.

PAINTING A PICTURE

Most of our communication about an event or incident takes place after it has occurred; we tell, text, email, and write what we have seen. In doing so, if we inadvertently omit a critical element, the recipient of our communication who was not present firsthand will never know the information was missing. As the primary source, we have a duty to include all of the important details while still capturing the big picture.

When I was a practicing attorney, to encourage us to relate a complete, detail-filled description that also incorporated the entire event —for judge and jury, who were not present—judges often asked us to think of information transfer as "painting a picture." The same terminology is used to get stories out of witnesses, when child welfare workers must fill out a home-visit report, or when an insurance adjuster investigates a claim.

To "paint a picture" of what we see, we must first realize that we are starting with a blank canvas. Only what we purposefully put on it will be "seen" by others. We must not leave it empty or incomplete; rather we must fill it with accurate, objective, descriptive facts using both broad strokes and fine details to record our observations.

For instance, I work with family protective services investigators to help them describe the residence they're visiting from the moment they pull up outside, not just from the front foyer. Is the grass overgrown? Is it near a busy or dangerous street? Is there trash piling up? Once inside, they should scan the entire environment. Is the floor clean? Are there animals about, and if so, do they look healthy and well cared for? What does the home smell like? Do the windows have curtains?

Then zero in on the details. What's on the coffee table? A cup? A bent spoon? A cigarette lighter? A Bible? Paper and crayons? A porn magazine? This is not making judgments; it's collecting facts.

When meeting children, look at their teeth. Are they clean or so decayed that it is evident the child has never been to a dentist? This small detail can tell a lot about the big picture of how well they are cared for.

I teach investigators to consider the reason they were called to visit someone—and then to look beyond. Focusing only on the reported incident could cause them to miss bigger warning signs in the home that could ultimately put a child at greater risk. The investigators need to diligently catalog the specifics but also have an appreciation for the rest of the family dynamics. In some cases, this practice leads to reward.

When caseworker Joanna Longley first visited a home in rural Pennsylvania to investigate a charge of possible child neglect, she noted all of the pertinent details of her visit in a report that painted a picture any other colleague could pick up and follow. The house had boards over a broken front window; the mailbox slot had duct tape covering it; and the woman who answered the front door and identified herself as the mother of the house refused to let Longley in. The mother displayed defensive body language as she wedged herself in the door's small opening, she smelled of cigarette smoke, and she ignored Longley's request for shelter from the snow that fell heavily overhead.

Although the mother was less than accommodating and Longley herself was far from comfortable, she stayed focused on the facts of the situation, not the subjective emotion behind the exchange. She also kept the bigger picture in mind, knowing that if she simply turned and left, the chance of a professional evaluation for the children left with her.

Instead of getting sidetracked by insult or injury, by cold toes or a client's lousy attitude, Longley remained observant and objective. Her goal was to see the woman's children in person, to note the details of their health, development, and appearance. While not ideal, this could be accomplished on the front porch. She briefly interviewed each child at the door and determined that they were not in immediate danger. Longley also looked hard at the facts to sort out her subjective observations. While the mother's demeanor wasn't polite, it wasn't abusive either. Could her standoffishness stem from defensiveness? Perhaps she'd had a bad experience with authorities in the past. The mother was the adult of the house, it was her house, and she had a right to decide who could come inside.

Longley's conscious decision to seek out the important details of the children's safety while deferring to their mother's wishes to do so outside paid off. By acknowledging the mother's authority, Longley earned her trust and was welcomed inside on future visits. The mother even opened up and began to work with Longley to improve her children's lives.

Let's practice "painting a picture" with an actual painting, seeking out details big and small.

Look at the two side-by-side images below. For the sake of our blank canvas, let's pretend we don't recognize these gentlemen. We'll call them #1 and #16. Using the investigative model we learned in the last chapter and a modern recording system of some kind to stay organized — pen and paper, smartphone, or Post-it note — complete an objective surveillance of the two scenes. Write down as many factual details as you can muster: the who, what, when, and where. Compare and contrast the two; for instance, #1 is standing while #16 is sitting, and both are presenting three-quarter profiles facing left. Ideally, you should spend two to five minutes on this exercise. Go.

Gilbert Stuart, *George Washington (Lansdowne Portrait)*, 1796.

Alexander Gardner, *Abraham Lincoln*, 1865.

What did you find? Did you note the differences in dress? In background? In hair ownership? How about the similarity of their skin color or that they are both next to a table? Did you then include the differences in those tables, including height, location, and appearance?

What about body language? How would you describe their posture? In a class of intelligence analysts, I had one tell me that "number sixteen is passive, while number one is more open." The word *passive* is subjective, open to interpretation. I pointed out that his colleague at the back of the room, an outgoing, animated guy, was sitting with arms held in the same way and yet we would never call him "passive." Instead, try to be more objective and more specific: #1's right hand is held out, palm up, while #16's arms are in front of him, fingertips touching.

Did you list that #1 holds a sword in his left hand while #16 holds spectacles in his right?

Is there a line-of-sight difference? Where is each man looking?

How do their expressions vary? While I'm tempted to say that #16 is wearing a smirk, that's another subjective inference. More specific would be: the corners of #16's mouth are raised slightly. Other objective details could include that #16 has disheveled hair and bags under his eyes, his tie is crooked, and his suit is wrinkled. Just because he was a president of the United States doesn't mean he isn't a mess in this image. Acknowledge and make use of the human condition as you observe it. It's valuable information that can contribute tremendously to the viewer's overall impression of the portrait.

Now go back and search the two pictures specifically for details. List as many as you can find.

In recording the details, did you note the buckles on #1's shoes or the watch chain hanging from #16's vest? That the sword in #1's hand is sheathed and the spectacles in #16's hand are folded? Did you list the dust and scratches on the image on the right? The books stacked under the table in the image on the left — two large ones, almost the height of the subject's knee, leaning against the gold table leg?

Did you see the rainbow in the upper right corner of #1's portrait? If not, as with *Renshaw's Cow,* I bet you can't stop seeing it now. In many ways it's the "mahogany table" of this picture: it's hanging out in the background, doesn't seem very significant, but it exists, so it is worth noting. In this case, it's a telling detail: there are at least 25,000 paintings of George Washington in the history of American art, but only three have rainbows in them. Discovering it would help you place the time period of this work. It was painted in 1796, the last full year of Washington's presidency. The rainbow was added to symbolize that America's first president had brought the young country through the storms of the previous decades and that prosperous days were ahead.

If you missed the rainbow or the spectacles, the sheath or the oversize books, remember to engage COBRA when searching for details. Look specifically for things that might be *camouflaged,* concentrate on just the *one* task of looking, take a *break* and come back to the search, *realign* your expectations of what you thought you might see, and *ask* someone else to take a look with you.

Finally, what are the big-picture observations we shouldn't miss in these two images? The things so "obvious" most people assume they don't need to be noted? Step back and consider the facts that aren't so small. One image is black-and-white, while one is color. Another big-picture fact that many people miss: one is a painting and one is a photograph. Everything must be noticed — just like Mrs. Winthrop's mahogany table.

WHAT'S YOUR MAHOGANY TABLE?

The takeaway here isn't that people miss shiny furniture, the patient's wife at the end of the bed, the correct angle of elevation on a math test, or inside-out pants. It's that those invisible-yet-visible things were, as they often are, the linchpins to success. Sometimes we're so busy looking for the answer that we miss the information that can get us there.

To remind themselves not to miss what's right in front of them, one group of executives I taught adopted the phrase "What's your mahogany table?" There is a mahogany table (or more likely more than one) in all of our lives — something that could be instrumental to our work and we just don't see it.

Look around you, your home, and your workplace, and ask yourself the same question. What's your mahogany table; what can you find hiding in plain sight?

* * *

We've learned how to master the fine art of observation: to gather only facts, to sort the objective from the subjective, and to keep an eye out for both the small details and bigger, but sometimes hidden, information. Now we're going to unleash our inner intelligence analyst and figure out how to make sense of what we've found.

PART II

$\cdot$ $\cdot$ $\cdot$

Analyze

Discovery consists of seeing what everybody has seen
and thinking what nobody has thought.

— ALBERT SZENT-GYÖRGYI

6

Keep Your Head on a Swivel

Analyzing from Every Angle

ALTHOUGH IT SITS on a hill overlooking the city, Rio de Janeiro's oldest favela, Morro da Providência, a massive slum of shanty houses, is largely invisible to its cosmopolitan neighbors. Awash in extreme poverty and violent crime, its residents are isolated in every possible way: economically, geographically, and socially. Neither taxis nor ambulances will go there. If you need to get up or down, there are 365 steps to climb. Fearing for their personal safety, even news crews won't ascend the hill; instead, when necessary, they send helicopters to report from afar. Special paramilitary troops do patrol the area, but residents view them with as much suspicion and distrust as they do the local drug lords—for good reason, since the two have been known to work together.

In June 2008, eleven soldiers tried to detain five young men from Providência. Two ran away. The remaining three, ages seventeen, nineteen, and twenty-three, were charged with disrespecting authority, led away to an army barracks, and then reportedly *sold* to a gang in a neighboring favela. Their bodies were discovered mutilated in a trash dump.

Although the victims—two students and one young father—were mourned by grieving friends and relatives, the rest of Rio hardly took notice. The favela residents demanded justice and started a small riot to grab the city's attention. It didn't work. The world continued to look the other way.

Until the day the huge eyes appeared.

One morning the citizens of Rio woke up to something new: the ramshackle houses on the hill of Providência had been papered overnight with oversize black-and-white enlargements of extreme close-up photographs of human eyes.

JR, Women Are Heroes, Brazil, *Action in the slums Morro da Providência, tree, moon, horizontal, Rio de Janeiro,* 2008.

They looked out from the sides of buildings, unmoving, unblinking, wide open, waiting. The favela that no one wanted to look at was suddenly staring at them.

What did the eyes mean? Whose were they? How did they get there? Reporters, still afraid to go and see for themselves, took pictures of the pictures and beseeched the public for answers.

The eyes were the brainchild of a self-titled *photograffeur* (*graffeur* in French means "graffiti artist") from France who goes only by the initials JR. A tall, thin man who is never seen in public without a hat and sunglasses to hide his identity, JR learned about the young men's murders and flew to Brazil to see if he could help. He walked up into the favela and introduced himself to the first person he saw.

He stayed for a month, meeting as many people as he could—community leaders, drug dealers, teachers, teenagers, and local artists—winning their trust and enlisting their help.

"The favela is in the center of town, but when you look at a map it is like it is not there," JR explains. "The people were saying, 'Hey, we are there, we are right there in front of you, and you pretend that we don't exist.'"

To give them a voice, he photographed women from the favela up close and unflinching. To JR, eyes are everything. He notes how often we avoid looking people in the eyes, something he hopes his in-your-face art can remedy. He had the pictures printed on waterproof vinyl and showed the residents how to hang the colossal portraits. Then he disappeared, so the now curious international media would have to actually interview the subjects, including family members of the young victims.

"I left Brazil right after we were done with the pasting," he says. "Down the favela, all the TV stations were there, waiting for an explanation as they'd seen those portraits appear, and wondering why or who had done it. It was the women who talked to the media about the project—their project—and I was very moved to see how each one translated it into her own words."

JR's plan to make people see the humanity behind the headlines worked. "For once, the media didn't cover the violence, the trafficking in the favela, but listened to the voices of the people," he recalls.

With his project, named "Women Are Heroes," JR was able to help change the way the rest of Rio de Janeiro, and the rest of the world, viewed the blight in their backyard by changing their perspective. Crumbling concrete houses are harder to write off as an inevitable side effect of civilization and corruption when they are shellacked with larger-than-life images of the people who live within.

The project also changed the way the favela residents saw themselves. Being international models gave them a new sense of pride; being part of a global movement changed their perspective on their ability to effect change. The Morro da Providência now has its own website, while locals continue to manage and host weekly events at the cultural center JR left behind.

The photographs even changed the perspective of the local government. The mayor of Rio confessed to JR that the exhibit had influenced subsequent political decisions. The Brazilian officers involved in the original crime were arrested, and the victims—Marcos Paulo da Silva, Wellington González, and David Wilson—properly named and memorialized by news outlets around the world.

The story of JR and the forgotten favela illustrates the paramount importance of perspective. Without it, we have only a partial picture of anything. To simply read the police report on the Providência incident and stop or alternatively only speak with the mother of a victim and then walk away would mean leaving information behind. Comprehensive assessment and analysis require examining things from all angles.

In art, perspective refers to the actual angle from which a work will be seen. It is carefully considered and in many cases manipulated by the artist to purposefully direct the viewer's eye. For instance, many Renaissance painters arranged their compositions to make sure the vanishing point, or where all lines seem to visually converge, fell exactly on the Virgin Mary's womb to emphasize her importance as the mother of Christ. We are also going to use perspective to our advantage, consciously taking control of it to make sure we are following every lead possible.

Perspective, from the Latin word *perspicere,* meaning "to look through," is defined as the point of view from which something is considered or evaluated. Originating in the fourteenth century, the word *perspective* was initially used to describe a physical object, specifically an optical glass that would change the way you viewed something. A telescope's perspective, therefore, was an actual piece of curved glass inside it. We can use this definition to think of perspective in a similar way, as another lens through which we see.

In the first section of this book, we learned how to gather information; now we will begin to look through what we have uncovered. We'll start by appreciating and analyzing perspective both from without and within.

PHYSICAL PERSPECTIVE

Dr. Wayne W. Dyer, author of one of the best-selling books of all time, says the secret to his success is the maxim he lives by daily: Change the way you look at things, and the things you look at change. Where we stand, figuratively and literally, when we view things can dramatically change the way we see them; therefore it's critical that we approach data from every possible physical angle. Look behind, underneath, in the corners, and off the page. Step back, crouch down, and walk around everything. Things are not always what they appear to be, especially at first glance from one angle. Take this bowl of food:

Giuseppe Arcimboldo, *L'Ortolano (The Vegetable Gardener)*, c. 1590.

What do you see? An onion, carrots, mushrooms, a turnip, parsnips, garlic, a sprig of mint, that furry thing near the middle (a chestnut — I had to look that one up), and a few varieties of lettuce — basically the fixings for a really good meal. Everything is in a dark bowl that appears to be made of some type of reflective metal and rests on a flat surface.

Now let's look at the same image upside down:

Giuseppe Arcimboldo, *L'Ortolano (The Vegetable Gardener)*, c. 1590.

With a new perspective, the image changes entirely. Instead of a collection of edibles, we now have the outline of a person.

Go back and look at the original picture. Would you have guessed that a bearded man was lurking inside? If we had committed to looking at the image from every angle, including sideways or upside down, we would have seen it. In all of my years of teaching, I've only ever had one student, a young journalism major from Columbia University, lie down on a bench in a museum, hang his head physically over the edge, and peer at a painting upside down. We should all be so committed.

Recently, I was waiting by the foreign baggage claim in an international airport terminal for a colleague to meet me. I did my best to stand out from the bustling crowd: I sat down. As everyone around me was walking, grabbing their bags, consulting their dictionaries and maps, or queuing up for the dozens of lines, sitting down gave me an instantly distinct profile.

I've sat, and unfortunately slept, in airport terminals before, but always by the gate where others were doing the same thing and discreetly against the wall. This time I plunked myself right in the middle of baggage claim with my back against a large pillar, so I wouldn't miss my colleague. Seeing things from the ground in this way, I noticed details I never would have otherwise. In an instant I became an expert on contemporary luggage, as large rolling bags obscured most of my field of vision, but I also noted socks and footwear, ankle tattoos, how people trod, what they dropped, and if they shuffled nervously. I was so deep in observation that I was startled when a face suddenly filled my view. A little girl, delighted to finally find someone else at her eye level, smiled and babbled at me in a language I sadly didn't speak. When she toddled away, she left her perspective with me, as all I could suddenly see was how the world must look in the strange and noisy environment when you only come up to everyone's knee and no one looks you in the eye.

Michelangelo, *David*, 1501–1504.

That's part of the magic of changing our physical perspective: that it will not only give us new factual information but can also change our perceptions. Let's experience just how dramatic this shift can be by analyzing one of the world's most famous works of art: Michelangelo's *David*.

The who, what, where, and when of the work are fairly well known: it is a sculpture of a muscular, nude man meant to depict the biblical hero David just before his battle with the giant Goliath. Carved from a single slab of white marble, he stands facing front, head turned to the left, counterposed with his weight on his right foot, left arm bent, right arm at his side. He holds a sling and a rock, and can be viewed under a skylight built just for him at the Accademia Gallery in Florence.

He's frequently been called strong, heroic, relaxed, languishing, contemplative, peaceful, even ethereal. Sixteenth-century historian Giorgio Vasari wrote, "Nor has there ever been seen a pose so easy, or any grace to equal that in this work, or feet, hands and head so well in accord, one member with another, in harmony, design, and excellence of artistry." Art critics have written that he "transmits exceptional self-confidence," is "the perfect man" and even "the standard by which male beauty has been judged."

Beauty is a subjective opinion, but let's examine the photograph of *David* on page 121 to verify if the other popular characterizations —graceful, peaceful, relaxed—are in sync with our own observations. His face does appear smooth, free of wrinkles, lips closed, possibly even turned up in a slight smile. His stance is casual, his right shoulder slightly slumped, his right hand gently resting against his thigh.

But how will our assessments stand when we view the statue from a different angle? As the iconic statue is almost seventeen feet tall and sits on top of a six-foot pedestal, most of us, whether we've seen *David* in person or in a photo like the preceding one, have viewed it from the front at an upward angle and from quite far away. If we walk around it, get eye level with it, and investigate it from other viewpoints, it tells a different story.

Michelangelo, *David* (detail).

The peaceful, relaxed image of *David* disappears when we get higher and closer. If we could view it from above, as Michelangelo did when carving it, we would find a face full of tension. His nostrils are flared, his eyes wide open, the muscles of his eyebrows furrowed. Close up, his stare is intent, possibly worried. In fact, a 360-degree computer study revealed the opposite of a relaxed man in repose: every visible muscle in David's body is tensed. Anatomy professors at Florence University assert that every detail of the sculpture "is consistent with the combined effects of fear, tension and aggression."

Close scrutiny also dispels the illusion of David's physical perfection. He is actually slightly cross-eyed and has a squint. He also has a flat spot on his head and is quite abnormally proportioned. David's hands are freakishly large, while his *pisello,* as they say in Italy, does not correspond in size. His head seems too big for his body, and Florentine doctors have discovered that he is missing a muscle in his back.

Viewing the statue from other angles calls into question other "facts" as well. The stone he holds in his right hand? A view from behind reveals the end of a flat cylinder in his fingers that some believe is the handle of a sling rather than a rock. His hand curves tightly around the object, obscuring much of it from our view, and as with the contents of the bag Linda Stein's personal assistant was carrying, we cannot presume to know what it truly is by guessing at a shape.

We must also take into account a perspective many often miss: that of the artist. How did Michelangelo intend for people to view *David*? Many scholars believe that the current placement of the statue is incorrect, and that to really stand in front of *David,* you need to move to the side into his line of sight. The statue faces as it does because in 1504, city leaders decided that its "malevolent stare and aggression" should be directed not at "peaceful passersby" but at Florence's true enemy, Rome. Regardless of what Michelangelo might have wished, *David* was originally positioned outside with his back against the Palazzo Vecchio, turned so that he was looking south toward the eventual capital of Italy. When it was moved inside in 1873, the orientation was kept the same; however, museum pillars and display cases installed to the right blocked a proper frontal view.

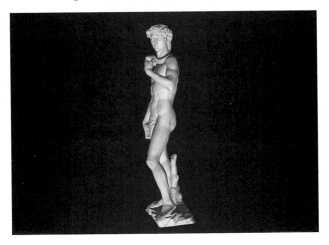

Michelangelo, *David*, digital image.

Stanford University's Digital Michelangelo Project provided a computerized remedy that allows us at last to see *David* from this alternate view (above). With this new perspective, the statue almost looks like a different person entirely. Our eyes notice different things: the curve of his abdomen is more pronounced, the sling over his shoulder easier to see, the knots on the tree stump behind him readily visible, and the focus shifts from his genitals upward to his face.

Looking at the statue from Michelangelo's point of view, we would also learn that the physical imperfections were deliberate. While David's eyes don't line up perfectly, scholars believe the mathematically inclined Michelangelo deliberately skewed them in a trick of perspective so that from the ground, where he knew a viewer would be standing, they would appear aligned.

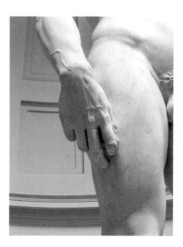

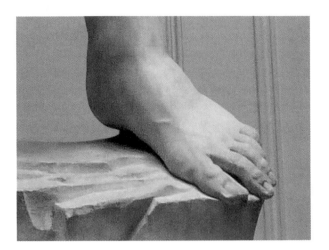

Only a close and careful inspection will reveal the veins in David's hand, the length of his fingernails, the gap between the first and second toes on his left foot. Why would something as small as the spacing between toes matter? In a criminal investigation, the exact placement of bodies and evidence, indeed everything in the surrounding scenes, is critical, but minute physical data matter in many other disciplines as well: manufacturing, medicine, archiving, insurance claims adjusting, scouting for an ABP on an airplane. In this case, the toe gap is important because that particular appendage separation was a signature of Michelangelo's work. In the absence of his name scrawled over David's backside, it is a nuanced hint to the viewer that we are looking at an authentic masterwork. But we would never have found it if we hadn't looked around.

To remind one another to keep looking constantly in every direction, World War II pilots came up with a phrase still used in the army (I've heard that football coaches are also fond of it): keep your head on a swivel. Instead of defaulting to what's right in front of us, we must keep shifting our perspective. Doing so can help us find more information, more of the story, the missing piece, the right path, the true intent, or even the way out.

I personally employ a practical head-swivel trick I learned from the FBI. They teach their agents to frequently turn around and survey the scene behind them when walking in unknown territory — an unfamiliar city street, a field, even an airport parking lot — since that's the view they'll have when they need to find their way back. Not doing so can mean that when you exit or try to retrace your steps — especially in an emergency situation such as a mall evacuation — you can get confused because the scenery is different; you're suddenly looking at the backside of the things you passed when you entered. By consciously acknowledging the lay of the land from all angles when you approach a new location, you capture a more complete picture of your surroundings that you can recall no matter what direction you're headed.

GO AND SEE

The importance of seeing things from all angles doesn't begin and end with investigative work; it's just as critical for any business that trades in process, products, or people. It's the key principle behind Toyota's famous *genchi genbutsu* concept — which translates to "go and see": the idea that the only way to get the comprehensive picture of a scene, see a process as a whole, and absorb as many details as possible is for managers to leave their offices, get out from behind their computers, and physically go to where the work is being done. Many manufacturing companies have adopted this in a practice called "*gemba* walks" — *gemba* in Japanese meaning "the actual place." In *gemba* walks, employees go to the place that matters most to their job, be it where the product is made or sold or even used, to better understand their work. Bill Wilder at *Industry Week* describes it as such: "Gemba is rarely found at an executive desk. Instead, you'll find it on the shop floor. Or in the marketing department. Or at a customer's place of business."

In another version of "go and see," some companies are sending their employees out to observe not where their work typically takes place but the opposite. In the search for efficiency, Detroit's Beaumont Health System hospitals have *kaizen* (Japanese for "improvement") teams of employees who walk around the grounds outside of their normal departments to find sustainable savings. One group saw that the sprinkler systems on the campus were watering unnecessary areas; fixing that and switching to low-flow sprinkler heads saved the company $180,000 and 500,000 gallons of water in six months. "Unless you go out and walk," says Kay Winokur, a nurse and Beaumont's vice president of quality, safety, and accreditation, "you won't notice these things."

Shifting our physical perspective can also help when we're stuck mentally. Just as the ancient Greeks purposefully carved grooves into their stone roads to make heavy wheeled carts easier for horses and oxen to pull, our efficiency-loving brains deliberately seek familiar patterns. Unfortunately sometimes we get stuck in those ruts.

Think of a time you stared and stared at a seemingly unsolvable problem or tried in vain to break a mental block. For me, it most often occurs when I have to write a technical proposal. I want it to be perfect. I need it to be perfect. But the words . . . just . . . won't . . . come. I sit hypnotized by my laptop while hour after unproductive hour ticks by, but I'm afraid to move on to something else, trapped in the vicious cycle of just-five-more-minutes and I've-already-wasted-so-much-time. Neuroscience and my author friends have taught me the simple solution for writers' or any other kind of block: get up and go.

"I limit myself to one hour without progress," Jess McCann, author of two dating advice books, tells me. "And then I'm out of there! I work on deadlines, so I can't completely abandon what I'm doing. I don't drop my project and go on vacation. All it takes is a quick change of physical location. Fifteen minutes outside, and I come back refreshed and usually with the answer I was looking for."

When you're ready to throw your computer (or coworker) out the window, go for a quick discovery walk around your office, around your building, or around the block.

"The very act of walking and moving about invigorates your brain," confirms neuroimaging experts Professor Roderick Gilkey and Dr. Clint Kilts, "because the brain is an interactive system." Any activity that stimulates one part of the brain, such as physical movement, simultaneously stimulates other parts, such as creative problem solving.

Even better than only walking is also observing what you see along the way. Scientists have discovered that just looking can have a profound impact on the brain's ability to perform. "Experience gained through observation activates performance-enhancing neurons which accelerate learning and the capacity to learn," Gilkey and Kilts say. To do this, seek and sort out objective facts — who, what, where, and when — while you're walking. The more unfamiliar the territory you traverse, the more potential there is for you to refocus your perceptions and break out of what psychologists call "functional fixedness," or the habit of seeing things from only one perspective.

Instead of banging your head on the wall thinking about the same thing, by getting up and going you'll engage your real-time observational skills, which will in turn ignite your critical thinking abilities, refresh all of your senses, and in many cases release your mental block.

A SENSE OF PERSPECTIVE

While we're on a perspective-changing walkabout, or any other time we're actively cataloging observations, we must remember to use all of our resources as data collectors, specifically to look with more than just our eyes. As *Discover* magazine editor at large Corey S. Powell writes, "Our appreciation of the natural world is bolstered not just in sights but in sounds, smells, and tactile sensations. A walk in the woods would not be the same without birdsong, the loamy odor of decaying leaves, the brush of branches."

Our perceptions are informed by observations from all of the senses, but we default to the visual too often. Objective analysis doesn't end with what we can see. We also need to catalog and analyze what we can learn from all five senses to develop a full picture of what we're observing; if we don't, we're leaving valuable information behind. The smell of the lobby in a hospital versus the smell in the emergency room, the decibel level of someone's voice, the strength in someone's handshake, whether they look you in the eye or look away: that's all important information.

Indeed, sight isn't always our most powerful or productive sense. Working with some of the finest law enforcement officials in the world, I am privy to some of the small yet significant behind-the-scenes details of major cases that don't always make the headlines. These details are often the most thought-provoking and revealing about the crime. Consider the murder of Annie Le, a pharmacology graduate student at Yale who disappeared in 2009 five days before her wedding. This investigation was hindered by sound and solved by smell.

Initially, sight wasn't helping the officers much. Surveillance footage and electronic key records showed Le entering the lab where she worked but never leaving. Her wallet and cell phone were left in her office. But authorities couldn't find her or her body; without either it's very hard to identify, much less indict, a suspect. After five days had passed with no discovery — no DNA, no confirmed crime scene, no Le — the FBI was called in.

One of the FBI agents was standing in the lab very frustrated that Le couldn't be found when he decided to do what no one else had done: go to the men's room down the hall. He didn't use the facility in the conventional way; instead, he was seeking someplace where he could ponder the case further and give himself a change of perspective. When he opened the restroom door, he recoiled from the foul smell. When the wall between the restroom and the lab was excavated, the victim's body was found stuffed inside.

Why didn't anyone smell the decomposition in the lab? Since the room held mice in their cages for experimentation, a built-in fan had been running nonstop to remove the animals' odor and circulate fresh air. The noise was so constant that no one even noticed it. If people had heard the fan, they could have turned it off and used their noses sooner.

We live in a very visual world, and it can be hard to cede our focus to other senses, and even more challenging since less used senses are harder to describe. We're not used to describing smells in concrete terms; we often resort to vague qualitative words like "nice" or "awful." But we need to be as thorough and precise when gathering information with our other senses as we are with sight. For instance, there is a distinct difference between a "musty" smell and one that is "musky." The same variation exists for sounds, tastes, and the physical feel of things.

To master this skill of differentiating with our senses, make conscious use of *all* of your senses in public and in private. When you're on the subway or at the grocery store or in your basement, note odors, and tastes, and sounds. I find the best way to get my other senses fired up is to close my eyes for a moment. On an airplane recently, I did just that and for the first time noticed the aromas of hand lotion, perfume, and bacon. How did I possibly miss the smell of bacon on a closed plane when my eyes were open? We were at cruising altitude; the bacon didn't just suddenly walk on board. My eyes were commanding all of my attention; I needed to turn them off so my brain would allocate resources to my other senses.

Thankfully, the more often you engage all of your senses, the more automatic the process will become. And you'll find that your other senses will enhance what you see. We can practice this skill using art, the same way we use it as visual data. We can look at a painting of a day at the beach and know what it sounds like: waves crashing, seagulls squawking, children shouting. To prove it, let's analyze the following painting by Édouard Manet. I'll give you a head start and tell you where we are: *A Bar at the Folies-Bergère,* a cabaret music hall in Paris.

What do you see?

Édouard Manet, *A Bar at the Folies-Bergère,* 1882.

This is a complicated painting, filled with people and objects. Let's catalog the facts, but this time we'll make sure to incorporate all of our senses: visual, aural, aromatic, and tactile. We don't have to be holding the orange to our noses to know it smells of citrus. We don't have to have our own hands on the white marble-colored bar to know it is rock hard and cool to the touch. We don't have to be in the room to know how loud it would be. These are facts we can deduce without being physically present in the scene.

How many people are in this painting? It's hard to tell, as many of them are reflected in mirrors, so let's estimate. Count one small section and then multiply; I'd say there appear to be around fifty people in the background, with one woman and one man in the foreground. Who is the main subject? The barmaid or the mustachioed man in the black top hat in the upper right corner? What about the woman in the far upper left corner of whom we can see only her pointed green shoes — the trapeze artist? She's the entertainment, one of the reasons the crowds have gathered: to watch her. She could be the most important part of the scene, but we'd never know if we hadn't spotted her.

Let's list some of the sounds we'd expect to hear. Glasses clinking. People talking. Most likely music. Perhaps the tinkling of crystals in the chandeliers from the movement of the air or the squeak of the hinges on the trapeze?

What might we smell? The oranges. The liquor. The flowers in the vase on the bar. What about the flowers in the woman's bosom? Perhaps she has them there as a nosegay, to help shield her from other unpleasant odors, the smell of a mass of people who rarely bathed in a confined space without air conditioning?

What would the air in the room feel like? We can't see any windows, but we can see clouds of smoke in the background, which suggests there isn't a breeze or good ventilation. What would the smoke smell like? Taste like?

Now let's study the different perspectives in the painting. We'll climb behind the bar and stand next to the barmaid to see things from her perspective. What does she see? Lights and chandeliers and smoke and people. According to the mirror behind her, she is quite far away from the crowd. The reflection behind her shows that the mustachioed man is the only one nearby. Where is he in real life? Shouldn't he be standing right in front of her, blocking our view? Since he is not, are *we* him? Is the viewer meant to be the man in the top hat standing right in front of her?

Let's step into the man's shoes. If we were him, what would we be seeking from her? A drink, attention, the answer to a question, perhaps. Our perception of her expression, stance, and response changes remarkably if we are him. When we actively insert ourselves into the scene, her vacant stare could take on an entirely new meaning. Instead of detached or downtrodden we might see her as rude or lazy.

Now let's zoom up and see things from an entirely different point of view: that of the trapeze artist. How different would this scene look, feel, smell, and sound from above? Both hot air and smoke rise, so the temperature would be higher, the air thicker. The noise would likely be the same, if not a little quieter, but the lights might be brighter as she hangs suspended above the shimmering fixtures and the crowds. Being at the top of the room, she has nowhere to look but downward. What does she see? The tops of a lot of hats. Like the little girl I encountered in the airport, the trapeze artist does not get a lot of eye contact. How might that affect her view of the scene? While the minutiae of so many individual conversations might roll over the barmaid, the trapeze artist is privy to none of them. Instead of being in the middle, she is truly removed and detached. Is she paying attention to the crowd or preoccupied performing her job?

Striving to see the world from other people's perspectives can make any scene more vivid. But its value is far more than aesthetic. In fact, the ability to imagine others' viewpoints, reactions, and concerns is one of the most important cognitive tools we humans possess, as it makes us not only more sympathetic to others but more discerning when dealing with them — or when imagining how we should deal with them.

We've seen how getting a new vantage point physically helps accomplish this; now for even more insight, let's put ourselves in someone else's shoes more completely. Instead of just standing where they're standing, let's examine what the world might look like from behind their eyes.

In *To Kill a Mockingbird,* Atticus Finch tells his daughter, Scout, "You never really understand a person until you consider things from his point of view . . . until you climb into his skin and walk around in it." To do so is to elicit empathy, which is a vital competency for collaboration, managing conflict, and creative thinking in both professional and personal settings.

Forbes magazine calls empathy "the force that moves business forward." Jayson Boyers writes, "The reality is that for business leaders to experience success, they need to not just see or hear the activity around them, but also relate to the people they serve."

I frequently work with professional fund-raisers, and I was called in to train a team that wasn't reaching the level of donations they had hoped for. They were confounded, since it was their charity's fortieth anniversary, a milestone they had proudly advertised in all of their literature. They couldn't understand why the celebration of their longevity didn't lead to increased contributions. The problem was one of perspective. They were looking at the yearly campaign from their own point of view: as employees. Their sense of pride, however, doesn't necessarily translate to anyone outside their organization. I told the fund-raisers to look at their pamphlet from the donors' perspective. A donor's first priority isn't a charity's age; it's knowing their money is helping someone. In their eagerness to advertise their anniversary, the employees had accidentally minimized the good works they had done that year. The problem of the decreased donations was solved by incorporating other points of view.

British philosopher and author Roman Krznaric asserts that empathy is also "the key to having a successful marriage, getting your teenager to talk to you, or stopping the inevitable toddler tantrum . . . Empathy is the demonstrative act of stepping into the shoes of another person and understanding their feelings and perspectives," he says.

Practice actively putting yourself in others' places both physically and mentally. What does a finger-wagging reprimand look like from so far above a child's head? What do department-trimming budget decisions mandated from the top look like from the manager's chair?

What does a missed bonus look like for an employee who lives paycheck to paycheck?

Depending upon how wide the gulf is between you and the person you're trying to understand, you might need to go a little deeper to get a good look at things from the other person's perspective. The Emmy Award–winning television show *Undercover Boss* does just that by disguising CEOs as new employees and letting them see what life is like on the front lines of the companies they own. While entertaining to watch, the social experiment has yielded real-world results the executives say they couldn't have gotten otherwise.

Rick Silva, the CEO of Checkers and Rally's, fast food burger chains with twenty thousand employees and more than eight hundred restaurants, says, "The circumstances are weird, but going undercover gives you the chance to really connect with your workers." Posing as trainee "Alex Garcia," Silva learned that some employees were abused by poorly trained managers, others worked cheerfully despite debt and "Dickensian struggles" at home, and many hourly staff members were frustrated by the incentive program that only rewarded managers. "They wouldn't be anything were it not for us," Johanna, an exceptional employee he worked alongside (and couldn't keep up with), told him.

Silva took many insights back to corporate headquarters and made many changes. "I call [my good workers] 'Johannas' now," Silva says. "And I've got a lot of 'Johannas' out there and they don't feel confident enough for all the right reasons in talking to management." To remedy this, a "coach-to-grow" pilot program to identify the best employees was introduced, and the company began giving bonuses directly to team members and not just their managers.

Many parenting and relationship experts recommend a similar trading-places experiment when imagination just isn't enough. Every Halloween, educational consultant and writer Jennifer Miller challenges her readers to participate in a *Freaky Friday*–like challenge in which caregivers and their children swap roles and act as each other for one family activity. After doing it with her own family, Miller reported, "I learned how uncomfortable and tough it is to really try and put yourself in another's place and perspective. It's hard work.

It requires actively thinking about the other person, their beliefs, their daily habits, and how they would authentically look and sound. There's immediate accountability too since the person you are attempting to imitate is watching you. After the game, I noticed I was thinking frequently about what [my husband] might say in a particular situation or how [my son] might react. Just this one activity has heightened my own awareness of my family members' outlooks."

Empathy isn't the only benefit of adopting someone else's perspective. Doing so can also help us with problem solving. Putting ourselves in the shoes of a fictional or famous person can help us shift our line of thinking when we're stuck. Individually or as a group activity at the office or at home, select a well-known person and try to find a solution using that person's personality, history, and viewpoint. How would Shakespeare approach your productivity problem? What new features would give your product or service a competitive edge according to Oprah? What would Spider-Man say about disrespectful language?

In our digital age, looking at things from all angles before we act is also imperative for our own protection. When Marlene Mollan's fifteen-year-old daughter was unsure if she should post a photo from a Halloween party on her Twitter account, she ran it past her mother to get a second opinion. In the picture, Mollan's daughter was standing, fully clothed and appropriately posed, between two friends, muscular boys her age who had their shirts off.

"I'm not doing anything wrong in the picture, and neither are they," the girl said. "But I just wanted to make sure it wouldn't look bad."

Marlene Mollan knew that once posted, the photograph would live online forever, so while she didn't personally have a problem with it, she encouraged her daughter to look at it from as many perspectives as possible.

"What does your boyfriend think of the photo, considering he's not in it?" Mollan asked.

"I showed him, and he's fine with it," she answered. "He knows those boys and I are just friends."

"What about how future boyfriends might perceive it?" Mollan asked.

"What do you mean?"

"It might scare someone off if they think you only date guys who look like that. What if your future Prince Charming can't bench-press two hundred pounds?"

"Mom!"

"How do you think your boyfriend's mother would view it?" Mollan continued. "Or your grandmother? Your principal? Pastor? Future college recruiter? Future boss?"

Possibly not well, her daughter conceded. After considering how others might see her differently because of the photograph, she decided not to post it.

Just as important as seeing things from others' points of view is making sure they are privy to ours. Letting other people know what we experience adds both to mutual understanding and to the aggregate of information that can be collected.

During the search for Annie Le, not a single person on the Yale staff thought to tell investigators about the fan running continuously in the lab where she worked. They just assumed the police would hear it or know about it and turn it off. How much sooner would they have found Le's body if someone had mentioned it?

Just because you see or hear or smell or know something doesn't mean that everyone else does. Be aware that things that are familiar to you may be unfamiliar to others. If you live in New York City, it may be the omnipresent noises of sirens. If you live in the country, it may be the chirping of crickets and birds. Make sure you're taking a complete inventory of your world when you need to share it with someone else. To do this, ask yourself these simple questions:

- What am I tuning out?
- What might I be taking for granted?
- What would someone else coming into my world not know?

The more information you can gather, the more opportunity there is for accurate assessment, which in turn leads to a higher chance of finding what we seek, whether it's the solution, the answer, or the truth.

We've explored how to assess the who, what, where, and when. Understanding other perspectives can also help us answer the elusive "why." Why did she do what she did? Why did he quit? Why did someone sabotage a system or throw a tantrum or break up with us or leave town or burn that bridge? In most cases, a problem is the result of a reaction, and reactions are caused by actions. Understanding how others see things, what facts of life they might be dealing with, can help to answer why they act as they do.

In 2013, I helped the Peace Corps design a training program for its sexual assault response team. The program included a section on seeing things from all perspectives in order to formulate the most effective response. To provide for their volunteers' continued safety, Peace Corps staff needed a better way to identify how information is presented and perceived in situations involving assaults of volunteers. For instance, if the facts of a volunteer's story change when she tells it to different people, this might seem to indicate that she's not telling the truth. Stepping into her shoes presents alternate explanations. Imagine being a traumatized young woman, overseas, separated from friends and family, trying to describe the nature of a sexual encounter to an older, male manager who might resemble the assailant or the stern father who warned her against leaving home in the first place. From this perspective, it becomes easier to see why she might not be so forthcoming. Discerning that the volunteer might not be comfortable relaying certain details to specific members of the team can help the staff adjust their reporting protocols.

Similarly, while it's imperative to find out what the victim knows about the perpetrator, it's just as important to look at things from the attacker's perspective. What facts about the perpetrator might have contributed to the incident? Does he or his family have connections in local law enforcement or influence in the local community? Does he have connections or influence with the people the victim works or lives with? To get a complete picture of the situation, the community's perception of the incident also must be investigated. What was their reaction? Are they supportive of the victim, and if so, will they continue to be? Ultimately the question that must be answered is whether or not the volunteer should return to her site. The only way to answer that question is to see things from the perspective of everyone involved.

After JR helped give the world a new perspective on residents of Morro da Providência, Rio's civic leaders took notice. They finally ventured up the hill, met with residents, and learned what it was like to live there under the thumb of gang leaders, isolated by geography, having to walk down 365 steps just to get to a grocery store. In 2010 the civic leaders implemented a revolutionary social services program that included Pacifying Police Units to reclaim the area from armed drug dealers and reestablish peace. Resident associations elected presidents to bolster community pride. And in July 2014, a new cable car system was inaugurated to connect the favela to the city below. The cable cars can transport one thousand people per hour up and down the incline and are free of charge. With beautiful 360-degree vistas from every cabin, the gondola is also attracting a new type of person to the favela: tourists. They are coming in droves for a beautiful new view of the city.

A NEW VIEW

Imagine that you are in a fishing village in the South of France, standing in front of a window that opens out to the clear, blue waters of the Mediterranean Sea. The same warm breeze that skims boats across the surface blows in through the open glass. The village is a riot of color, from the local flowers that bloom year-round to the brightly hued buildings that hug the pebbled beaches.

That's just what the artist Henri Matisse enjoyed for nearly a decade when he escaped the wet winters of Paris for a rented studio in the small town of Collioure. The studio's window, technically two large doors that opened onto a tiny balcony, looked out over the town's harbor. Matisse spent countless hours in front of the window painting what he saw, capturing the colors he called "explosives," such as in this piece from 1905 simply titled *Open Window:*

Henri Matisse, *Open Window, Collioure*, 1905.

In 1914 he painted the same scene, titled *French Window at Collioure,* shown here:

Henri Matisse, *French Window at Collioure*, 1914.

What happened? The scene outside the window hadn't changed: it still held the blue Mediterranean, colorful ships, and warm sunny days. In fact, according to art historians at Centre Pompidou in Paris where the painting hangs, a closer view reveals that trees and ironwork on the balcony are faintly visible, as they were painted before Matisse applied a black color wash over them. What scholars believe changed was the way the artist viewed the world.

Like perception, our perspective can change. It is not permanently fixed. Many things can manipulate it: time, state of mind, new experiences through which we filter the world. How a person feels about something today, how he describes something today, may be very different from how he will feel about it or describe it in the future. In a recent session I did with child abuse investigators, one investigator acknowledged that what is going on in her personal life can color how she "sees" the information on a site visit.

For Matisse, life in 1914 was very different from life nine years earlier. World War I had recently begun, and France was suffering great casualties. The German army had invaded Matisse's hometown, trapping his elderly and ill mother behind enemy lines. His friends were drafted, his brother was a prisoner of war, and although he had tried to enlist many times, he was repeatedly rejected for being too old to serve. Instead, the French military commandeered his house in Paris for their headquarters, and he was exiled to his summer studio.

The actual vista outside the open window in Collioure had not changed. The landscape wasn't decimated by bombs or the town overrun by a foreign military. Life continued in the Catalan village as it had. Except to Matisse, it didn't look the same.

Why is this important? Because our changing perspective can change our observations. If we interviewed Matisse and asked him what color the sea was in 1914, and he said, "Black," it would not be a lie. The sea might appear blue to us but truly black to him. I highlighted this in the Peace Corps sexual assault team training, that a victim could change the facts of her story simply because she might remember things differently over time.

Current research suggests that the more we recall something, the more we either remember or remake our memory of that thing, especially if it's connected to an emotional experience. Elizabeth A. Phelps, professor of psychology and neural science at New York University, believes this is because of a direct line of communication in our brain between the visual cortex, the amygdala, where emotions are encoded, and the hippocampus, where memory is stored. When something arouses our emotions, good or bad, the amygdala tells our eyes to pay closer attention, giving our hippocampus more to store. However, while emotional involvement heightens our confidence in our memories, it doesn't necessarily enhance their objective accuracy.

Being aware of this possibility can help us avoid making assumptions — someone isn't telling the truth now, or wasn't before — that can put off those we're called to serve.

A SERVICE PERSPECTIVE

No matter what our jobs might be, we're all in some sort of service to others: our customers, our coworkers, our boss, our children, our partners, patients, distributors, readers, end users, even our friends. Instead of describing only experiences from our own reference point, we need to be attuned to others' perspectives so that we'll be better able to accommodate their needs and desires.

A perfect example of how someone I taught put this into practice for the benefit of her clients and her career is oncology social worker Judy Galvan. Judy set out to visit a terminally ill patient at the woman's new hospice care facility armed with a bright, scarlet blanket. She had heard the woman often spoke of being cold, a common complaint of cancer patients. Judy had known the patient for two years, had previously visited her at her home, where she lived proudly and independently, and knew the woman resisted checking in to the hospital until there was no other option.

"When I entered her hospital room, I was struck by how white, how stark, and how vacant it seemed," she told me. "Even though I've visited dozens of patients in hospital settings exactly like this one, I took in this patient's environment differently."

Having analyzed different perspectives in art, seeing things from a barmaid's and favela resident's eyes, Judy stepped behind this patient and saw things from her point of view.

"I noticed right away she was asleep in bed with her glasses on," Judy recalls. "As I laid the blanket over her, the contrast between the red blanket and the whiteness of the entire setting reinforced my perception of her description: cold. *Cold* means so much more than just lacking in temperature. There was nothing on her walls, except a small activities calendar that was placed out of her line of sight. She had one small window that overlooked a bland, urban landscape. And her pallor matched the room."

Determined to bring more warmth than just a blanket, Judy helped create a more visually interesting environment in the room with colorful objects her patient could see. She also arranged with the nurses to have the woman regularly taken to a garden on the hospital grounds. The change in scenery dramatically increased the quality of the woman's final days.

Shifting our perspective lets us see things for the first time or see things anew. The process can help us find both tiny details and earth-shattering, paradigm-shifting ideas, and you can use that information to solve problems and uncover new possibilities.

The final definition of *perspective* is the ability to view things in relation to their true importance. To master this angle as well, we'll sharpen our prioritization skills by looking at a boat, a train, a bridge, a balcony, and a house on fire.

7

Seeing What's Missing

How to Prioritize Like an Undercover Agent

WITH THE GLOCK pistol in my hand, I had a terrible sense of déjà vu from my graduate school police ride-along, only this time I was the one holding the gun. And I was standing outside my own house.

My pulse was racing as I climbed the front steps. I had never even held a weapon before, but I had no choice. I had heard that my son was alone in the house with an intruder, and I was the only one nearby. As I entered the front hallway, a man dressed in black ran in front of me, through the open back door, and into the yard. I sprinted after him. I could only see him from the back. He was holding a brown bag that looked bulky and heavy. He said nothing. I said nothing. I simply pulled the trigger.

The kickback was loud and sudden; the gun almost hit me in the face. I had aimed at his heart and hit my mark. He was dead.

The North Carolina police sergeant who had given me the gun couldn't believe it.

"He was retreating, you weren't in any danger, and he didn't even have a weapon," he scolded. "And *that's* the only guy you shot?"

I couldn't explain my action; no one was more surprised by it than I was.

When I'd arrived at the Integrity and Accuracy Conference for the North Carolina District Attorney's Office that morning, I was excited; prosecutors, public defenders, and police officers would all be attending this event, the purpose of which was to reinforce that in law enforcement everyone is on the same side. I never expected that I'd end the day holding a gun, much less killing someone.

After I registered my attendance, I was led into one of the hotel's ballrooms and told it was time for my FATS (firearm training simulator) testing. I was informed that everyone at the conference had to do it.

They put a patch on my neck to measure my pulse, set me up in front of an elaborate, realistic video screen system, and handed me a real gun.

The sergeant gave me a quick lesson in firearm safety, assured me that it wasn't loaded with ammunition, just a sensor, and stood back to let me begin.

I still wasn't ready. "When do I shoot?" I asked.

"Ma'am," the officer drawled, "shoot *when appropriate.*"

How was I supposed to know when that was? Who's to say what's appropriate? And therein lay the lesson: the situation and stimulus for action are different for everyone.

The video lit up. I was suddenly standing in a dark alleyway lined with rough brick walls. I raised my hands in front of me as the officer had demonstrated; I was to anticipate danger. The screen moved to simulate me walking, the walls blurring as they passed my peripheral vision. An empty white plastic bag rustled past my feet. A can of bright blue spray paint rested beneath an unfinished work of graffiti as if someone had left quickly before completing it. As I walked, a mangy amber-colored cat sitting on top of a dented, gray metal trash can hissed at me. A man's back came into view. He was stopped in the middle of the passage a couple feet ahead of me. He wore baggy jeans and a leather jacket. Greasy brown hair curled over his collar from beneath a black skullcap.

I stopped and stood still, though slightly wobbly, unsure of what to do. The gun was cold and heavier than I'd expected; holding it at arm's length made my wrist ache faintly. Suddenly the man turned and lunged at me with a knife. I lowered the gun and pulled the trigger.

The video stopped and the officer reappeared. "Um, darlin'," he said, "you fired at his feet."

"I know," I answered.

"Why?" he asked.

"I didn't want to hurt him, I just wanted to stop him," I explained.

"Ma'am, he *did* mean to hurt you," he replied.

Without a pause, the second scene started. I was in a backyard. A wooden fence about six feet high encased the patchy grass area on all three sides, the slats so close together that the view beyond them was obstructed. An unplanted bed of soil lined with large rocks hugged the fence.

Two men stood in the middle of the yard, struggling over something I couldn't see. They wrestled for control of an object, hidden by their callused hands. I hesitated.

"You can talk to the video," the policeman called out to me. "It's interactive."

New information, good to know.

"What's going on here?" I said in my most authoritative voice.

The men stopped and looked at me. "Who is she?" one asked the other.

How did they know I was female? I wondered. Could they really see me? The simulation felt more and more real.

The man on the right, burly with a stubbly beard and a good six inches taller than me, let go of the scrawnier, clean-shaven man. "I'll take care of her," he said.

He bent down, picked up a large rock, and advanced toward me. I stood my ground. He lifted the rock and brought it down where my head would be. The video stopped.

"Why didn't you fire?" the officer asked me.

"He didn't have a weapon," I said lamely.

"A rock that size in the hands of a man that big is a weapon," he said. "He just killed you. And not in a pretty way."

Fantastic.

The third video rolled. This time I was driving a car. An odd sense of discomfort settled over me — in real life I don't drive. As I pulled up to my house, a plump, blond, middle-aged woman in a fuzzy pink bathrobe ran up to my car window, her face creased with worry.

"Someone's been casing your house," she said. "I think they're inside."

I jumped out of the car.

"Isn't your kid inside?" she said.

As if on cue, a small voice echoed from inside the house: "Mom!"

I went through the front door, arms raised, and saw the man with the bag running away. Without hesitating, I shot him in the back, killing him.

"So when someone actually wants to kill you, you either don't shoot or shoot them in the foot," the officer repeats, "but this guy, running away, without a weapon, without threatening you, *him* you kill?"

It turns out I was the only one at the conference who'd shot at the last man. When they asked me later to stand up and explain why I had, I still didn't have a good answer. It was a visceral reaction: if you hurt my child, I will kill you. I didn't have any proof that my child had been hurt, I didn't have really good justification for homicide, but I did it. I fired.

I spent many agonizing nights afterward trying to figure out why I pulled the trigger when I did. Everything happened so quickly, my thoughts had barely had time to catch up. My reactions were automatic and almost felt involuntary. But they were mine, and I would have had to take responsibility for them if this had been real life rather than a simulation. So what had shaped my reflexive decision to fire?

Even in the short time frame of each simulation, I'd gathered plenty of objective facts. I'd noted the gender, height, and facial features of my companions as well as what they were wearing and carrying. I hadn't made assumptions about their character or morality. I'd taken in my environment, both the big picture and small details. Although I couldn't smell a video, I'd used my other senses to take in textures and sounds. I'd heeded my own perceptual filters, recognizing that being behind the wheel of a car made me uncomfortable. Even my past experience came into play: not having any personal encounters with violence from a knife or a rock meant I didn't implicitly see them as fatal weapons.

Very quickly I'd collected a lot of data and sorted it for objectivity or subjectivity, fact or assumption, but what had made me act on only some of it and not all of it? What had caused certain items to rise to the forefront and influence my decision making? The way I prioritized the information.

The reason I didn't shoot at the first two attackers but did fire at the last, unarmed man begins and ends with my son. He is my number one priority. As most parents undoubtedly do, I value my child's safety even over my own life.

It's critical that we know how we prioritize information because what we label in our minds as most important is what we're going to *act* upon. Up until now, everything we've covered has dealt with assessing information and analyzing what we've gathered.

How we prioritize that information, however, whether consciously or not, will most directly affect our actions.

As soon as we have multiple data points, we have a choice: which will we act upon? Our resulting actions are not always as extreme and physical as deciding whether to shoot a stranger. We might have to make less life-threatening but still critical decisions such as determining which pieces of information we're going to dedicate resources to pursuing and in what order.

We can't physically or mentally follow up, hunt down, or investigate every single piece of information we uncover, at least not all at once. In reviewing the cognitive limits of the human brain and the myth of multitasking, we've learned that a single human cannot do multiple things at once. Walking and talking, yes. Reading a book about neural connections while interviewing a university professor and his orangutan puppet? No. If we don't consciously decide which task to deal with first, our brains will choose for us based on our built-in perceptions and biases. And that's not always a good thing, as we can see from the experience of Dr. Anna Pou.

When Hurricane Katrina hit on August 29, 2005, Dr. Pou, a respected surgeon, was on duty at the Memorial Medical Center in New Orleans. She volunteered to stay past her shift to care for patients and didn't leave the hospital for four days, while conditions within and outside the facility deteriorated. She carried supplies, helped ration food, and took two-hour turns manually squeezing ventilators to keep patients alive. All of her good deeds, however, were overshadowed by decisions she made when prioritizing.

As floodwaters surrounded the hospital, it lost electricity, the sanitation systems stopped working, food ran out, and the building's temperature rose to 110 degrees Fahrenheit. At night the hospital was pitch black and frightening.

"We started hearing stories about murders, about gangs raping women and children," Pou told the Associated Press. "The women that had their children there were really scared."

People had to make tough decisions about how to care for and then evacuate the more than two thousand people inside. Dr. Pou was one of those people. She prioritized who needed to be moved, and in what order, and who could be left behind based on the medical conditions she observed. For her efforts, she was subsequently labeled a hero and a murderer. Although she had stayed, at great personal risk, and for five days led a small cadre of healthcare workers to save and evacuate patients, a year later, as Dr. Pou pulled up to her house after a thirteen-hour surgery, she was arrested, handcuffed in her scrubs, and charged with second-degree murder for the deaths of some of the elderly patients, all with do-not-resuscitate orders. She had decided to sedate them in order to "help [them] through their pain," and they had subsequently died. The case was eventually dropped when a grand jury refused to indict Dr. Pou, but not before the charges had wreaked havoc on her personal and professional life.

Catastrophic events and emergencies can quickly, and without warning or remorse, expose any foundation's underlying flaws to you, your business, your family, and sometimes the entire world. Following deadly accidents in 2013, the New York Metropolitan Transportation Authority released a report that found the Metro-North Railroad prioritized on-time performance over public safety. Riders were understandably outraged. Also in 2013, the Arizona Division of Occupational Safety and Health announced that nineteen firefighters lost their lives in the previous summer's Yarnell Hill fire because the Forestry Division had prioritized protection of property over the safety of their workers, a finding that devastated the victims' families.

Mistakes from poor prioritization can follow us. Although he has moved on to become the head of a wireless charging company, any future success Thorsten Heins finds will always be accompanied by the postscript of his folly as the former CEO of BlackBerry, Ltd. CNN reports that he was ousted for his "one, crucial, overarchingmistake: he didn't prioritize BlackBerry's core business-focused customers." Instead, he tried to mimic the mass consumer success of Apple and Android, a decision that led to a disastrous $1 billion writedown on unsold inventory. Similarly, the reputation of the Daughters of the Republic of Texas, the patriotic women's group that has managed the locally revered Alamo historical site since 1905, took a hit when the state attorney general's office revealed — and the *New York Times* reported — that the organization failed to prioritize the preservation of the very site it was dedicated to. While $10 million was allocated to expand the Alamo's library, only $350 was reserved for preservation-related projects each year, and the roof was allowed to leak for fourteen years. The furor resulted in the governor and the Texas General Land Office ending the Daughters' 110-year reign as caretakers of the property.

After my own experience behind a Glock, I will never again judge anyone for life-or-death decisions, but I cannot control whether I will be judged. Dr. Pou was called to account for her decisions months later and was judged for them outside the context in which she made them. We all run the same risk all too often. Everything from managing relationships to budgeting finances can quickly spin, or be spun, out of control. Having a clear understanding of our priorities ahead of time can help alleviate much of the damage.

Conscious, planned prioritization is critical for more than just law enforcement and medical professionals. Being able to rank information from most important to least is essential for business, education, parenting, job interviews, and even the SAT. Prioritization allows us to be more focused, more efficient, and more decisive.

Many people are unaware of what their personal prioritization techniques are; that is the case with most of the professionals I train. During a program I taught that included 911 operators, I had all the participants pair up. One person would face a screen at the front of the room, and the other would look away from the screen and take notes. I put up a photograph and gave the observers one minute to describe what they saw to their partner, who was instructed to make a sketch based on the information the observer gave. Here is the photograph.

Joel Sternfeld, *McLean, Virginia, December 1978*.

To see your baseline prioritizing skills, take one minute and write down as many objective facts as you can.

After I called time, we reviewed how successfully the duos had cataloged the facts. Everyone told me about the pumpkins, some mentioning that they were smashed in the foreground. I heard wonderful descriptions of fall colors and leafless flora. Many had the full signage correctly noted: McLEAN FARM MARKET, SWEET CIDER. Some even mentioned the red apple painted on the sign at the right.

Unbelievably, some observers had completely neglected to mention *the house on fire*. They assured me that they hadn't missed it; they just hadn't gotten to tell their partners about that part yet because, as one of them explained, "we started on pumpkins and worked our way back from the foreground, and then you called time."

Let me repeat: this group included *911 operators.* I'm not trying to single them out, they were terrific participants, but I think it indicates the enormity of the challenge—and possibly the danger—we face when we lack a prioritization plan. We should all have one. And simply going front to back isn't a good one. It's a way to list information, but just listing information isn't good enough. At work or at home, we can't just dump everything in no particular order onto another person or into a report. We can't assume anyone else has the time or desire or skill to parse mountains of data from various sources. We need to give the information some order, or someone else will, perhaps incorrectly. We need to make sure that the important information doesn't get lost or buried by everything else.

To do this, we need a system to prioritize information. There are dozens of methods, some with arcane monikers: high/medium/low, MoSCoW, tops and bottoms, Pareto charts, Kano, matrices, scattergrams, and timeboxing. In the medical world, they use the triage system to find and care for the most injured first. In the military, reverse triage—which Dr. Pou employed in her hospital—is used to evacuate first those most likely to live. Six Sigma has a project prioritization matrix. SAP product integration uses value mapping. And while the Pentagon uses the CARVER matrix, the National Association of County and City Health Officials simply uses colorful poker chips dropped into shoe boxes at meetings. It doesn't matter which method you choose to prioritize; what matters is that you *do* prioritize, making sure that you put the most important information first.

To remind themselves to start a story with the most salient piece of information, journalists say: "Don't bury the lede."

In order to prioritize, we must first sift through all available data and bring the most important facts to the top. We can't do this successfully unless we've first collected everything that could possibly be collected, but once that's done, we need to whittle it down.

For instance, say you've just completed a home visit for a welfare check. You've collected every fact you could find, from the nap of the carpet to the contents of the magazine basket. You don't, however, need to pass every bit of information on in the formal written report. You don't need to include that the curtains in the living room were blue, but if they had bullet holes in them, you need to note it, and you need to note it first.

The Baltimore Police Department does a great job of this in its sexual assault investigation training. While its "Interviewing the Victim" guidelines packet is detailed and thorough, including information such as where the victim should be interviewed, how the report should be written, and if background checks should be run, it begins with a single sentence: "Interviewing the Victim Detectives shall prioritize the needs and comfort of the victim." Placing this directive first clearly and concisely highlights what an important part of the process it is. And it is, since according to Captain John Darby of the Philadelphia Police Department Special Victims Unit, the better a victim is treated, the more likely the case will end with justice for the perpetrator.

Like observation, perception, and perspective, priorities will differ for each of us and for each scenario. Different prioritization systems will work better for different people. The one I've found to be the most helpful to the widest range of people I teach is the three-prong approach outlined in the CIA training manual *The Psychology of Intelligence Analysis* by Richard J. Heuer. To help organize data and find the most important elements of any situation, you ask three questions: What do I know? What don't I know? If I could get more information, what do I need to know?

WHAT DO I KNOW?

To answer this question, we'll use the assessment skills we've sharpened in the previous chapters. We'll start at ground zero and just observe, then work on collecting the who, what, when, and where. We'll pay attention to our perceptual filters and make sure we're only drawing objective conclusions. We'll then change our perspective physically and mentally, reorienting ourselves to better see both the small details and the big picture. Once we finish that process, we'll analyze all of the data and decide what's most important.

Let's practice with the following painting, called *Time Trans-fixed* by René Magritte, currently in the collection of the Art In-stitute of Chicago. Use all of the observation and perception tech-niques we've learned so far and list all the facts you can find. You can write them down or just catalog them mentally; I just want you to articulate what you notice. And I want you to notice what you no-tice, so don't keep reading until you've given it a really thorough once-over.

René Magritte, *Time Transfixed*, 1938.

Now check off everything you saw:

_____ a train coming out of a fireplace; more specifically, a black
and gray steam locomotive traveling out of a fireplace and
suspended several feet above the floor

_____ smoke or steam emerging from the engine's front-most
smokestack

_____ a mottled grayish white fireplace with a mantel

_____ a black clock with a round white face containing Roman
numerals on the mantel

_____ two brown metallic-looking candlesticks flanking the
clock

_____ a large gold-colored framed mirror mounted above the
fireplace

_____ the wood-grain floorboards; bonus points if you counted
fifteen

What about the smaller details? Did you note any of the following?

_____ that the locomotive has ten wheels, only six of which we
can see

_____ the red stripe along the side of the train and the red
bumper on front

_____ the light-brown wainscoting on the walls surrounding the
fireplace

_____ that the time on the clock appears to be 12:42

_____ the shadow of the train in the fireplace pointing
southwest

_____ that only the left candlestick is reflected in the mirror

_____ that the steam from the train flows up into the chimney
instead of out into the room

Now let's order the facts from both sections by numbering them
in the chart on page 157 from most to least important. Since the level

of importance will change for each situation and each person evaluating it, I'm going to give you some parameters:

1. Let's say you were called into an apartment, such as Linda Stein's, to investigate a murder. In column 1, number each fact according to what might be the most important.
2. Imagine that this is the house of a missing person, such as Annie Le. How would the order of importance change? In column 2, number each fact according to what you now believe to be the most important.
3. Now it's the drawing room of a billionaire and the scene of a massive art heist. In column 3, number the facts in order of importance.
4. Let's shift gears and imagine you're an interior designer called in to completely gut and renovate this space. Use column 4 to number the facts according to what might be the most important.
5. Finally, if you'd been hired by a historical society to renovate and preserve this room, what would be the order of importance of what you've seen? Fill in column 5.

We can see how prioritization changes depending on circumstances. For a murder investigation, the most important items would be the candlesticks as potential weapons. For a missing-person search, it would be the time on the clock. For an art heist, it would be the train that was left behind. Even when the order of importance remains the same — both an interior designer and a historical preservationist would be most concerned about the wood floor, wainscoting, and fireplace surround — the reasons for those priorities are different: a designer is looking at the scope of demolition, while a preservationist views the same things with an eye toward refurbishment. Ultimately, there's no single right answer, as long as we are prioritizing what we know with a specific purpose in mind.

That said, we must still catalog and list the facts that may not be relevant to the purpose at hand. We might have no idea what a train is doing in a fireplace, but that doesn't mean we can ignore it.

1. MURDER INVESTIGATION	2. MISSING PERSON	3. ART HEIST	4. INTERIOR DESIGNER	5. HISTORICAL RENOVATION	
					a train coming out of a fireplace, or more specifically, a black and gray steam locomotive traveling out of a fireplace and suspended several feet above the floor
					smoke or steam coming out of the engine's front-most smokestack
					a mottled grayish white fireplace with a mantel
					a black clock with a round white face containing Roman numerals on the mantel
					two brown metallic-looking candlesticks flanking the clock
					a large gold-colored framed mirror mounted above the fireplace
					the wood-grain floorboards; bonus points if you counted fifteen
					that the locomotive has ten wheels, only six of which we can see
					the red stripe along the side of the train and the red bumper on its front
					the light-brown wainscoting on the walls surrounding the fireplace
					that the time on the clock appears to be 12:42
					the shadow of the train in the fireplace pointing southwest
					that only the left candlestick is reflected in the mirror
					that the steam from the train flows up into the chimney instead of out into the room

Sarah Grant, *The Furniture City Sets the Table for the World of Art,* 2009.

During an assessment exercise I showed the photograph above — which is an actual, unaltered photograph of an outdoor art installation in Michigan — to one of my classes and asked a young man to describe it. He did a great job, except that he failed to mention the table and chairs on top of the bridge. He left them out not because he didn't see them but because he "didn't know what to make of them." That is not a valid reason for omitting a fact. It doesn't matter if you don't understand it; someone else might. Ignoring the unknown can be dangerous.

When email had just started to become mainstream in the mid-1990s, many companies didn't know how to handle the sudden influx of new customer contact. One well-known corporation — a large, public entertainment destination for happy families — simply ignored it. For months. Executives told their customer communications department not to worry about email and not to respond at all because they believed people were just sending comments "into space" and didn't expect a reply back. Two things quickly changed their minds. The *New York Times* ran a front-page article about how Fortune 500 companies were bungling their email policies; this company was not mentioned, but management realized it could easily have been. And a tech-savvy employee who was working on the company's first website discovered that bomb threats were being sent via email. Immediately, the company put together a team to figure out how to manage this new reality of modern communication effectively. It was lucky that ignoring the unknown didn't literally blow up in their faces.

So we're cataloging and still prioritizing what we see even if we don't know what we're looking at. Now let's look at what to do about the things we don't see.

WHAT DON'T I KNOW?

Answering this question takes skills very similar to the ones we used to answer the previous question, but instead of searching for what's there, we'll search for what isn't. In many instances, what is not present is as important as what is. This concept is called the "pertinent negative" in emergency medicine, and it's defined as "the absence of a sign or symptom that helps substantiate or identify a patient's condition." For instance, a doctor with a patient complaining of shortness of breath might listen for a crackling sound in the patient's lungs. If it's not found, it can help rule out pneumonia. The crackling sound is the pertinent negative: it's usually present, but in this case it isn't.

Knowing that Sir Arthur Conan Doyle studied medicine under the tutelage of the notoriously observant Dr. Joseph Bell, it should come as no surprise that his most famous fictional creation was exceedingly adept at using the pertinent negative. We can see this skill in an exchange between Sherlock Holmes and Scotland Yard's Inspector Gregory while they're investigating a murder in the short story "Silver Blaze." Inspector Gregory initiates the dialogue quoted below, and Holmes responds:

> "Is there any point to which you would wish to draw my attention?"
> "To the curious incident of the dog in the night-time."
> "The dog did nothing in the night-time."
> "That was the curious incident."

The dog's failure to bark was the clue that broke the case and pinpointed the murderer as someone the victim (and the victim's dog) knew.

Within and beyond the world of medicine, the absence of an object, event, or behavior can help identify or substantiate a situation. When we are observing what we see, we must also note the important information we *don't* see, especially if we're expecting it to be there.

Look again at the painting on page 154 and list what's missing. Did you note the following?

____ no candles in the candlesticks
____ no tracks under the train
____ no fire in the fireplace

Identifying the pertinent negative helps give our observations more specificity. By articulating what is conspicuously absent, we are giving a more precise description of what we perceive. When we purposefully state the pertinent negative, we are more accurate. It isn't enough to say that there are candlesticks on the mantel. If we just say "candlestick," at least half of our listeners will assume there are candles in them. We have to specify that there are no candles to debunk assumptions.

Most of my classes notice the missing candles, whether they state it or not, but almost everyone forgets to mention that there is no fire in the fireplace. If you ask people to draw a fireplace, sight unseen, chances are they will put some logs and a fire in it. That's what fireplaces are for. So the absence of a fire is important information.

The pertinent negative can lead to the big break, the elusive solution, or a clue we might otherwise never have gotten. In fact, it's so powerful that just hearing about it from a three-minute online video on my website helped solve a homicide.

North Carolina District Attorney's Office investigator Gerald Wright was called to investigate a fatal boating accident. The report filed by the witnesses on board claimed that their boat had unexpectedly rolled in the water, causing one of the occupants to be ejected and killed. All the officers on the scene knew that something about the situation wasn't adding up, but they didn't know what. When Wright arrived to search the vessel, he found on the deck in the bow a mesh bag that contained a collection of documents: ownership papers, electronics manuals, insurance information. Nothing about

Visual Intelligence

them seemed out of the ordinary until Wright recalled my lesson on the pertinent negative. What was missing from the boating accident that should have been there? Water. He realized that if events had played out as the witnesses claimed they had, the papers in the boat would have been wet, and they weren't.

His observation led to a complete investigation, including a forensic download of the vessel's navigation system that ultimately proved that it hadn't rolled over. Instead, it pitched to one side and ejected the passenger, who was then struck by the propeller as the boat was steered back around to circle the victim. The "accident" was reclassified correctly as a homicide.

I work with resident advisor programs on college campuses, and one of their biggest problems is "Velcro parents" who can't seem to let go of their children. These parents can consume an inordinate amount of an RA's time with anxious phone calls: "I haven't heard from my son in twenty-four hours. Is he safe?" The RA can go look in the room, but RAs aren't keepers or concierges; if the student isn't there, the RA generally has no idea where he is. Colleges are big, and college students are exploring their newfound freedom; they often don't check in with their parents.

An RA can't simply tell parents that their child is gone; it won't ease the parents' minds or stop the check-ins. Instead, I teach them to employ the pertinent-negative search that investigators use when trying to determine if a missing person is a kidnap victim or a runaway. Aside from the person, they look at what else is missing. Where is the student's phone, laptop, wallet, keys? If those things are gone, the person most likely chose to leave and isn't in danger. RAs can employ the pertinent negative when assessing the big picture of what might have happened: Is the student a loner, not checking in with others regularly, or is a lapse in connection with parents and friends completely out of character and therefore a real sign of danger?

Medical personnel can also tell a lot from who is missing; the absence of relatives and friends in the hospital speaks volumes about a patient's life and support system. Teachers can note the same in parents' level of involvement in their child's classroom, or lack thereof.

Actively cataloging what's missing can also help us zero in on what we need. Organizational consultant Terry Prince recommends looking at who, what, where, and when from a "missing perspective" when project planning. "Who do we *not* need? What should we *not* include? Where are we *not* going? When are we *not* doing this?"

A teenager in Michigan used the pertinent negative to help the less fortunate in her city. While walking through downtown Detroit for a Martin Luther King Jr. Day procession, Hunter Maclean noticed something missing from her fellow marchers. Although the temperature on the January morning was well below freezing, most of the people walking, including many children, lacked hats and gloves. Determined to fix the problem, Hunter started a collection at her high school. Her charity, Warm Detroit, has since expanded to five other schools and delivered more than two thousand hats and gloves to homeless and women's shelters in her area.

Acknowledging what we don't know can be as important as identifying what we do. This doesn't just include the pertinent negative or what's missing, it also includes the information we gathered that is subjective, unclear, or based on an assumption. We cannot act as if these things don't exist. Admitting them up front and labeling them correctly can lead to the extra data necessary to turn a "not sure" into a "definite."

Many people leave out what they don't know because they mistakenly think it shows ignorance or a lack of hard work. Asking the question "What don't I know?" is not the same as throwing out an "I don't know." In truth what you are saying is, "No one right here right now knows, and I was observant enough to notice this important fact and open it up for others to help me find the answer." If we reframe our attitude about it, others will follow.

Our boss or project manager or partner wants to know if something isn't heading in the direction that was anticipated, if something isn't working, and what's missing. The sooner we find out about an issue, the sooner it can be fixed. Letting others know what's missing shouldn't be looked upon as a shortcoming by us or our superiors. Instead, view it as an opportunity to further investigate and collaborate.

Managers need to remove any stigma to allow their employees to feel comfortable bringing unknowns to their attention. A corporate culture that doesn't support honest and objective observation and reporting because of executive expectations will lead employees to fill in the gaps, which isn't good for anyone. For instance, in chapter 4 when we studied the risk of assumptions, we reviewed some of the findings of the Iraq Intelligence Commission's report about the events leading up to the Iraq War. The report concluded, "Perhaps most troubling, we found an Intelligence Community in which analysts had a difficult time ... identifying unambiguously for policymakers what they *do not know*. Too often, analysts simply accept these gaps; they do little to help collectors identify new opportunities, and they do not always tell decision makers just how limited their knowledge really is ... Analysts must be willing to admit what they don't know in order to focus future collection efforts. Conversely, policymakers must be prepared to accept uncertainties and qualifications in intelligence judgment and not expect greater precision than the evaluated data permits."

Imagine that your organization faced the same internal scrutiny the intelligence community did. How would it rate in employees' willingness to admit what they don't know and managers' willingness to accept that information? In analyzing data, collaboration is key. Everyone needs to know what we know as well as what we don't.

WHAT DO I NEED TO KNOW?

The final question to ask in any situation: if I could get more information about this scene or situation, what specifically would I want to know? Asking this question can help us prioritize potential follow-up work by showing us where to dedicate our time and resources. Of course, our needs for additional information will vary depending upon our personal experience, job, and reason for looking; a law enforcement officer will seek to fill different holes than a potential employer will.

Let's practice with Edward Hopper's *Automat* painting on page 60. In chapter 4 we assessed it in detail, and in the end, there were many things we did not know.

We did not know the following:

- the identity of the woman in the green coat
- her age
- where she lives
- where she works
- why she is in the Automat
- what she's drinking
- what's she's already eaten or drunk, if anything
- her mood and overall personality
- her reason for being out alone
- her marital status
- the name of the Automat
- where it is located
- what time it is
- where the woman's missing glove is
- why it is missing

Look back over this list from the point of view of your job or primary daily responsibilities. Now prioritize by number which answers would be the most important for you to find out—which answers might lead to other answers. You now have a personalized priority list explicitly showing what things you would need to work on finding out first.

PUTTING IT ALL TOGETHER

To see the three-question prioritization method in action, let's revisit my surprising shoot-to-kill experience at the North Carolina FATS session and see how I prioritized information in the third scenario with the man holding a bag running out my back door. I've been doing this a long time, and it's second nature to me now, but here's what transpired automatically in my brain:

What do I know?
- My son is home alone.
- There is a strange man in my house.
- He's running away carrying something.

What don't I know?
- Where in the house my son is.
- If my son is safe or hurt.
- Who the stranger is.
- If the stranger has a weapon.
- What the stranger is carrying in his bag.

What do I need to know?
- Whether my son is all right.

In this instance, the home was my own, my son was crying out, and I had a loaded gun. Without me even realizing it at the time, my priorities informed my actions and resulted in the death of an unarmed man. The outcome might not have been the same for someone with different priorities, but I'm grateful that the simulated experience gave me a chance to review and practice prioritizing outside of a real-life incident. Knowing what our priorities are ahead of time or as soon as information presents itself will help everyone involved, before, during, and after an event.

Now let's practice prioritizing using our three-question method on the following photograph:

What do we know? As we learned in the assessment chapters, let's start with who. There are four white women standing at a rough-hewn wooden railing. Easy enough, yes? However, we don't want to jump to conclusions, even on the simple stuff. Are they women? Yes, they appear to be. Are there four of them? Look again. Unless one of them has a bionic arm, there is a fifth person we cannot fully see with her hand across the right shoulder of the woman to the far left. So there are five people. Each woman we can see has a hand to her face. One of the women is wearing glasses. All of the women have on long-sleeved dresses and are wearing their hair swooped back from their face in a similar style. The woman third from the left wears a watch on her left wrist.

I've had participants tell me that the women belong to a religious organization. One was positive they were "Amish," since she grew up in Pennsylvania and knew what the Amish were like. While it might be a good guess, it's still an inference. Based on our observations alone, we have no proof that they are Amish or religious in any way. They could be historical reenactors.

What other facts do we know? What about where? They are outdoors. We can't assume that they are in a rural setting or what kind of building they are in front of, as we can't see it. What about when? Someone told me that it looks like a modern photograph even though the women are wearing old-fashioned clothing. I agree. The photo was not taken one hundred years ago but is more recent. How recent —1980? 2014? We don't know because of their old-fashioned dress. We can see that it is daytime, but that is all.

Let's look at the second prioritization question: what don't we know? We don't know these women's relationship to one another. We don't know where they are. We don't know when this photograph was taken; what they are looking at; why their faces are registering emotion that could be grief, horror, disbelief, or sadness; or what they are feeling.

Finally, what do we want to know? Everything, of course, but let's prioritize. Looking back over what we don't know, what one fact would answer the most of our unanswered questions? The single most important question that would give us the most answers is: what happened?

As it turns out, I can tell you. In April 2008, Texas authorities raided the Yearning for Zion Ranch outside Eldorado, a compound owned by the Fundamentalist Church of Jesus Christ of Latter-Day Saints, a polygamous sect led by Warren Jeffs. More than four hundred children were taken into custody. This photograph shows some of the mothers watching the scene unfold. By prioritizing all of the information we don't know and boiling it down to "we'd like to know what happened," we just answered the majority of the other questions: who the women are, what their relationship to one another is, where this happened, and why.

While other people might have scrambled in different directions trying to track down who the women were or where this took place, by narrowing our focus to what we most wanted to know, we obtained the most answers in the shortest amount of time.

URGENT VERSUS IMPORTANT

As you prioritize information, be aware of the difference between urgent and important. Urgent concerns scream for our attention, but they usually offer only short-term solutions. Important things contribute value in the long run. While sometimes urgent tasks are also important, more often the urgent obscures the important.

President Dwight D. Eisenhower was well known for prioritizing his daily duties by sifting the urgent from the important; time management experts today still recommend the Eisenhower Decision Matrix. Brett McKay and his wife, Kate McKay, authors of the bestselling *Art of Manliness* advice book series, explain why it's so effective: "Urgent tasks put us in a *reactive* mode, one marked by a defensive, negative, hurried, and narrowly focused mindset . . . When we focus on important activities we operate in a *responsive* mode, which helps us remain calm, rational, and open to new opportunities."

Almost everyone today operates under resource constraints—a

lack of time, people, or money. Urgent is not likely to ever go away. Recognizing this stress can help you cut through it.

Let's look back at the pumpkin patch photograph on page 151. The house on fire is definitely an urgent fact, but is it the most important? Let's use our three-pronged prioritization technique to find out.

What do we know? There's a two-story, yellow painted house on fire being attended to by a fire truck with a telescoping ladder behind a pumpkin patch at McLean's Farm Market in the autumn.

What don't we know? Where the pumpkin patch and house are located. How the fire started. Why the customer shopping for pumpkins seems so unconcerned about the blaze in the background.

What is the most important piece of information we need to know that will help us answer the most questions? The house on fire is urgent, but the more important mystery concerns the dispassionate shopper.

Examining the shopper more closely might help us figure out why he's so blasé about the nearby fire. He is wearing a bulky, yellow coat, which considering that the temperature might be chilly in autumn isn't that striking. He is also wearing a helmet and boots: rubber boots with the telltale colored stripe on top. He is a fireman. Let's analyze this new fact.

Why of all people would a fireman be casually picking pumpkins in the face of a house fire? Could he possibly not know about it? In rural settings such as this, the fire departments don't comprise thousands of people as in a big city, so chances are that he knows about the fire. And he's still shopping. When is a fireman not concerned about a fire? When he knows it was set on purpose as a training exercise.

Photographer Joel Sternfeld happened upon this scene when he was traveling across the country in his Volkswagen van. The title of his famous photograph, published in *Life* magazine, revealed nothing more than a time and place: *McLean, Virginia, December 1978.* Viewers and critics alike took it at face value: damning evidence of professional incompetence, Nero hunts for pumpkins while Rome burns. Sternfeld confirmed only later in his career that the photo did in fact depict a controlled training exercise and a fireman taking an honest break. Had someone, anyone, followed up on the most important fact — a browsing firefighter — the truth could have been discovered much earlier.

WHAT OUR PRIORITIES SAY ABOUT US

What's important to one person might not be important to another, but make no mistake, how you prioritize can tell the world — your bosses, coworkers, partners, friends, children — a lot about you.

Over the holidays a photographer in Erie, Pennsylvania, hoping to get a heartwarming shot, visited a charity warehouse where local children were allowed to pick any three things they wanted. Most chose toys or dolls. A few chose new tennis shoes. But one child's choice stood out: he selected Cheerios, toilet paper, and toothpaste. Without saying a word, the child communicated his priorities, and in doing so offered a peek into his personal life. Unlike the other children, who were part of an after-school care program, this boy was homeless.

Before it was acquired by Delta, Northwest Airlines had a reputation for prioritizing passenger comfort over the cost of fuel. Aviation enthusiasts who tracked Northwest's flight patterns recorded that the airline gave a wide berth to turbulence, while other planes flew right through it. Knowing Northwest's priorities helped customers decide whether or not to use the airline based on their own priorities: whether a smooth ride was more important to them than a quick flight.

We must be conscious of what our priorities tell others. Does our boss know the lengths we'll go to to secure a new deal? Do our loved ones know they rank higher than our professions? Does our date know she is more important than that phone call? Do our kids know that spending time with them outweighs everything? Whether we're aware of how we advertise our priorities or not, we are advertising them.

I took a group to see the painting *Dowager in a Wheelchair* by Philip Evergood in the Smithsonian American Art Museum. It's a very large — 3 feet by 4 feet — very busy painting of a well-dressed elderly woman being pushed down a crowded New York City street by a well-dressed younger woman. They pass mothers with baby carriages, shoppers carrying parcels, people walking dogs. They are bordered on the left by cars and a taxi, and on the right by an apartment building.

Philip Evergood, *Dowager in a Wheelchair*, 1952.

The painting is a cacophony of color and movement and is painted from an unusual perspective. Flowers bloom from window boxes. The naked backside of a woman in red high heels can be seen through the window. The woman in the wheelchair herself is covered with details. She wears a flower-patterned orange and purple hat with a gauzy veil over her face, a purple choker, long black gloves that creep well past her elbows, and three bracelets on one wrist. She has on low black heels with a Mary Jane strap. Spectacles sit on her lap. And her filmy lavender dress, hemmed with lace or revealing a petticoat underneath, is see-through.

There's a lot going on in the picture. How do you prioritize it? If the first thing you say is "nipples" instead of "old woman in a wheelchair," people might wonder why. Be honest about what you see, but know that the order in which you present that information reflects upon you. Take the time to organize your observations and what you believe is critical, and be able to back up your reasoning before you make your thoughts public.

Prioritizing information, especially if we're not used to doing it, might feel at first like it's slowing us down, but it's an integral step in the organization and analysis of information. Thankfully, as with all of the other skills described in this book, the more we consciously prioritize, the quicker and more automatic the process will become. And in the end it will save time and energy because it helps to focus future action in the right direction.

Prioritization helps us order what we've already collected. We just need to think carefully, especially in a professional context, about what we believe is important before presenting our findings. The next step: learning how to effectively articulate what we've discovered.

171

·

Seeing What's Missing

PART III

· · ·

Articulate

The difference between the almost right word and
the right word is really a large matter — 'tis the difference
between the lightning-bug and the lightning.

— MARK TWAIN

8

Making Your Unknown Known

How to Avoid Communication Breakdowns

IN 2001 THE DISAPPEARANCE of twenty-four-year-old government intern Chandra Levy sparked a media frenzy when the investigation revealed that she'd been having an affair with married congressman Gary Condit. In the absence of information about her whereabouts, Levy became fodder for popular culture including jokes on late-night talk shows and a name check in a hit song by rapper Eminem ("How can one Chandra be so Levy?"). Her body wasn't discovered for over a year, her killer wasn't prosecuted for eight years, and as most of his case is tied to an alleged jailhouse confession, he has been granted a new trial.

It was a sad, prolonged, and unfortunate situation for everyone involved, but one aspect stuck with me for a long time: that a single word might have derailed the entire investigation.

After Levy left her house, her friends and family had no idea where she was headed. She literally disappeared without a trace, leaving behind her phone, credit cards, and driver's license. It took over a month to recover the last search results on her laptop, which indicated an interest in Washington, DC's, Rock Creek Park, a 1,750-acre enclave nearly four times the size of New York City's Central Park.

On July 25, 2001, eighty-five days after she disappeared, dozens of DC police officers assembled to search the sprawling natural area. Orders were to look one hundred yards off all of the park's roads. By the end of the day, they called off the search, having found nothing.

It was later determined that the actual order was to explore one hundred yards off all of the park's *trails*. Someone in the chain of command had changed a crucial word. The assumption that "roads" and "trails" were the same thing dramatically shrank the search area. Levy's body wasn't discovered for another ten months—seventy-nine yards off one of the park's trails. A single miscommunicated word likely led to the delay of discovery and meant most of the forensic evidence that could have positively identified her killer was gone.

Seeing what others don't or what could change everything is only half the battle. We can have prodigious observational and analytical skills, but if we're not effective communicators, it doesn't do us or anyone else any good. A discovery is useless to society until it's communicated to others. We can spend all the time in the world gathering and analyzing data, but if we don't articulate it correctly, no one else, including ourselves, will ever benefit from it. And yet every day around the world lack of communication and miscommunication cause problems that could have been avoided, including lost evidence, lost opportunities, lost loves, even lost lives.

After an operation in southern Afghanistan on June 9, 2014, a special ops group of American soldiers was returning to base when insurgents ambushed them. A United States–chartered B-1 bomber answered their call for support by swooping in and deploying two missiles . . . directly on top of the troops they meant to protect. In one of the worst instances of friendly fire in Afghanistan in over a decade, five Americans and their Afghan ally died. The official cause: miscommunication.

In a three-hundred-page report released by the Pentagon, air force major general Jeffrey Harrigian concluded that "had the team . . . communicated effectively, this tragic incident was avoidable."

I recently took a group of analysts to a museum in Washington, DC, and we stopped in front of a large—over 6 feet high by 15 feet wide—painted image by James Rosenquist called *Industrial Cot-*

tage. It shows a gray-framed window in the middle. To the left against a bright red background two strips of bacon hang from a clothesline next to a steam shovel. The right side of the work has a mostly bright yellow background punctuated by four drill bits. It's odd and colorful and a lot to take in, but the group I was with *analyzes situations for a living.*

"How would you describe this?" I asked. Having already been through the "#1 and #16" painting and photograph exercise we covered in chapter 5, they were ready to point out all the details, both small and obvious.

"There are three panels," one participant declared.

We were standing inches from the work. Being so large, it was painted across five separate canvases that were hung one beside the other. The gaps were not painted over; they were clearly visible. Five panels. Not three.

"Well, it's painted to look like three," he amended. "Same difference."

"Same difference" isn't just a colloquial and ambiguous oxymoron; in this case it's incorrect. There is a difference. Physical panels are not the same as thematic panels. Three is not the same as five.

Think about all of the situations where three versus five would make a huge difference: in information that passes between military commanders and their officers, doctors and their patients, pharmaceutical companies and their customers. Precision in objective description is just as important to accountants, journalists, teachers, architects, engineers, chemists, analysts, stockbrokers, human resource managers, researchers, archivists, assistants, even delivery people. No person or business can afford to waste time and resources getting it wrong.

In 2008 the global analyst firm IDC surveyed four hundred companies in the United States and the United Kingdom and calculated the total estimated cost of poor communication to be $37 billion a year. The loss in productivity per employee per year resulting from communication barriers: $26,041. IDC maintains that these figures are low, as they don't include the cost of miscommunication on brand, reputation, and customer satisfaction. A full 100 percent of the companies also reported that miscommunication put their employees or the public at risk of injury, while 99 percent revealed that it put their sales and customer satisfaction at risk as well.

Of course, our job isn't the only area of our life that demands precise communication. The same is true for our academic pursuits, personal interests, and relationships. Sometimes our words are misunderstood or accidentally repeated incorrectly; other times they come out wrong to start with, buried in emotion or simply tossed out without proper thought or precision. The importance of getting it right is compounded by modern communication technology, since our instantaneous, continuous, universal connectivity increases the likelihood of simple but devastating miscommunication. And those errors aren't likely to go away, since the Internet has an infinite memory. Whole Foods CEO John Mackey is still living down the 2007 discovery that he created a fictional identity on Yahoo message boards to compliment his company and himself. In a March 21, 2015, broadcast, the host of NPR's *Wait Wait . . . Don't Tell Me,* Peter Sagal, reminded his listeners, "Among [Mackey's] many posts about Whole Foods and what a great company it is, he said, quote, 'I like Mackey's haircut. I think he looks cute.'"

A message as short as a tweet can be ruinous. People fired for their tweets include a law fellow at New York University, a senior editor at CNN, a director at the National Security Staff at the White House, and the chief financial officer of public retail company Francesca's Holdings. Firefighters, actors, teachers, journalists, IT consultants, waiters, and even mechanics are among the people who have found themselves holding a pink slip after sending out a single tweet. A damning online post can not only hurt an employee, it can also bring derision and damage to an entire company—just ask (or Google) Qantas, McDonald's, Vodafone, Kenneth Cole, or Chrysler.

In March 2015, former major league baseball pitcher Curt Schilling sent a tweet congratulating his teenage daughter for committing to a Catholic university's softball team. College student Adam Nagel and recent college graduate Sean MacDonald tweeted Schilling back with what *USA Today* politely labeled "sexual violence and innuendo." Nagel was suspended from his college, scheduled for a conduct hearing to determine further disciplinary action, and turned over to the police. MacDonald's former fraternity publicly condemned him, and he promptly lost his job with the New York Yankees. Headlines across the country proclaimed YANKEES FIRE EMPLOYEE OVER VULGAR TWEETS without mentioning that MacDonald was a new hire, only part-time, and had worked for the team for a mere eighteen hours.

Even when they don't originate on the Internet, communication missteps will likely be recorded there for the world to read and judge ad infinitum. For this reason, it's more important than ever to be able to communicate effectively in any form because whatever we write or say in public will also end up replayed, ridiculed, or rewarded in cyberspace.

Effectively articulating what we see allows us to correct misperceptions before they continue any further. We'll never know if the person next to us saw something differently if we don't give voice to our observations and inferences in both personal and personnel instances. Our partners can't read our minds. We might have deduced something about the job candidate incorrectly. We might be misreading a potential donor. Expressing our perceptions gives other people the opportunity to address or redress them. Effective communication also helps set expectations. If we can't articulate what we expect from others, we're setting them and ourselves up for frustration at best and failure at worst. Giving others clear instructions, requirements, and goals helps us achieve progress, completion, and success.

To hone our skills and help avert potential information-dissemination disasters, we'll turn again to the art world — although this time we'll dig a little deeper and discover that the secrets to good communication can be unveiled by studying how art is created.

THE ART OF COMMUNICATION

I don't think it's a coincidence that two of the twentieth century's most famous and ferocious communicators — Winston Churchill and Adolf Hitler — were avid painters. Throughout their lives, Churchill and Hitler produced hundreds of works: landscapes, seascapes, still lifes of flowers spilling from vases, and even the occasional portrait (Hitler painted Jesus' mother, Mary, while Churchill captured his wife, Clementine). It makes sense because artists are inherently communicators, most compelled to share their message with the world no matter what the cost. Or as Georgia O'Keeffe put it, the life of an artist is not driven by success; rather, "making your unknown known is the more important thing."

Artists know they are artists not because they've been recognized as such or have a degree or win certain awards. They identify as artists because they can't help but create. Sculptor and MacArthur Fellowship recipient Teresita Fernández articulated it this way: "Being an artist is not just about what happens when you are in the studio. The way you live, the people you choose to love and the way you love them, the way you vote, the words that come out of your mouth, the size of the world you make for yourselves, your ability to influence the things you believe in, your obsessions, your failures — all of these components will also become the raw material for the art you make."

To enhance our communication skills, we must do the same thing: recognize that we don't have to have the word *communication* in our job title or department name to be a full-time communicator. We are all communicators because we all have a constant need to communicate. Everything in our lives, including what we see and how we choose to see it, becomes the raw material for our communication. We can make sure we are using it wisely to make masterpieces and not mistakes when we approach communication the same way an artist prepares for, executes, and exhibits a work of art.

Regardless of how easy or effortless the finished product might seem, a painting, sculpture, or any other work of art relies on a specific and almost standard process. While the details of the process might vary from person to person, those differences are only superficial; for instance, while a sculptor will require different tools than a photographer, they will both need to learn the best way to work with them, that is, wield a hammer or arrange a camera. The underlying process is ultimately the same: the artist must marry a concept with a medium, or what she wants to say with the mode she uses to express it. Likewise, we will learn that regardless of what we are communicating and the methods we use to communicate it, we can build the best message with the same study of planning, practice, and thoughtful execution. The first step: prudent planning.

CHOOSE WISELY

Although the finished product, particularly in modern and avant-garde artworks, might seem to have required little thought, even Jackson Pollock's abstract drip paintings were not done haphazardly. Pollock famously stated, "I can control the flow of paint: there is no accident."

The artist must deliberately choose what materials to use. Pollock had to decide what kind of paint would work best for his vision — choosing consistency, color, amount, availability, durability, even price. Similarly, even though they can come to us spontaneously and seemingly without thought, we should view our words as the artist views paint: as a tool that must be carefully pondered and selected before use. The single decision of what colors to use is extremely important for artists. In the same way, we must decide ahead of time which words we will use when communicating to make sure we are painting the most accurate picture possible.

Think about the words you regularly use. What color are they? And are they the best choice for your message? Are you covering your employees with a dark red when a sky blue might be more effective? Do you wash your teenage son in neon green when he might respond better to a subtle gray?

Of course, no color is inherently bad or good; it all depends on when and where it's used. Yellow might be perfect for a birthday party but not for a funeral. The words we say to our friends at happy hour would probably not work as well in a boardroom. To determine if we've chosen the right hue for the right situation, we need only to ask ourselves if we're using objective or subjective words. Subjective words can be used, albeit still carefully, in social settings, while objective should be used for everything else.

Just as we must be objective in our observations and inferences to keep our investigation focused on facts, when we're in professional or public situations, we need to communicate using only objective language. This is especially true in employee evaluations, human resources, and educational settings, and heartbreakingly so in instances involving children.

One of my past participants, Anne Charlevoix, a special education teacher and a member of her school's multidisciplinary evaluation team, recalled how a teacher once came before their committee insisting they create an intervention plan for one of her first-graders. Asked to describe his need for assistance, the teacher offered the following: "He is so lazy, he complains constantly, and he never does his work." When the team asked for specific examples of these behaviors, the teacher struggled to provide them. She had made up her mind about the child but was at a loss to explain why. She didn't think she needed any more reasons than that he was lazy and complained, but those reasons were her subjective opinions. When Charlevoix completed an in-class assessment of the student and recorded objective information about his performance, behavior, and actions, the committee determined that the child had a personality conflict with his teacher but that he didn't need special services.

"Your class made me so much more aware," she told me later, "of the power of the language we use and how easily we can create an inaccurate impression when we speak subjectively."

The easiest way to ensure that we're communicating objectively is to consciously choose objective words. Surefire, always safe objective words include numbers, colors, size, sounds, position, placement, materials, location, and time. Instead of saying "too much," give the actual amount. Instead of "big," include a measurement, estimation, or comparison.

In most cases subjective language is easy to spot: it's opinionated and not based on fact. There are, however, some tricky subjective signal words that can cause our listener to tune out or, worse yet, turn against us if we're not careful. Here are a few of them:

SUBJECTIVE WORDS AND PHRASES TO AVOID	WHY?	HOW TO AVOID THEM
Obviously Clearly	Because many things in this world aren't obvious, and even fewer are clear. (Remember *Renshaw's Cow?*)	Instead of saying "Clearly it's *x*," or "Obviously *y*," try using "It appears that *x* is based on *y* and *z*."
Never Always	*Never* and *always* are not precise and are statistically very improbable, therefore often used in exaggeration.	Instead of saying "never" or "always," give a concrete, definitive number. If that isn't possible, it is better to use "frequently" or "seldom."
Actually	In cases of correction, *actually* signifies that the speaker is very sure the other person is very wrong before an explanation is even offered. Leading with a possible insult is not a great way to get results.	Instead of saying "actually," try using "I don't believe . . ."
It goes without saying . . .	If something is important, then it goes *with* saying.	Just eliminate "it goes without saying" from your vocabulary altogether.

It can be especially easy to slip into the subjective when we're critiquing, correcting, or upset with the person we're communicating with, but in doing so we run the risk of alienating the very person we're meant to help. For instance, consider the word *bad*. *Bad* is an opinion, is open to interpretation, and has a negative connotation. Using the word *bad* to describe how your child acted when you were on the phone isn't objective or particularly helpful to anyone involved because kids can't fix *bad*. (And feeling bad about themselves might make them act even worse.) Instead, communicate using objective facts: "You were yelling when I was on the phone." Yelling is a concrete action, a behavior that can be changed. Reporting that someone was yelling doesn't convey personal judgment. There's no room for argument either: the child was yelling or wasn't. The same goes for a work situation. Rather than calling an employee's quarterly sales "terrible," use indisputable facts: "You missed your sales quota by 30 percent."

Another trick to help curb the subjective is to replace exclusive words with inclusive. Instead of saying, "This doesn't work for me," instead use "What if you tried . . . ?" or better yet, include yourself in the team with "Why don't *we* try . . . ?"

Like the artist who has chosen a color palette, we've chosen the words that will work best, but we must go further. The artist will not go to the paint store and ask simply for "blue paint"; a true artist will be more specific. Paint can be watercolor, oil, or acrylic. Paint can come in a can or a tube or spray from an aerosol. Paint can be thick or thin, toxic or even edible, fast- or slow-drying. Blue can be indigo or cobalt or ultramarine.

To avoid similar confusion with our words, we must add specificity. Instead of saying "car," be more specific and say "SUV"; instead of "dog," try "German shepherd." Similarly, we shouldn't say "mother" if we can't prove it; instead use "woman with child." Saying "on this side" isn't specific enough, especially for someone not standing where you're standing and seeing what you see; instead, give a position: "to the far left." Rather than "thing" or "stuff" or "colorful," elucidate more precisely.

A lack of specificity in communication cost artist Christian Alderete dearly. When Alderete was chosen by the city of Pasadena, California, to participate in the pilot Neighborhood Enhancement Mural Program, he was thrilled. Backed by a government grant, he spent over two months creating a colorful, Mayan- and Aztec-themed, sixty-foot masterpiece and got thirty local kids involved as well. Arts and Culture Commission chairman Dale Oliver called the mural "spectacular."

But just a couple of months after it was completed, someone painted over it entirely, kids' signatures and all.

The shopkeeper of the store decorated by Alderete's art had received a letter from Pasadena's Planning and Community Development code compliance program warning her to remove extraneous signage and repaint a wall in disrepair or face being shut down. Which wall wasn't specified.

Jon Pollard, the city's code compliance manager, admitted that there was "some miscommunication."

Alderete put it differently. "It's like a kick in the face," he said. "It was something living. Something I hoped to see become a landmark in the city."

Businessman Joe Lentini also learned an expensive lesson about the importance of specificity when he dined at Bobby Flay Steak at the Borgata Hotel Casino in Atlantic City, New Jersey. When ordering drinks for his table of ten, he told the waitress he didn't know much about wine and asked her to pick a bottle for him.

"She pointed to a bottle on the menu. I didn't have my glasses. I asked how much and she said, 'Thirty-seven fifty,'" Lentini recalls.

Bobby Flay Steak has a twenty-four-page wine menu that offers more than five hundred choices. The majority are less than $100 a bottle, with a selection of "50 under $50" highlighted on the first page, so when Lentini received the bill and saw that instead of the $37.50 he was expecting, he was charged $3,750, he was aghast. He called the waitress over immediately and explained that he would never have ordered such an expensive bottle of wine. She in turn brought over the manager.

"I said the waitress told me it cost 'thirty-seven fifty,' not 'three thousand, seven hundred and fifty dollars,'" Lentini said.

While the waitress disagreed, other diners confirmed Lentini's exchange. Don Chin, the patron sitting on Lentini's left, recalled what was said when the wine was ordered. "Joe had asked for a suggestion on the wine and the waitress pointed to a wine," he said. "Joe asked the price and she said 'thirty-seven fifty,' not 'three thousand, seven hundred and fifty,' which is what I would have said, so we all thought it was $37.50. We all had a heart attack [when the bill came]."

Instead of removing the item from the bill, the restaurant's management offered to discount the price of the bottle of Screaming Eagle wine to $2,200. Lentini reluctantly paid, then took his story to the press.

When the story was picked up nationally, Borgata executive vice president Joseph Lupo responded, "Borgata is confident there was no misunderstanding regarding the selection. We simply will not allow the threat of a negative story that includes so many unaccounted and questionable statements to disparage our integrity and standards, which Borgata takes great pride in practicing every day."

The restaurant explains that another person at the table was made aware of the exact price of the bottle before the check was delivered, which that person confirms; however, he asserts that the revelation occurred only after the bottle was opened and drunk and the damage was done.

Simply because the Borgata management claims that there was "no misunderstanding" doesn't make it so. The fact that the two sides—business and customer—do not agree about why the incident occurred is the very definition of a misunderstanding. So let's look at the miscommunication involved.

According to multiple accounts, the waitress signified the price of the bottle of wine using a vague shortcut: "thirty-seven fifty." Without the specificity of dollars and cents, there is room for misunderstanding. Saying "three thousand, seven hundred and fifty dollars" or "thirty-seven hundred fifty dollars" would have removed any room for error.

The restaurant wine list is also not as specific as it could be to alleviate potential problems. The prices of the hundreds of bottles of wine are listed without dollar signs or decimal points or commas. Does "900" mean nine hundred dollars or nine dollars? Especially considering that the steakhouse is located at a tourist destination popular with foreign visitors, the lack of specificity lends itself to miscommunication.

When the manager was called over to sort out the situation on the spot, before it became public, he had further information about his restaurant's wine list: of the more than five hundred regular-size bottles of wine listed, only seventeen are priced over $1,000, and only one bottle is more than $3,750. He knew that the waitress served someone who professed not to know anything about wine the second most expensive bottle among five hundred choices.

While it can be argued that Lentini and the Borgata and Bobby Flay Steak all paid dearly for the miscommunication — was $2,200 worth the cost of negative publicity? — the incident did produce one example of exceedingly good communication in the form of the original article by reporter Karin Price Mueller. In her piece for NJ.com, she reported only the facts of what happened, where it happened, when, and with whom. She interviewed the people involved directly, and didn't name anyone who didn't wish to be named, including the waitress. She even pointed out possible perception errors to her readers: "We weren't at the table so we don't know what was said when the wine was ordered" and "We don't know what the waitress did or did not say. We only know what Lentini remembered, and what Borgata said it learned when it asked the employees who were there."

Specificity not only protects against miscommunication, it can also lead to greater success. After taking my class, Lieutenant Tom Holt, who coordinated the NYPD's Grand Larceny Task Force, changed the way he communicated with his twenty-four plainclothes officers. "Instead of telling my people that the guy who keeps looking into one parked car after another is dressed in black," he explained, "I might say he's wearing a black wool hat, a black leather coat with black fur trim, a black hoodie sweatshirt, and Timberlands." This new specificity helped his department apprehend more of the shoplifters, pickpockets, and purse snatchers who regularly stalked the Times Square area.

In the quest for specificity, however, remember to be wary of assumption. When describing a painting out loud in one of my sessions, a student said that the subject was "standing next to European architecture." Sounds specific, yes? "How do you know the man in the painting is in Europe?" I asked. He didn't. It could be a museum or a pavilion at Disney World. Instead of assuming a location you can't verify, describe the pillars and sconces that you see.

CONSIDER THE AUDIENCE

Although many artists and writers dream that their work will be seen by everyone, the reality is that it can't. Some audiences are larger than others, but "everyone" is not a realistic goal. The viewer of a commissioned portrait of a loved one will likely be a different person from a Coachella Valley Music and Art Festival attendee, with a very different mind-set.

An artist's knowing her audience and planning for it is a marker of competence to seasoned agents, publishers, and collectors. Literary agent Susan Ginsburg notes that one of the most common mistakes she sees in query letters, especially from first-time authors, is the promise that a book will appeal to "everyone."

"Publishers need to know that they can position a book so that it sells well in a particular market," she says. "They can't do that if the author doesn't even know who his audience is."

Just as a sculptor must plan a piece based on where and how it will be installed and exhibited—a work placed outside in a public space might require different materials and viewing angles than one designed to be seen in a gallery—we must plan for our audience when crafting good communication. Not everyone will see the same way and not everyone will hear the same things either, especially if we're not tailoring the message to the person with whom we are communicating.

After one of my classes, a medical student named Josh Bright came up to me and shared how fine-tuning communication is an essential part of patient interaction.

"I never thought of myself as a translator, but that's essentially what we're all doing when we communicate effectively: we're translating our message to one another. When I see patients, they describe their complaints and concerns to me subjectively because it's about how they're feeling. I then translate that into objective symptoms that can be treated," he said. "However, if I speak to them from my own reference point, they might not understand. In fact, the medical terminology generally confuses or alarms people. I have to translate my own message of diagnosis into something that's easily understood from their perspective."

The same applies to almost every exchange we have. To make sure our communication is tailored to the people we're trying to reach, research who they are. In 2001, when Sara Blakely first created footless panty hose for her new company, Spanx, she flew to London to cold-call the buyers at Harrods, Harvey Nichols, and Selfridges as she had done successfully a few months earlier in the United States with Neiman Marcus. Since her only product at the time was a novel concept—*you cut the feet off your control-top stockings?*—she spent much of her energy trying to explain what Spanx was and why people needed it.

While in London, she also landed a live interview with the BBC. Slightly punchy from a combination of jet lag and nerves—the interview would reach more than a million people—Blakely hoped to cover any anxiety with her trademark thousand-watt smile.

Her male interviewer, as confused as everyone else to whom she had tried to describe her new naughty-sounding shapewear, cut right to the chase: "So Sara, tell us what Spanx can do for women in the UK."

Blakely answered with a huge smile of confidence, "Well, it's all about the fanny. It smooths your fanny, it lifts your fanny, and it firms your fanny."

Fanny wasn't a word she regularly used, but she thought it sounded safe and British and would help ease the minds of any uptight listeners. As the color drained from her interviewer's face, she got the feeling that she'd chosen the wrong word.

"I think you mean *bum*," the interviewer said, interrupting her.

"Yes, sure. Bum," she conceded, recognizing the polite British word for "bottom."

When Blakely got off the air she found out that while *fanny* was a quaint way American grandmothers might refer to a bum, in England it was a very crude slang term for "vagina." While she meant to simply describe how her product would discreetly transform the appearance of cellulite on a woman's buttocks, she had instead announced on live radio that it would smooth, lift, and firm women's vaginas . . . and used a dirty, dirty word to do so.

Think about your audience. Do they call their customers guests, patrons, members, or users? Are there certain words that are off-limits in their environment, like *fanny?* Tailor your message accordingly.

When the Colorado Bureau of Investigation wanted current inmates to help solve cold cases, they communicated the pertinent information of the unsolved cases in an unusual way: by printing it on playing cards that were then distributed for free in the county jails. The hope was that inmates would be more receptive to the information if it was presented in a way that was accessible, easy to read, and literally at their fingertips. CBI cold-case analyst Audrey Simkins says the strategy worked. "We have gotten about four dozen calls, and are opening the doors on those cases." Currently used in seventeen states across the country, the cold-case playing cards have been credited with solving forty cases and generating hundreds of tips.

Just as we did with perspective to gather as much information as possible, before we communicate we should step into the shoes of our potential audience and make sure we're including all of the facts that would be pertinent to them but also translating that knowledge into a language that can readily be understood and accepted.

CONCRETE PRACTICE

Once the artist has selected his materials and considered his audience, he is ready for the next step: practicing. Practicing actually straddles the stages of planning and execution, since it's a little of both: we are planning for the final product with an early execution of it.

While practice efforts are called different things in different creative professions — the sketch, the rough draft, the model, the dress rehearsal — they share a physical reality. Practicing art isn't just thinking about something, it's doing it. Author Dani Shapiro writes, "Think of a ballet dancer at the barre. Plié, elevé, battement tendu. She is practicing, because she knows that there is no difference between practice and art. The practice *is* the art."

In the same way, we must practice our communication skills if we are to master them. Practice will not only help us fix the things that aren't quite ready for prime time but can also help us become more comfortable delivering our message.

Not everyone is a born orator. Some of us are just naturally quiet, some are paralyzed by the thought of opening our mouths, while many of us are more comfortable behind our computers or in our laboratories. Thankfully, speaking in public, speaking when we're nervous, and speaking when we're not used to doing so are skills we can master with practice. And for those with a fear of speaking in public, media trainer Bill Connor has good news: practice can trump personality. "I've seen supremely self-confident men and women swagger up to a podium full of bravado but lacking in preparation, only to completely bomb," he says. "They try to wing it, and find they've run out of material in 30 seconds. I've also seen shy people take the time to prepare and practice, and then deliver moving, funny, impactful messages in a way that influences audiences and advances their own agendas."

Quiet author Susan Cain's number one tip for public speaking, especially for introverts: "Practice it out loud, until you're comfortable." To do that, we just need to speak.

It sounds elementary, and in many ways it is. We tell children to "use their words," but we frequently don't, relying instead on electronics, photographs, and vague gestures. We need to say what we see.

My son's preschool teacher told me years ago that she didn't think he was verbal enough. She warned me of the well-documented links between language development and literacy, and confessed that children with inadequate communication skills were harder to test not just for kindergarten readiness but also for other possible underlying issues such as developmental language disorders or autism. She suggested that to encourage his verbal communication I practice my Art of Perception exercises out loud with him. So I did. Everywhere we went, instead of just talking to him as I normally had, I would encourage him to describe to me in detail what he saw. We started talking about all the things we saw and why we thought they looked that way, and he hasn't stopped talking since! In a great role reversal, as we walk the streets of New York City together today, my son will say, "Did you just see who walked by?" or "I bet you didn't notice what just happened across the street." He catches me at my own game and often asks, "Could you explain that a bit more clearly?"

To practice our out-loud communication skills, look at the

following painting. What do you see? Write three or four objective sentences that best distill the important information.

René Magritte, *The Key to Dreams*, 1927.

The painting is by René Magritte, who often painted words onto his images. (We've already looked at two of his other works, the ham on the plate with an eyeball in chapter 2 and the train coming out of the fireplace in chapter 7.) Magritte once said that he aimed to make "everyday objects shriek aloud"—a fitting goal for better communication.

This painting, *The Key to Dreams*, is part of a series in which Magritte explores the nature of representation. Of the four pictures, three are incorrectly identified by their captions; only the one in the lower right corner is correct. A bag is labeled "the sky." A knife is labeled "the bird." A leaf is called "the table." Only the sponge is as it says it is. The juxtaposition of images and words, especially presented in the style of a vocabulary primer or flash cards, gives us pause. We are forced to take a step back and rethink what we are seeing.

Now let's get you talking. Take the sentences you wrote about the painting, go find someone, and read them aloud. Don't show the person the painting, as that's often how we're communicating: conveying what we see to someone who can't see it. This is simple yet valuable practice in verbalizing our findings.

To test how well you communicated the objective facts, ask the person to draw the painting based on your description. If you find you haven't included enough information for the person to replicate it, go back and write a different description that conveys the information more accurately.

THE IMPORTANCE OF EDITING: WHY SAYING TOO MUCH CAN BE AS BAD AS NOT SAYING ANYTHING AT ALL

Those two little words at the end of the previous section — "go back" — represent the third, and perhaps most important, stage in creating both art and communication: editing.

Art is about more than just adding paint to canvas; many times it's equally about subtracting. Teresita Fernández's advice to graduating art students, which MIT Fellow Maria Popova called "an ennobling moral compass for being a decent human being in any walk of life," included the tip: "Purge regularly. Destroying is intimately connected to creating."

Amsterdam-born painter Jan Frank, known for his intricate ink drawings and massive, modern plywood paintings, agrees. His goal with every work is to apply "as little to the surface as possible . . . The more complex it becomes," he says, "the more I dislike it." How does he know when a painting is finished? "When I get the feeling that adding one more stroke would be one too many."

Ralph Steiner, *American Rural Baroque*, 1930.

Editing includes knowing how much is too much and when to leave well enough alone. As I was writing this chapter, I kept thinking of a famous photograph from 1930 of an empty chair. The work, Ralph Steiner's *American Rural Baroque* (see previous page), captures an empty wicker rocking chair casting a shadow on a porch. The image is simple yet striking: the ornate patterns from the rocking chair contrast with the straight lines of the wall, floor, shutter, and column. We don't expect an unoccupied rocking chair to make a statement, but it does. It narrates a story about the eloquence of emptiness, about the romance of a past era. To include a human presence would have ruined it both figuratively and literally, as the wonderful design of the chair back would disappear.

Likewise, when we communicate, we need to make sure we aren't obscuring our message with "too much" by talking too much, using too many words, or including unnecessary information. Former sales executive Jess McCann, author of *Was It Something I Said?*, believes that our tendency to go overboard in both professional and personal communication comes down to discomfort; we're uncomfortable either because of the act of speaking — due to our personality or because we're in a high-pressure situation — or because of the information we're meant to impart. We might have no trouble conversing with friends in a casual setting, but when asked to deliver a poor quarterly earnings report or answer our child's questions about sex, we suddenly come down with a case of what McCann calls "verbal vomit." To counter this common problem, she recommends using the KISS principle, an acronym adopted by the US Navy in 1960 to remind its designers that in many cases less is more. KISS stands for "keep it short and simple" and is applicable whether we're composing an email at work or turning someone down for a date afterward.

Paralegal Cara W. was filled with anxiety about her first date with Dan. She considered herself "unlucky" in love and was nervous that she would doom the relationship before it ever started. How should she talk about her past relationships? Keep from nervously monopolizing the conversation? Let him know that she didn't want to move too fast? McCann gave her the same answer for every situation: prepare with KISS.

"Most of us stumble into self-talk because we don't take any time to sit down, think, and prepare," McCann tells me. "We feel this innate need to say more, but in most cases, we don't need to elaborate. When we do, we just end up confusing the person we're talking to."

She counseled Cara to make a list of the questions she was most worried about, helped her edit the answers until they were short and simple, and then made her practice answering them. Instead of telling Dan that she had gotten physical too soon in past relationships and regretted it, McCann instructed Cara to simply say, "I really like you, I just want to get to know you a little bit better. I hope that's okay?" Instead of answering the question "Are you seeing anyone else?" with a long explanation about who and for how long, her fear of dying alone, or how she had dated half the college football team, they crafted a simple two-word answer: "Not exclusively." When the night of her big date with Dan finally came, Cara wasn't her usual nervous self because she had prepped and practiced what she was going to say. Armed with her edited answers, she was able to enjoy the evening and really focus on connecting with her new friend.

Excellent communicators are concise. They make every word count. To practice the skill of precisely distilling language, look at the following photograph and describe it in just one sentence. Write only your observations, devoid of assumptions and inferences.

Did you include any of the following words: "woman," "child," "church," "pew," "sitting," "hand," "face"? Good, as those are the most important. Hopefully you didn't write "mother" or "her child," as that would assume a relationship that might not be true. What about "twelve," the number of people we can see? Great. You could have further differentiated the scene by stating that of the twelve people we can see, ten are standing, while two, a woman and a child, are sitting.

You might have noticed other details that are true but not important enough to warrant inclusion in a single sentence, including: circular light, boots, striped shirt, jeans, and cross-legged. Remember to prioritize.

Did you use the term "African American" in your sentence? Most people do, but that's a subjective inference, not an objective observation. You are assuming that the people are in America and are in fact of African descent. Can you tell where this photograph was taken? Are there any clues that would suggest location such as a flag or writing of any kind? No. So, we cannot assume. The people might be in Haiti, or they might be in America but of Jamaican descent. Many people worry that using the term "black" would be construed as racist, and "African American" would be more politically correct. I understand those concerns, and we need to be thoughtful and never offensive, but going too far with political correctness and perceived politeness can also keep us from specificity and accuracy. Unless we know it for a fact, "African American" is an assumption, and if the people are Haitian citizens, it's incorrect. Don't worry about being politically correct, worry about being *correct*. "Black" is a descriptive term. Black is an observation of what we see. It's perfectly acceptable and a more objective observation to describe the people in this photograph as "black."

Did you include any of these words to describe the woman: "upset," "crying," "sad," "agitated," "distressed"? The little girl *does appear to be* comforting the woman; her hand to the woman's cheek is gentle, her face is calm, possibly worried. But remember that the little girl is a child. She might not understand what she is witnessing. The woman has her own hand to her face, which is contorted by emotion, but can you tell what kind? Is she upset, sad, or agitated? Is she crying? She might be, although we can't see tears.

It's tempting to immediately see the woman on the ground, her face contorted, and assume she has collapsed in distress, but that is an assumption. It might be true, but we need facts to back it up. Let's look at the rest of the photograph. What are the other people around the woman doing? Are they distressed? We can only see the faces of four of them, but none of them appears to be upset. Two look expressionless, and two others are smiling, one with hands in the air, open, by her face. Maybe she's clapping?

The body language of everyone besides the woman and child is also telling. They are all looking forward, past the woman. No one looks at her or reaches down to help her. If someone was in distress, wouldn't the people around her react? What about the man in the background center? What is he holding? I've had people say it was a "gun," but that's incorrect. Look closer. It's not a gun. Also, the pews signify that the setting is most likely a church. The likelihood of an unconcealed weapon in a church is small. The man is in fact holding a microphone, possibly attached to a camera.

What is going on in the photo? The people are in a church, but are they participating in a service, or is it just a meeting? Where is the church? Why are the people gathered? Who or what are they looking at? When is this taking place?

This is the important information that we do not know, that if we could find, would help us tremendously. Since this is a photo and we have access to the photographer, David Goldman, we can get answers to some of those questions. Let's see if we can piece the story together with some missing facts.

Who is it? The woman seated on the floor is Latrice Barnes. The child is her daughter Jasmine Redd, age five. So we have confirmation of their relationship. Do we know what is going on in the photo yet? No, but now that we have a positive identification, we could possibly contact her.

Where is it? The First Corinthian Baptist Church in Harlem,

New York. So we are in the United States, but we still can't assume everyone in the photograph is African American.

When is it? Tuesday, November 4, 2008. Does that date have any significance? Yes, it does. From the *New York Times*: "On Nov. 4, 2008, Barack Obama was elected the 44th president of the United States, defeating the Republican nominee John McCain. Mr. Obama, a United States senator from Illinois who was the son of a Kenyan father and a white mother from Kansas, became the first black commander in chief." Notice the *New York Times* does not call Obama the first African American president, it calls him the first black one.

Latrice Barnes is on the floor of the church because she was overcome with happiness at the historic election results. She might be crying, but they are tears of joy and hope, not despair or anguish.

We are not expected to know more than we can observe, but we need to correctly observe what we can. Our reporting should not include assumptions or incorrect information that would lead someone else down the wrong path.

Let's try another photo, but this time I want you to describe it in only five words. You may not think you can say much with just five words, but that's exactly what the headline writer did when this image appeared in the *New York Times*. If the headline writer could do it, so can you!

Did you use any of the following words: "teenagers, young peo-ple," "sitting," "stoop," "smiling," "flip-flops," "five"? All are good! I've heard "summer" because of the teenagers' dress, but it could be an unseasonably warm spring or fall day; "warm" would be more ac-curate. Hopefully you didn't include any of the following assump-tions: "NYC," "flirting," or "family." Some of the examples I've been given include "teenagers at stoop flip-flop party," "teenagers out en-joying warm weather," and the witty but not terribly descriptive "four teenagers and fifth wheel."

The actual five-word headline for this photograph shocked me. It read: "Teenage Summer, the Fasting Version." What? Reading the accompanying story enlightened me in many ways. The photo showed five teenagers who were observing Ramadan, a monthlong period during which Muslims fast from sunup until sundown. The article explained that to conserve energy many young people wear flip-flops during Ramadan so they aren't tempted to participate in sports. The headline was brilliant in that it was correct, objective, and provocative. It made me read the article to see what was go-ing on (which is generally the purpose of a newspaper headline), and I changed my assumptions when I did. All because of five little words.

DON'T LET BAD PAINT DRY

Even with preparation and editing, artists aren't always happy with their finished composition. However, when they find that some-thing they've painted isn't working for whatever reason — a hat is too large, a hand is slightly askew, a beached whale is found to be an unappetizing addition to a seascape meant to hang in a dining room — they don't just shrug it off and leave it be. They correct and rework. This process happens so often in the art world that there's even a name for it: *pentimento,* from the Italian word for "repen-tance." Whether the offending strokes are painted over or scratched off, they must be remedied as quickly as possible lest they become permanent.

When John Singer Sargent was trying to make a name for himself in France, he convinced the society celebutante, fellow American Virginie Amélie Avegno Gautreau, to pose for him. Like the rest of Paris, he was enamored with her pale, powdered skin, and what he called her "unpaintable beauty." This seven-foot-tall portrait debuted at the Paris Salon in 1884 to instant scandal in part because the strap of Gautreau's dress hung loosely off her right shoulder, a suggestion of sensuality inappropriate for a married woman. Gautreau's own mother demanded that the painting be removed from the exhibition before the end of the first day, crying, "My daughter is lost! All of Paris mocks her!"

Afraid the family would destroy it, Sargent took the painting into his own studio and amended it to have the strap sit securely on Gautreau's shoulder, as it does today. But it was too late; his career in France was finished. Sargent had hoped his enthusiastic model would be buoyed by its reception and pay him a higher price than he could normally command. He was wrong. The Gautreaus, and the rest of Paris, wanted nothing to do with him. He fled to London, telling friends that he considered giving up painting altogether. Sargent kept the portrait in his private studio until 1916, a year after Gautreau's death, when he sold it to the Met under the condition that it be renamed to erase all reference to the model. Three decades later, the revised *Madame X* finally received the critical and public praise it deserved.

Likewise, we must fix our communication mistakes as soon as we're aware of them. If we don't, the long-term consequences can be damning.

In 2006, after thirty long hours of searching for thirteen miners trapped after an underground explosion in Sago, West Virginia, the International Coal Group finally had news for the families gathered nearby in a local Baptist church: twelve men were recovered alive; only one had died.

"We were told they would be coming to the church to greet their families," the Reverend Jerry Murrell recalled. "They even told us which door they would come in, and how to prepare, that immediate

Albumen print from a scrapbook of photographic
reproductions of paintings by John Singer Sargent.

John Singer Sargent, *Madame X (Madame Pierre Gautreau)*, 1883–1884.

family members should line up first. People were singing songs. Kids were dancing in the aisles. The exuberance just began to build; it was just unbelievable."

As the reported "miracle" set the church bells ringing at midnight, company executives learned the devastating truth: the opposite was true — only one man had survived, and the other twelve had perished. Unbelievably, they waited *two and a half hours* to correct the miscommunication. When the families were told the truth, without an apology, according to one miner's son, celebration turned to pandemonium. People fainted, others lunged at officials, some threatened to go home and get their guns. The long delay in correction made a terrible situation even worse. A family friend told CNN, "We waited and waited. Loved ones and families stood out on the porch wrapped in blankets waiting for their fathers or brothers to come up and give them a hug."

"In the process of being cautious, we allowed the jubilation to go on longer than we should have," Bennett K. Hatfield, International Coal Group's chief executive, admitted.

The mishandling of sensitive information caused the media to come down even harder on the mining company and label it a "crisis upon a crisis." International Coal Group never recovered. The company's stock, trading for $11 a share before the accident, fell to just above $1 in 2009. The company no longer exists, having been acquired by Arch Coal in 2011.

Public relations executive Scott Baradell says it didn't have to be; "Hatfield should have met with the families as soon as it was evident that false hope was spreading and told them this: 'We've found the men, but we do not yet know how many of them are alive. We are checking their vital signs. As soon as we learn more, we promise you'll be the first to know. Please be patient with us.'"

People will be more forgiving and patient with us when we own up to our errors and correct them as soon as we discover them. Don't let the paint dry or the dust settle on a communication mistake. Instead, make it right as soon as possible.

MAKING SURE THE MESSAGE IS RECEIVED

Once the work is finished, the artist has a final decision to make: how it will be displayed so that it is best received. Should it be hung at eye level or rest on the floor? Should it be framed or not? Will a frame enhance or distract from the work?

Georges Seurat, known for his pointillism painting technique — using tiny dots of color to create large scenes — left nothing to chance. He designed special frames for his massive works, and even restretched his original 6-foot-by-10-foot canvas of people relaxing on the shore of a lake, *A Sunday on La Grande Jatte,* so he could add a border of red, orange, and blue dots to provide the perfect visual transition between his work and the rest of the world. Van Gogh, too, famously obsessed about how his paintings would be framed, painting plain wooden frames with yellow crosshatches when he couldn't afford traditional gilded ones. Matisse called the four sides of a frame "the most important parts of a picture."

In many ways, the most important part of our message is also how we convey it so that it is correctly received. All the preparation in the world won't help if we turn off our audience or make them tune out. The first thing we must pay attention to is how we're framing our message with our body language and nonverbal communication.

Albert Mehrabian, professor emeritus of psychology at UCLA and a pioneer researcher of body language, calculated that "the total impact of a message is about 7 percent verbal (words only), 38 percent vocal (including tone of voice, inflection, and other sounds) and 55 percent nonverbal." Like a giant, gilded frame that completely overshadows a subtle work of art, our tone, facial expression, and posture can change the way someone receives our message. Our subtext, intentional or not, can make the difference between engaging a listener and driving her away.

Joe Navarro, body language expert and the author of *What Every Body Is Saying,* advises that to deliver good communication with good nonverbal communication, at least in America, we need to greet others with a firm handshake and look them directly in the eyes.

When shaking hands, a confident grasp is firm, not limp and not crushing. Shaking too loosely can give the impression that you are weak or can't be bothered; alternatively, shaking too hard can give an impression of dominance or aggression. Looking someone in the eye when communicating, whether as speaker or listener, is also important because it tells the other person that you are engaged and paying attention to him. Of course, we don't want to stare someone down or just glance fleetingly at him; the right amount of time to look someone else in the eye is as long as it takes to note eye color.

If you deal with people from other countries, you should research the basics of acceptable nonverbal communication cues for that culture. I had a colleague who often spoke to Japanese audiences and was mystified as to why, unlike every other group, they never had any questions after her presentation. When she found out that often in Japan, people don't raise their hands to be acknowledged, they simply look at the speaker and hope to be recognized, she felt awful. For years she had seen people look expectantly at her, probably burning with unasked questions, and she had never called on them. Every country and region has its own etiquette, and the Internet makes it easier than ever to research what's proper and what's not before you communicate with someone outside your culture.

There is one gesture that we should universally avoid: pointing. Employees at Disney are trained never to point in public because in many countries the gesture is considered rude, but perhaps even more important, because it is ambiguous, and lazy. If a guest asks, "Where is the nearest bathroom?" and the employee just points into the distance, that employee is conveying that she doesn't care, that she hopes the guest will ask someone else a little farther down the way, and she isn't giving the guest any real guidance. Instead, Disney employees must use specific instructions that include nearby landmarks. A more complete, more helpful answer would be "The nearest restrooms are about twenty feet down on the right, just past the bamboo gate. If you run into the spitting camel, you've gone too far." Pointing leaves far too much open to interpretation that can't be translated into the written word. "See that thing? Right there?" What thing? Where?

Relying on pointing also short-circuits vital deductive analysis.

Forcing specific articulation increases our focus, will deliver a more detailed account, and creates a superior memory of the observation. That's especially important when information is disseminated for years, such as when an eyewitness or an officer, a caseworker or a teacher, has to repeat her description of an experience later in court.

Most of the people I teach have real trouble with the no-pointing rule. Even groups who you would think would naturally be more descriptive speakers, such as journalists, can't stop pointing, especially in a visually stimulating environment such as a museum. It may take a little retraining of your hands, but keep them lowered when you speak.

When I tell people they can't point, invariably someone tries to circumvent the rule by motioning with his head. No good. We must be aware of our nonverbal communication, but we cannot let it replace our words. Body language is not an acceptable substitute or shorthand for saying what we see.

THE SECRET

I was on a flight recently when the cabin crew told a joke: How do you keep a secret from a flight attendant? Announce it over the intercom. As my son would say, "It's funny because it's true." Unlike the passengers, who hang on every word from the cockpit, flight attendants tune out intercom announcements because they're not messages meant for them. They communicate with the captain in different ways, generally with lights and those doorbell-like chimes coded to avoid raising public concern.

Even though we can do our best to tailor our message to our audience, tailoring content is no guarantee that they will listen. To help ensure that our communication is received, we need to take a few final steps in our delivery. The secret for doing this successfully entails what I call the three Rs: repeating, renaming, and reframing.

The First R: Repeating

Andy Warhol established himself as the king of pop art with a simple idea: the repetition of images. Whether it was Campbell's soup cans or a grid of Marilyn Monroe faces, once you saw a Warhol image, you couldn't forget it — because you saw it more than once in the same place. We can apply this concept to communication, not by repeating ourselves but by asking our receiver to echo us.

Simply asking our listeners if they've heard us isn't enough. Organizational psychologist Dr. David G. Javitch advises, "Do not ask the person if he or she heard you or understood you. The answer to both questions is almost always yes. Why? Because no one wants the boss to think she's ignorant or wasn't paying attention, or that she misinterpreted the message." Instead, do what air traffic controllers do with their pilots to make sure your message was received: ask your listeners to repeat it in their own words. If the waitress at the Bobby Flay Steak restaurant had the customer repeat the price, hearing "thirty-seven fifty" said out loud again might have sparked him or one of his dinner companions to question it and ask for a clarification.

If you're uncomfortable asking someone to repeat the information verbatim, you can prompt him by asking him to rank it. Javitch recommends, "Ask the receiver what the most difficult, easiest or complicated steps will be to carry out the task."

The Second R: Renaming

Nine years after Picasso completed a large oil painting featuring five nude females with angular and disjointed bodies, he was finally ready to let it out of his studio for public display. As the work depicted prostitutes on the street outside a brothel in Barcelona, Picasso had named it simply *Le Bordel d'Avignon* (*The Brothel of Avignon*), calling it *mon bordel* ("my brothel") for short. The work itself was shocking enough thanks to the primitive, carnal poses of the women, so Picasso's friend André Salmon, the poet, rechristened it for the 1916 Salon to *Les Demoiselles d'Avignon* (*The Young Ladies of Avignon*), to make it more palatable to a scandal-shy public. The name stuck, and the painting, now on permanent view at the Museum of Modern Art, is considered one of Picasso's most influential works. Changing the name of the painting didn't change the content or composition in any way, but it did allow it to be better received.

When we reach a barrier of understanding, a simple name change can be all that's required to overcome it. *New York Times* best-selling author Harvey Mackay suggests, "Sometimes you can get what you want by calling it by another name. Let's say your opponent does not 'renegotiate' contracts. Okay. What if we call it a 'contract extension'? Your opponent says no to severance pay? Okay, it's a 'consulting contract.'" As long as it's an accurate synonym and doesn't change the meaning, think Shakespeare: "A rose by any other name would smell as sweet."

The Third R: Reframing

The curators at the National Gallery of Art in Washington, DC, have always been proud that so many works in their collection are exhibited in their original, artist-designed frames. However, they were shocked to discover in the 1990s that not every frame was correctly matched to its intended artwork. Upon closer examination, they found that the original Winslow Homer frame displaying his work *Right and Left* was actually too small for the painting and obscured important details. The frame was a perfect fit for a different Homer work that lacked an original frame, *Hound and Hunter.* The frame was swapped and a new, larger one created that allowed *Right and Left* to be fully appreciated.

If the information you're trying to convey isn't resonating with your audience, try to reframe how you are presenting it. I'm reminded of an anecdote from the mid-twentieth century that perfectly illustrates the impact of reframing our communication.

An elderly blind man was sitting on a busy street corner at rush hour begging for money. He had a cardboard sign next to his tin cup that read: BLIND. PLEASE HELP. The cup was empty.

A young advertising copywriter walked by and saw the blind man, his sign, and his empty cup, and noted that people walked right past him unmoved. She took a pen from her pocket, turned the cardboard sign around, and scribbled a new message on the back. She left it with the blind man and went on her way.

Immediately, people began putting donations in his cup. When it was overflowing, the blind man asked a stranger to tell him what the sign now said.

"It reads: IT'S A BEAUTIFUL DAY," the stranger said. "YOU CAN SEE IT. I CANNOT."

Changing the way we present our information can drastically change how it's received. People are always surprised when I tell them that the average Art of Perception seminar is three hours long. Three hours is a long time to listen to one person speak, and while I do have a lot of information I want to impart, I'm careful in how I frame it: with lots of interactive visuals, collaborative exercises that require participants to get up and talk with their colleagues, and frequent museum tours. By the end, most participants tell me they could stay with me another three hours.

AN INVITATION

I recently attended an art exhibition in New York titled *In the Studio,* which explored how artists represented their own workspaces in art. While vastly different, the works were all personal statements on the artists' relationship to the sacred place where they create their messages.

German-born British artist Lucian Freud, grandson of Sigmund, depicted his studio in a painting called *Two Japanese Wrestlers by a Sink.* Instead of showing a serene room with large windows, easels, or a single brush, the image is almost entirely taken up by an ordinary, rather dirty basin; the titular painting of wrestlers is off to the side and severely cropped. The sink is more central to this painting and to the process that produced Freud's art than perhaps any other single element. By showing it front and center, Freud reminds us that his art, his creative communication, didn't appear by magic but was the product of planning, practice, and purpose.

In another piece, *The Painter and the Buyer,* a sixteenth-century self-portrait sketch by Pieter Brueghel the Elder, Brueghel stands in his studio holding a brush before an unseen canvas while an onlooker hovers over his shoulder. It's significant that Brueghel incorporated the viewer into a self-portrait, as it confirms the artist's recognition that his communication isn't just about what he wants to create but is equally about how others will see it. While an artist's end product

Pieter Brueghel the Elder, *The Painter and the Buyer,* c. 1565.

might seem effortless and universal, it is neither. Rather, all works — at least the good and memorable ones — are created deliberately with consideration for the buyer, end user, or viewer.

Richard Diebenkorn, *Studio Wall,* 1963.

Finally, I had to stop before Richard Diebenkorn's painting from 1963. I found it remarkable because unlike his abstract landscapes, *Studio Wall* is more representational and accessible: it shows the artist's work hanging on the wall and appears to offer the viewer an empty seat, inviting him into the studio, as it were. That's what both art and communication are: an invitation. An invitation to let others into our brain, to let them know what we see and how we see it.

Now that we've reviewed good communication skills in regular situations — product launches, press conferences, social media interactions, theme parks, restaurants, and even first dates — let's explore how to keep our cool and keep communicating effectively in times of stress and duress.

9

Big (Naked, Obese) Sue and the High School Principal

How to See and Share Hard Truths

WE'VE COVERED THE tenets of good communication for day-to-day situations, but what about when we need to communicate but we really don't want to — when we're confronting the difficult or stressful, the unsavory or even taboo, the things that make us inherently uncomfortable? As much as we want to, we cannot ignore them. If it's real and concrete and factual and happened and is in front of us, we have to deal with it.

For centuries philosophers and psychologists have debated why humans, as Scottish skeptic David Hume put it, "avoid uncomfortable truths." Is it egoism, hedonism, or an attempt to maximize self-survival? No one has a definitive answer. However, as we've learned in honing our observation skills, just because we don't know why doesn't mean we can't deal with our conscious ability to turn away from things we don't like. And turn we do. We deny and deflect, pretend and pass the buck, but none of those evasive actions will erase our having been presented with something and not dealing with it.

To avoid leaving information behind, we have to be able to describe things accurately no matter what the situation. That need, however, is even more pressing when it comes to troubling information because refusing to acknowledge the information — let alone observe, analyze, or articulate it—can make it worse. Ignoring things that trouble us will not make those things go away. Like a spark that becomes a forest fire, they may even escalate or even explode. And we may be held accountable for turning away from the problem when it was smaller and more easily solved or contained.

To avoid being the captain of the *Titanic* who ignored the warnings of ice, we have to face even the seemingly unfaceable head on. We have to, as the Navy SEALs say, get comfortable with the uncomfortable. Combat veteran turned digital marketing agency manager Brent Gleeson explains, "There have been many times as a business owner that I have been in very uncomfortable situations. That could be a difficult conversation with a team member, a lawsuit, or dealing with a demanding board member. Discomfort comes in many forms. But the more you embrace that as a reality, the wider your comfort zone becomes."

The more we confront and communicate about what makes us uncomfortable, the better we'll be at it. Let's start by dealing with the paintings below and on the facing page. We're just going to catalog their similarities and differences. (Don't feel bad if you're thinking, "Before marriage and after" or "Wife and mother-in-law." I've heard them all. Just don't say them out loud!)

Goya, *The Naked Maja*, c. 1795–1800.

Lucian Freud, *Benefits Supervisor Sleeping*, 1995.

Both paintings show women reclining on a couch, although in opposite directions. The woman in the painting on the left has her eyes open, head lifted, and is looking straight ahead. The woman in the painting above has her eyes closed, her face slack and collapsed into the couch. Both women have brown hair. It appears that the woman in the painting above has uncombed hair.

What about the couches? Don't say one is "fancy" and one is "trashy"; those are judgment words. *Fancy* and *trashy* mean different things to different people. Instead, be specific. Talk about satin and velvet versus missing cushions and stains. The couch in the painting on the left is technically a dark green, one-armed chaise longue with ivory sheets and two pillows edged in lace. The picture above shows a traditional two-armed, floral-patterned couch without any cushions and dirty, ripped upholstery.

The painting on the left features a brown and amber background; we cannot see the floor. The painting above has a wrinkled, gray sheet of fabric in the background; the floor is wood-grained.

Anything else? I show these two images all over the country to thousands of professionals and leaders every day, and one of the very last observations ever uttered is that *both women are naked.* You can say "naked"; it's a fact. They are both turned in an almost full-frontal position with nary a scrap of clothing or clever camouflage to hide their nudity. The first woman has her hands behind her head; the second woman has her left hand on top of the couch and is cupping her right breast with the other.

What about their weight? No one ever wants to mention that either. "Isn't it a social thing to say one is slender and one isn't?" a participant asked me recently. No, there is a major objective difference in their weight. To be more specific, the second woman is more than just overweight, she is obese.

Obese is a clinical term defined by the Centers for Disease Control to describe the weight of an individual with a body mass index (BMI) of over 30. For a five-foot-nine-inch woman, that would be 203 pounds or more. It's safe to say that the woman in the second painting is obese. At the time of this painting, the model, Sue Tilley, was 280 pounds. You're not casting judgment or making fun to say so, you are simply saying what you see.

I did have a doctor raise his hand and tell me that one woman was "perfectly healthy" while the other was "morbidly obese." I objected to his description, but not for the reason you might think. "Morbidly obese" is the medical terminology for anyone with a BMI of over 40, or over 35 with obesity-related health conditions. And it's not even the highest obesity rating; a BMI over 45 is referred to as "super obesity." The physician didn't say "disgustingly" obese; he gave a clinical definition. It's his word choice for the woman in the first painting that was an inference. Perfectly healthy? How could he tell? Maybe she had schizophrenia! (He subsequently apologized for his incorrect inference.) The comparison of the two works of art is as much about choice of words as it is about tackling sensitive subjects.

We've become so afraid to say anything, we forget what facts are. Facts are proven truths, not opinions. A good way to quickly sort through the difference? Say what you see, not what you think.

SAY WHAT YOU SEE, NOT WHAT YOU THINK

It bears repeating not only because you need to stick to objective facts, but also because you need to say what you see, even when you don't like what you see. Effective communication means being able to talk about any pertinent subject, even that which is uncomfortable, unusual, or unsettling. You may not like something, you may have a personal aversion to it, but that doesn't mean you can ignore it.

As I mentioned, I show these two paintings to every group, even religious organizations. One time I was presenting to educational leaders from at-risk high schools when a principal raised his hand and told me, "I don't want to look at those pictures. They disgust me!"

I explained that while it is never my intention to offend anyone, whether he liked the pictures or not was irrelevant. We cannot turn away from things we don't like. The fact is, the women are naked. You have to deal with that. You don't have to like it. I can only imagine the difficult and even distasteful things a principal at an inner-city high school is faced with. Turning away from them is never an option.

Art, like life, isn't always pretty. The images on the preceding pages aren't private pieces of pornography; they are iconic paintings that took the art world by storm for different reasons. The first one, Francisco de Goya's *Naked Maja*, is said to be one of the first instances in Western art of an artist painting a nude woman who wasn't a mythological, historical, or allegorical figure. For his crimes of "depravity" in painting it, the artist was brought in front of the Inquisition. Painted around 1800, it has hung in the Museo del Prado in Madrid since 1901. The second painting, *Benefits Supervisor Sleeping*, is a 1995 work by Lucian Freud. It's often colloquially referred to as *Big Sue* in honor of the real-life model, Sue Tilley, a social services worker who spent three years posing for the portrait. When *Big Sue* sold at auction for $33.6 million in 2008, it broke the record for the most ever paid at auction for a work by a living artist.

Art is the perfect vehicle for learning how to communicate when we're uncomfortable. Of course the subject matter of art can be controversial or unpopular, but more important, art is what it is to each and every viewer. It doesn't move, it doesn't talk back, it won't follow you home. It is static, timeless, and does not judge you for how you interpret it. And therein lies its power. Installation artist and photographer JR explains that art is about "raising questions, and giving space to interpretation and dialogue. The fact that art cannot change things makes it a neutral place for exchanges and discussions, and then enables it to change the world."

In 2013 I took a group at the Met through a temporary exhibit in an interactive gallery called *The Refusal of Time* by William Kentridge. I gave them no warning, we didn't stop and read the labels, we just walked through a doorway into a darkened room featuring a five-channel video installation with sound, megaphones, and an "elephant" breathing machine. It was extremely dark and very loud. Darkened screens filled the walls playing flickering, mostly black-and-white movies of shapes being blown around, silhouettes of people dancing, and scribbles. A booming, lumbering soundtrack of music and spoken word played, while a moving sculpture resembling an Industrial Revolution–era factory machine with exposed gears and a giant head endlessly and noisily pumped its bellows in the center of the room.

We walked straight through the exhibit, and when we got out I turned and asked the class what they had observed. It was a good test of short-term situational awareness, as even though they were in the middle of a class about honing their observation and perception skills, more than half the class was completely tuned out, since I hadn't given them explicit instructions to tune in.

One participant offered that it felt like being trapped in an old Silly Symphony black-and-white cartoon where the giant flowers bend their knees and dance in a disturbing rhythm. Creative, yes, but I didn't want to know how the artwork made them feel, I wanted to know what they saw. In the absence of a wealth of observational data, other students filled in the gaps with their opinions. "Uncomfortable," said one. "I have no idea what that was," said another. Another participant got claustrophobic and "couldn't wait to get out." Another simply declared, "I hated it."

Yes, it was an assault on the senses. It could easily make anyone uncomfortable. That's true for a lot of things in this world. But we can't let our discomfort override our need to observe and be aware.

Let's look at a painting that could be described as overwhelming. Five hundred years before *Where's Waldo?*, Dutch artist Hieronymus Bosch painted *The Garden of Earthly Delights*, a massive triptych painted on three oak panels almost 22 feet across and 13 feet high symbolically depicting the garden of Eden, the fall of man, and hell. (It's in the permanent collection at the Museo del Prado, and well worth seeing in person if you can.)

Hieronymus Bosch, *The Garden of Earthly Delights*, c. 1500–1505.

Since the painting is so large, we're going to zoom in on the detail in the very bottom right corner:

Hieronymus Bosch, *The Garden of Earthly Delights* (detail), c. 1500–1505.

It does not matter how we feel about this depiction. It is definitely strange. But rather than talk about what we think, let's talk about what we see.

I'll start with the most important: in the upper left-hand corner, there's what appears to be a man, who looks like he could possibly be deceased, being attacked by two rodent creatures. On the far right we have an anthropomorphic pig wearing a veil resembling a nun's habit. The pig is sitting upright and leaning its snout against the ear of an adult human male, also sitting, who has his right hand on its cheek. The man has what appears to be a piece of paper with writing on it draped over his left thigh but otherwise doesn't appear to be wearing any clothes. In front of the man and the pig is a creature with the beak of a bird, thighs like a human, and reptile feet wearing a large closed helmet favored by medieval knights that covers most of its body. The creature has the end of a feathered arrow sticking out of its right thigh and a severed foot hanging from a curved spike protruding from the top of its helmet. An inkwell hangs from the creature's beak, which protrudes from the helmet's visor, into which the pig is dipping a quill held in its left front foot.

See, it's not so bad if we just stick to the facts. Let's try another painting. What do you see?

William-Adolphe Bouguereau, *Dante and Virgil in Hell*, 1850.

This is generally the point where the people who were okay with the nude women and the pig dressed like a nun begin to squirm a little. It doesn't matter if the painting makes you uncomfortable or brings up things you'd rather not think about. It's *especially* when we don't like something or wish to avert our eyes from it that it becomes essential that we're able to describe it objectively, putting aside both assumptions and emotions.

Really look at the painting. What's going on? Does your perception of the facts change the more intently you look? While at a cursory glance it might seem that two nude men are wrestling out of playfulness, a show of strength, or attraction, when we look more closely we instead see signs of aggression: a knee in the back, fingers clawing at flesh, an open mouth at another's neck. The 1850 painting by William-Adolphe Bouguereau is titled *Dante and Virgil in Hell*, and it depicts a passage in Dante's *Inferno* where Dante and Virgil are touring the eighth circle of hell and witness a heretic fighting a con artist:

> *They smote each other not alone with hands,*
> *But with the head and with the breast and feet,*
> *Tearing each other piecemeal with their teeth.*

It's fine to be uncomfortable looking at this painting. It's fine to not like it. It's not fine to ignore it, because it exists. It's in front of you. It's when we ignore the facts or choose not to believe what we see that bad things happen.

BELIEVE WHAT YOU SEE

Sometimes the facts that are presented to us are so uncomfortable or unbelievable, we block them out, to disastrous results. Psychologists have borrowed the legal phrase "willful blindness" — in which someone tries to avoid liability for a wrongful act by purposefully being unaware of the details — to denote the things we purposefully choose, even unconsciously, not to see. Like our other cognitive blindnesses, it can be overcome with conscious awareness. Unlike the case with our other cognitive blindnesses, failing to overcome it can have far-reaching consequences, as seen in the case that rocked Coventry.

In England, the idiom "sent to Coventry" refers to someone whom you can't talk to anymore because that person deserves complete isolation. Sadly, this proved to be true for four-year-old local resident Daniel Pelka. In March 2012 the little blond boy was found starved and beaten to death by his parents — despite authorities having been called to his home *twenty-six times.*

School officials had noted that on separate occasions Daniel showed up with a broken arm, two black eyes, and "four dot-shaped bruises" around his neck. He winced when a teaching assistant playfully ruffled his hair. Teachers noticed that he was "wasting away," all skin and bones with sunken eyes, his clothes "hanging off him." They documented that he was stealing food from other children's lunch boxes and eating scraps covered in dirt from the school's garbage cans and sandpit.

His stepfather claimed that the boy had broken his arm when he jumped off a couch. It was determined that he had an "obsession with food." His seemingly caring mother claimed he had a medical condition that made him so skinny. His pediatrician explained his poor growth and weight loss as symptoms of a medical condition. Although the police frequently visited his house to deal with violent domestic disputes, they never talked to Daniel or considered child abuse (a perfect example of what happens when we don't ask questions, as we learned in the last chapter).

The official review of the case found, "The practitioners involved were not prepared to 'think the unthinkable' and tried to rationalize the evidence in front of them that it did not relate to abuse [*sic*]."

Daniel didn't die because people failed to notice his condition. They did notice. They did document. They did care. But they didn't want to believe what they saw in the aggregate. They didn't want to confront the distressing reality of abuse when analyzing the facts in front of them.

We need to believe what we see even when it means we might have to think the unthinkable and say the unspeakable. We cannot ignore warning signs because they seem to portend the impossible. The belief that she couldn't sink contributed to the *Titanic*'s tragedy. The belief that Lehman Brothers was too big to fail contributed to its collapse. We can't gloss over facts that we find distasteful, distressing, or disturbing because the unimaginable happens every day. We need to be able to communicate when it's business-as-usual but also prepare our business for the unforeseen, for the emergency, for the impossible.

To practice objectively analyzing both the "impossible" and the uncomfortable, let's move a bit closer to Bosch's *Garden of Earthly Delights* and analyze this detail:

Hieronymus Bosch, *The Garden of Earthly Delights* (detail), c. 1500–1505.

It doesn't have to make sense or relate to our lives for us to assess and analyze it thoroughly. What's going on in this picture? Write down a few sentences to describe it.

Here's what I saw: an anthropomorphic creature with the head of a small bird sits in a circular chair on stilts while eating what appears to be a nude human body. The creature has a cauldron on its head and its feet inside two urns and is holding the bottom half of the human body in its mouth with its right claw around both of the human's thighs. Two more human forms appear to be in a bubble underneath the creature's chair. And five black birds, seen only in silhouette, are flying out of the half-devoured human's backside.

I don't find it a particularly pleasant scene, but that doesn't matter. Nor do I find it very realistic, but it is real — that is, it's an image that actually exists in the world, so I can use it as visual data and describe it. And so can you.

More important, we can translate this skill of precisely assessing art that is out of our comfort zone into handling difficult communication, because while looking at paintings is most likely not part of your daily routine, managing sensitive information is. We all have to deal with difficult situations and discuss uncomfortable topics. Professionally, at some point we're going to have to ask for a raise, challenge a new company policy, reprimand an employee, or resolve a dispute. Personally, at some point we're going to have difficult talks with our partner, our child, or our parents. Once again, the problem with ignoring something is that it's dangerous. Training surveillance agents in the intelligence community is a constant reminder that things you don't talk about won't go away. In fact, they may escalate, cause more damage, and increase your own exposure. In contrast, the willingness to tackle difficult subjects and situations can earn you the admiration of your boss, your customer, your potential donor, and even your loved ones.

Children in particular need direct, forthright communication, especially concerning troubling issues. Minimizing, sidestepping, or denying others' concerns will not make the problem go away and can hurt the relationship we have with them.

I once coached the headmaster of an elite Manhattan private school who had the unenviable task of telling the parents of a teenage honors student that their beloved baby girl had been giving sexual favors in the boys' bathroom. The conversation did not go well because the parents refused to have it.

"That is an outrageous accusation!" the mother fumed. "Our daughter would *never!*"

The headmaster explained that it wasn't an accusation or an assumption. The girl had been caught by a trustworthy, tenured faculty member. The parents stormed out, refusing to continue a conversation that might ultimately help get their daughter the counsel or discipline she needed.

They were taken aback and possibly taken over by their emotions and disbelief. However, turning away from it didn't make it go away; in fact, it possibly made the ordeal worse, especially if they swept the situation under the rug at home the same way they did in the headmaster's office. According to family therapist Ron L. Deal, when caregivers turn away from an upsetting situation concerning a child, the child often interprets it as the adult turning away from her. This can lead to the child permanently turning inward, acting out with negative behavior, or losing long-term trust in the parent figure. Deal says, "Over time this goes a long way to increasing emotional distance in the parent-child relationship and diminishing the parent's voice with the child." To prevent this, the parents needed to rise above their discomfort with both their daughter and their daughter's educators and have an objective conversation about the facts.

When we are emotionally overwhelmed and can't seem to think straight, we can always fall back on the same investigative model we've learned to use to gather facts: who, what, where, and when. Instead of letting their emotions dictate their response, the student's parents could have asked: "Who was involved in our daughter's activities?" "What exactly did the incident entail?" "Where did this happen?" and "When did it occur?"

True leaders can handle an uncomfortable conversation as easily as a crisis. They know how to digest and deliver bad news without displaying subjectivity or emotion, even when they don't like it. And in every course I teach, I can spot these people immediately. They're the ones who when everyone else says, "I don't like this," or covers their mouth with their hands, or turns away, say with a definitive nod, "Interesting." Their brains are engaged, overriding their guts and their body language.

Here's how to be that person.

OUTSMART YOUR EMOTIONS

Just as with observation skills, the most important thing we can do to sharpen our communication skills, especially in times of stress or duress, is to separate the objective from the subjective. In assessing, we separate fact from fiction. In analyzing, we separate inference from opinion. In stressful communication, we must separate the message from any and all emotion.

Humans are emotional beings. Emotions are a natural part of who we are. As the psychologist and emotion researcher Paul Ekman explains, we developed emotions to deal with ancient threats such as saber-toothed tigers, and as a result we often experience them unconsciously. "They have to happen without thinking or you'd be dead," Ekman says.

Emotions are also what we're wired to pay attention to. If we didn't have an instant fear of becoming a tiger treat, our legs wouldn't move us out of harm's way in time. Particularly in stressful situations, people will be emotionally sensitive. Communicating emotionally with them will make them answer in kind. Emotional volleying does not accomplish concrete work. Instead of focusing on the information or task at hand, emotions can cause us to stew over the personal.

When you convey information, especially to people who report to you, choose your words and requests with care. If you include even a hint of negative emotion — disappointment, disgust, disbelief, condescension, sarcasm, passive aggression, or veiled insults — that's what your listeners will hear first and hang on to the longest.

I once worked with a woman who was particularly skilled at demeaning her subordinates with corrections wrapped in insults. Unfortunately, while her criticisms may have been valid, her reproachful tone and the wounded reaction of the recipient made it very difficult for them to register. One person on the receiving end of a red-lined rampage wasted days wading through and fixating on the unnecessary censure before she could get back on track and fix the factual issues.

Comments such as "Work on tone!" came across as in-print yelling. "You need to do better" was taken as an insult. The writer obsessed over the reprimand "This isn't the way to do this. Google and Wikipedia are not valid sources." As a corporate communications specialist with a degree in journalism, the writer knew Google and Wikipedia weren't credible references, and she didn't use them. Did her boss think she did? Or was it just a derogatory censure? Instead of bolstering her research, as the writer agreed she needed to do, she spent hours prepping a defense of her skills. She was defensive and angry and eventually reluctant to change anything.

Both the writer and her boss had the same goal: a well-written, well-researched report done in a timely manner. Miscommunication that threatened to undermine that was ultimately detrimental to both parties. It wouldn't have taken the boss any extra time to construct more helpful edits such as swapping "That's not what 'ambivalent' means!" with "'Ambivalent' means having mixed feelings about something, no?" Doing so would have saved the entire team from the resulting wasted time and interoffice drama.

That's not to say that we can't ever express emotion. If you need to convey a feeling — *I love you* — use emotion. When you need to convey a fact — *your performance is below par* — eliminate emotion unless that's all you want in return.

Since our own emotions can seemingly come out of nowhere and take us by surprise — "You might not even know it until someone says to you, 'What are you getting so upset about?'" Ekman notes — the first step to mastering them is getting to know them. Just as with our subconscious perceptual filters, introducing a conscious awareness of our emotions into the communication process will help us overcome them.

To start, Ekman recommends being aware of our facial expressions, our body language, and any tension we might be carrying. If you catch yourself clenching your jaw or tightening your shoulders, use it as a sign that you might be emoting unwittingly. If you find that to be the case, do the same thing we do when looking at art: step back, assess, and evaluate. Ask yourself, "Why am I emotional? What could have triggered it? Did I misunderstand something?"

We must be aware of our own emotional triggers and signals because other people around us can see them, sometimes before we do. Patients can tell when we can't wait to get out of their room. Kids can tell if we hate helping them with their homework. That client can tell if we secretly think he's ignorant. And the minute they see it, we've compromised the quality of our relationship, the care or advice or instruction that we can provide, and possibly even our professional or personal integrity.

Pretending our emotions don't exist isn't a solution. Trying to suppress them might be not only futile — researchers at Queensland University of Technology in Australia found that people who attempted to suppress negative thoughts in fact spawned more of them —but harmful to our health. A 2012 experiment at Florida State University recorded stronger stress responses based on heart rate from people who tried to restrain their negative thoughts than from those who didn't.

When it comes to negative emotions or thoughts, experts advise: let them flow to let them go.

When you first approach a situation, before you communicate anything, give yourself a few moments to work through your emotional response. In a session with medical students at The Frick Collection, I split up the group into pairs and assigned each pair a work of art to observe, study, and then present to the class. I could tell from their body language that two young men—first-year medical students—didn't appreciate the portrait of a woman, Jacques-Louis David's *Comtesse Daru*, I asked them to assess. They stared blankly. They shifted their weight. I finally said to them, "If you don't like it, that's fine. Just be able to tell me why."

Suddenly they found their tongues. They told me they thought the subject was unattractive; she was cross-eyed, her hat looked like a shower cap, and her dress was ugly.

Jacques-Louis David, *Comtesse Daru*, 1810.

"Great," I replied. "*Now* tell me what you see objectively."

Acknowledging and getting their subjective thoughts out allowed them to break free of their reluctance and reticence and do what they needed to do. They could then state that the woman's gaze didn't quite meet theirs, her cheeks appeared overly puffy, her necklace of large green gemstones was prominently featured; that she had horizontal creases in the flesh of her neck that contrasted with the vertical earrings she was wearing; that she wore a white dress with an empire waist and ornately patterned sleeves; and that her right arm was draped in a patterned fabric and the viewer could see the suggestion of a folded fan in her right hand.

In life as in art, we're not going to like everything or everyone. When you meet somebody you have to work with, a coworker or witness, a student or supplier, and you instinctively just don't like him, step back and ask yourself why. Why don't you like him? Specifically what don't you like? You might discover it's because he looks like an ex-boyfriend or the teacher who humiliated you in second grade. But once you recognize that, you'll be able to see how subjective and unimportant it is and move on.

MOVING ON

We can prepare and practice and do our best to be objective, but there will still come occasions when we find ourselves in the thick of a heated, emotional discussion. How did we get there? The possibilities are endless: a misperception, a misunderstanding, a few poorly chosen words taken the wrong way. But whatever the reason, we're there. We're staring at the uncomfortable painting of the bird creature eating the man with more birds coming out of his backside. And we need to get out. But how? By using the same techniques we learned in the previous chapter: repeating, renaming, and reframing.

Repeat It

Just as we seek confirmation that our message has been received by having the other person repeat it back to us, we can use the same strategy to turn the tide of a heated debate. To do this, philosopher Daniel C. Dennett advises, "you should attempt to re-express your target's position so clearly, vividly, and fairly that your target says, 'Thanks, I wish I'd thought of putting it that way.'" Dennett suggests then stating any points of agreement and anything you have learned from the other person.

Charles Richards and his wife, Caroline, put this advice into practice and found it kept them out of countless circular and painful arguments. They told me how one day, Charles heard Caroline call his name from the bottom of the stairs. There was no mistaking the tone: she was upset. He rushed out of their bedroom and stood on the landing above her.

"What's wrong?" he asked.

"I can't take it anymore," she said.

"What?"

"This," she replied, pointing to a pair of socks and a book on the first step.

"What?" he repeated, slightly confused. He saw the items, but he didn't see the problem.

"These are yours, yes?" She sighed. "You left your socks by the back door when you got home from the gym, and your book was in the living room. I picked them up when I was cleaning and put them here for you to take upstairs."

"Sorry," he said, "I didn't see them there."

"But you walked right by them," Caroline insisted. "Why do you always do this?"

"Do what?" he said. "Not take my stuff upstairs?"

"Yes!" she answered. "You never do. You just leave it there for me every time."

"I do?" he said doubtfully. "You put stuff on the stairs purposefully for me to take up?"

"Not specifically you," she answered. "Whoever's going up next. But you walked right by it."

"I honestly didn't see it," he said.

"How could you not see it when you had to step over it?" she replied.

Charles and Caroline admitted that they were both getting increasingly agitated. To defuse the situation, Charles decided that instead of defending himself or telling his wife how wrong she was, he would try to simply repeat her concern.

"So you leave stuff on the steps for the next person going up to save you from having to always run up and down them," he said, "and when I walk right by it without picking it up, it aggravates you, yes?"

"Yes," she said. "A lot."

"I really don't notice it. It might as well be invisible to me," he said. Then he dug deeper into her concern. "But it's not to you, is it? It's the opposite. You not only see it, you see it as an insult or something I'm doing on purpose?"

Caroline hesitated because he was right — that was how she saw it. For further clarification, she then repeated his words.

"You really don't see things on the stairs?" she asked. "Like it's invisible? That's crazy to me because the pile on the stairs is so obvious to me, it might as well be glowing. It practically shouts at me."

"Really?" Charles answered. "It bothers you that much? It's like visual pollution to you."

"Yes," she said, relieved that he understood. In fact, he explained it better than she had. It was like visual pollution to her. And he didn't see it at all. "I had no idea you didn't see it," she continued. "The stairs are your blind spot, then?"

Now it was Charles's turn to be relieved. Piles of socks on the floor really didn't register in his field of vision, and he was glad his wife understood.

Instead of allowing the conversation to degenerate, Charles and Caroline consciously chose to communicate better by repeating each other's concerns. In doing so, they not only avoided having a fight, they came to better understand each other and learned something new about the way the other saw the world.

Rename It

Another way we can try to extricate ourselves from the entanglements of a he said, she said, what-did-they-really-mean debate is to rename it. Instead of slogging through what exactly happened to get you there and whose fault it was, wrap everything — all comments and feelings and innuendo and assumptions — into a single package and give it a new name. Call a time-out, and then sum up the entire messy situation for what it is and label it accordingly. Instead of referring to the problem as a mess or disaster or even a problem, rename it a miscommunication.

I've been on the receiving end of bungled plans, missed connections, and confusion probably as often as I've caused them. We aren't perfect. Sometimes we forget or screw up or just say the wrong thing. In one of my latest calamities, a new client flew all the way to New York City from Los Angeles to attend one of my sessions for a future business opportunity, and no one showed up to my presentation. No one. As if I hadn't even been scheduled. I had been thorough — booked and confirmed! This nice woman from California came all the way across the country to see me in action, and instead she got to watch me show up in an empty room. I was many things: embarrassed, upset, disappointed, even a little angry, and I believe she was as well. But none of those subjective emotions were going to change reality. The Art of Perception wasn't going to happen that day. And the client was leaving town the next. Screaming at the scheduler wasn't going to fix that. Nothing was.

Unfortunately, as much as I wanted to, I couldn't wish the situation away or pretend it never happened. It had. And I was worried about the resulting damage: would she think I was unorganized or unprofessional? I could have made a big deal about how it wasn't my fault and tried to pinpoint whose it was, but that would risk my relationship with the company that had hired me. To leave the situation unaddressed could invite further confusion or stoke unspoken animosity. I had to face the issue and put it to rest in a way that didn't compromise anyone's reputation. To do so, I quickly labeled the entire event a miscommunication.

A miscommunication is a fact. There is no blame or shame in a fact. When you find yourself in a highly charged situation, drop all of the drama and opinion and what-ifs — the "you didn't tell me" or "we wouldn't be here if" — and agree to call the entire scenario a miscommunication. Doing so gives everyone a way out and a reason to let go of the emotional attachment to any subjective points at the same time. Once we're dealing with a fact, we can move forward.

The client and the company and I were all relieved once I stepped up and renamed the situation. The pressure was suddenly off. Miscommunications happen. To everyone. Thankfully, we can usually fix them and try to prevent new ones.

Reframe It

Finding a solution takes just one more step: reframing any outstanding concerns as questions rather than problems. Questions make communication a give-and-take; there's a query and an answer. Questions give the person you're communicating with options and an out. Questions also protect you, the asker, from the possibility that you have incorrect information or are working with an assumption.

Instead of saying, "X is wrong," reframe it: "Is it true that . . . ?" or "Did you mean to . . . ?" Instead of asking someone, "Can I talk to you for a minute?" which immediately implies a conflict or problem, ask instead, "Can you help me with something?" Reframe the issue in the best possible terms, and the response will be more positive.

I did want to know what happened to my group so I could be better prepared should it happen again, so I asked the person who scheduled the session about it. Instead of saying, "They should have been here!" I reframed it as a question: "Where did everyone go?" And I learned that this company's employees periodically get called out on department-wide emergencies that can't be predicted. Knowing this didn't help get my session back and wouldn't guarantee that it wouldn't happen again, but it will keep me from inviting guests to that venue next time.

I thanked the company representative and left, taking the client out for lunch. In the end we had a great day, we got to know each other better, and I flew out to Los Angeles the following month to conduct another session, which she was able to attend.

Once we've learned to recognize and then eliminate emotion in our information delivery, we can apply the good communication techniques we learned in the last chapter.

If repeating, renaming, and reframing doesn't work and the person you're communicating with still won't let go until blame is assigned, go ahead and assign it—to the situation. Try "I'm sorry *there was* a miscommunication/misinterpretation/things weren't clear." Some people won't quit until they hear "I'm sorry," and while you're not saying it was your fault, you are giving them a truthful concession, since chances are you're more than sorry to be stuck in this situation with them.

Also keep in mind Mary Poppins's famous advice: "A spoonful of sugar makes the medicine go down." Coating our words with sweetness can help the other person receive them more easily. While writing anything—a report, a press release, a book—has its fair share of challenges and deadline pressures, there is perhaps none so nerve-wracking as showing someone your first draft. Thankfully, unlike other people I've had the misfortune of working with, my editor, Eamon Dolan, is great at delivering difficult news with a liberal dose of kindness. Early in my first communication from him, he wrote, "My notes take a very matter-of-fact tone, but please imagine a 'please' in front of all of them. I use a very direct style in my marginal notes for the sake of clarity and efficiency, and I apologize in advance if any of them veer into brusqueness." Those two sentences at the start of our professional relationship made months of otherwise hard-to-hear critiques not just bearable but many times delightful because he had dismissed any doubts I had about his intentions.

THE RECEIVING END

We're on our way to becoming objective-communication experts. But it's equally critical to address good communication when the tables are turned, when we are on the receiving end of an emotional tirade and need the perfect response to salvage an otherwise untenable situation.

First and foremost, no matter how upsetting the communication is, do not react emotionally, orally or in writing. Instead, do what you did when you were becoming emotionally self-aware: absorb, process, let the negative feelings flow, then let it go. It's probably harder to put emotion aside when you're the one who's feeling insulted, especially if it's coming from someone above you, but it's the only way to get ahead and win respect.

If the people communicating with you haven't taken the time to segregate their emotions, you have to do it for them. Ignore the subjective aspect of whatever they're telling you, and focus on the facts. Defend yourself from any actual accusations, but forget the emotion they're wrapped in. Letting the insult go unanswered does not make you a lesser person. It makes you the opposite.

If the emotional upheaval keeps coming from the same person, try assessing and analyzing that person objectively. Look for the facts. Ask yourself: Who is this person? Where is he from? Why would she do this? You might uncover an obscure fact — about his upbringing or home life or job history — that helps explain his actions. The person might not change, but at least you'll have a new perspective to help inform your perception of him — which just might be enough to defuse any future emotional bombs.

Bruce Vincot, a sales manager at Unicore, a manufacturing company, couldn't believe what he was seeing. When he got the call that a major customer was canceling its contract, the rep in charge of the account didn't handle the news well.

"It's not my fault!" the salesman screamed at his boss. "I'm not taking the blame for this!" The young man then jumped out of his seat and left Vincot's office, slamming the door behind him.

Vincot's emotions were instantly ignited. "The salesman is a punk," he thought. "That's not how we did things twenty years ago. The amount of disrespect . . ."

While Vincot's initial reaction was to go after the rep and fire him on the spot, he knew he needed to give himself a few minutes to calm down. This wasn't the sales rep's first temperamental display, but he was the highest performer in the entire company. Firing him would be an emotional relief but a financial mistake. Vincot knew he would have a hard time explaining to his own bosses that he let the number one salesperson go because he'd thrown a tantrum.

As he pondered how to handle this situation, an image from his Art of Perception training came to mind: the two men fighting in *Dante and Virgil in Hell*. While he didn't connect to the painting when he'd first seen it, he could suddenly relate. He felt his sales rep was attacking him while his bosses stood by, coolly detached and watching, which rendered him helpless.

To defuse his emotional response, Vincot got out a piece of paper and used the training; he would look at the exchange exactly as he would a painting and simply list the objective facts. He began with the ones that bothered him the most:

- The sales rep slammed my office door.
- The sales rep raised his voice and acted unprofessionally.

He caught himself. Was designating the yelling "unprofessional" objective or subjective? He was fairly sure it would be considered unprofessional by most professionals, but since it was not something he could prove, he crossed it off.

- The sales rep raised his voice.

That fact could speak for itself, and anyone who read his report could choose to label it unprofessional or immature or crazy. So, what had caused the outburst?

- Customer X canceled its contract.
- Customer X was the sales rep's account.

Both true and objective. Now, what about why?

- Customer X felt our prices were too high.

Writing that fact down gave Vincot pause. It was a fact; he had spoken to the customer himself. The customer canceled the contract because of price, not because of the sales rep, not because the sales rep had yelled at him or slammed the door of his office. Was there a connection between the cancellation and any of the sales rep's actions? Yes, there was. Vincot wrote it down:

- The sales rep did not present new pricing in person, sent via email instead.

He knew because the rep had told him when he asked — admittedly with disgust — "how in the hell" the contract was lost.

Writing down the objective facts did several things for Vincot. It gave him time to calm down and let his own emotions subside before he acted; indeed, the act of writing just the facts defused a lot of his own feelings. It highlighted his own part in the exchange — *Had he yelled first? Had that triggered his sales rep's explosion?* — and systematically separating the objective from the subjective put everything in perspective. The facts weren't that bad. The sales rep hadn't assaulted him or yelled at him in front of a customer or his coworkers. He had raised his voice and slammed a door. Was it really such a big deal? Vincot himself had been in the trenches cold-calling for twenty-five years; he knew the stress of the sales rep's job. He took a moment to remember the rash things he had done in his younger days when his emotions got the best of him.

Most important, the exercise made Vincot realize he'd been prioritizing the wrong things. He had listed the sales rep's behavior first, when the more critical fact was that a major client had been lost. Focusing on that fact helped Vincot create a secondary list of steps needed to rectify the true problem and keep it from happening again. Was the company's standard sales procedure of presenting price in person clearly communicated to his team? Did it need to be reviewed? Did they need more training?

By cataloging the objective, Vincot was able to eliminate emotion, find a new perspective, and prioritize what was really important for the success of his company, his team, and himself.

Approach the difficult in life the same way you approach the difficult in art. Take your time and gather the facts. Analyze them and prioritize them. Take a step back and consider things from alternative perspectives. Consider your body language and nonverbal communication and that of others. Be objective, accurate, and precise. And know that the result of learning how to separate the subjective emotions from objective communication is confidence.

I was having dinner with one of my former students recently, a manager at a pharmaceutical company, who revealed that she was no longer intimidated by difficult conversations.

"I used to dread it when I knew I had to have one," she told me. "If I had to give a bad performance review or terminate someone, I would be sick for days beforehand, worrying about it. But what I learned from concentrating on the objective and leaving the subjective by the wayside is that facts give confidence. Facts are the truth. I found security and confidence knowing I was going to only have to deal with facts."

If we can factually describe a pig in a nun's habit kissing a naked man, a bird creature eating a human with more birds coming out of his backside, two nude men wrestling in front of the devil, and Big Sue cupping her own breast, we can likely navigate corporate downsizing, quarterly budgets, bad medical diagnoses, employee evaluations, and even talking to our teens about sex.

Now that we have mastered the tenets of good communication even in bad situations, in the next and final section, we'll look at what unintentional behaviors we might need to reconsider and which we might need to change. We've learned how to assess, analyze, and articulate information. Now we must use those skills in the real world, a world that isn't still or objective. To do this, we need to adapt. Adapt to our surroundings, adapt to less-than-ideal circumstances, by adapting our own thoughts and behaviors.

PART IV

· · ·

Adapt

We don't see things as they are. We see them as we are.

— ANAÏS NIN

10

Nothing Is Black-and-White

Overcoming Our Inherent Biases

EVEN THOUGH SHE had been a nurse with the New York State Health Department office for more than ten years, Lucy Agate had never had to investigate a case like this. She arrived at the East Neck Nursing Center in Long Island, New York, with a manila folder containing the accusations — NURSING HOME STRIPPER SCANDAL, ELDER ABUSE, and GEEZER TEASER, the headlines screamed — along with a copy of the lawsuit against the home filed by the son of one of the residents.

The *New York Post* had just run the story — "The elderly residents of a Long Island nursing home saw their shuffleboards replaced by washboard abs when they were subjected to a low-rent Chippendale's striptease in the facility's rec room" — along with a large color photograph of an elderly woman in a wheelchair seemingly placing dollar bills in the waistband of the large, muscular man leaning over her wearing nothing but briefs.

"The outrage!" Agate tells me in her distinctly Long Island accent. "We got angry letters all the way from California. The owners of the nursing home were horrified: 'We had no idea this was going on!'" Agate was called in to investigate what had actually happened.

According to the lawsuit, Franklin Youngblood had been visiting his mother at the nursing home when he discovered the offending photograph in a bedside drawer among her belongings. When he confronted the staff about it, Youngblood claimed they lunged at him and tried to take the photo away. He also wanted to know how his mother had access to money when her cash was supposed to be locked up in a commissary account.

Youngblood, members of his family, and his attorney held a press conference outside the nursing home. Youngblood claimed that his mother, "a traditional Baptist, hard-working lady," had been "defiled" by the incident. The lawsuit stated that when "nursing home employees subjected her to this disgraceful sexual perversion," the woman "was placed in apprehension of imminent, offensive, physical harm, as she was confused and bewildered as to why a muscular, almost nude man, was approaching her and placing his body and limbs, over [her]." It further stated that the "vile" occurrence was done for the "perverse pleasure and enjoyment of the Defendant's staff."

Attorneys for the nursing home held their own, competing press conference, during which they claimed that the residents had wanted the event, and that Youngblood's own girlfriend had accompanied the woman to it. The Associated Press reported that Youngblood's family denied this but wrote in a decidedly opinionated fashion: "In any case, that does not mean Bernice Youngblood was not harmed by what she saw."

Much hinged on what nurse Lucy Agate would see when she arrived to determine whether the facility had failed to meet New York State standards for quality of care.

Agate interviewed everyone involved: the residents, the caregivers, the nursing staff, the managers, the owners of the home, Apollo the stripper, the stripper's agency, and the old lady in the photograph, Youngblood's mother. The objective facts surfaced when she systematically asked questions to find out what she didn't know and needed to learn.

How did a stripper get into the nursing home? The residents

voted on their monthly activity, and they voted to have a male stripper.

"A committee of residents requested it, and then all of the residents democratically voted to have it," Agate says. "The residents are adults. They're allowed to vote."

Were the residents forced to go? No. In fact, the nursing home offered an alternative activity for those who didn't wish to attend.

Was the entertainment discriminatory against the male residents? Were only females allowed to attend? No, men were invited to attend as well, and one did.

Were the residents taken advantage of financially to pay for the stripper? No. The residents didn't pay for it with their own money; the nursing home footed the bill. Does that mean there was a fiscal misappropriation of taxpayer money? No, the money came from the nursing home's activities budget. The staff asked corporate for permission for the stripper, and it was granted.

What about the tips the residents were doling out? Did that money come from their commissary accounts? No again. Agate discovered that the residents do have their own pocket money.

"They have the right to stick a dollar bill in a gentleman's waistband if they want to," Agate says. "*Not* allowing them to would be a violation of their resident rights."

Most important, even though they had voted for it, did the residents feel abused? Agate interviewed every one of them.

"They all said the same thing of the show," Agate reveals, "that the home should get a refund. Even the lady in the wheelchair said it was the worst lap dance she'd ever gotten! They said the guy was terrible. He had been instructed not to bump, grind, touch anyone, or basically do anything. They were all disappointed!"

How did media outlets across the country fall for the salacious story of a stripper forced upon elderly nursing home residents? Because our perceptions and internal biases affect how we act and how we expect others to act.

"Everyone was so quick to believe the photograph proved elder abuse because we don't want to see an elderly woman in a wheelchair as having sexual desires," Agate concludes. "The fact is, the residents are all adults, they all have rights, and they are allowed to see a male stripper if they choose to."

Up until now, we've dealt with our perceptual filters as blindnesses and studied how they can affect our observations. We now know that when something we see is not in sync with our expectations, we can subconsciously make it align, either by missing important details or making assumptions that fill them in or simplify them. To refine our model for improving observation and communication skills, though, we must look at how these inherent filters can do more than just make us miss something based on our background, mood, or political affiliations. We need to examine how our perceptions can lead to biases that affect our actions, and learn how to adjust for them accordingly.

Before we can learn to overcome our biases, however, we must understand what they are. *Bias* can mean many things — although its connotation is usually negative, and thus, no one wants to acknowledge a known bias. I ask almost all of my classes to raise their hands if they are biased. Eventually some hands will go up, but not without hesitation. I tell them what I'll tell you: we *all* have biases, we were born with many of them, and they're not all bad.

* * *

In scientific and sociological terms, a bias is a perceptual filter that doesn't just change how we see things but can affect our *actions.* For instance, our bias toward sci-fi movies will cause us to buy a ticket for the newest blockbuster regardless of the early reviews. Our bias against mall food courts will make us go somewhere else at dinnertime. A bias can be that which we avoid and that to which we're drawn.

We're biologically wired to have biases, and they aren't inherently negative. The problem arises when we refuse to recognize our biases, sort through them, and then overcome the ones that are based on beliefs that are untrue, unhelpful, or unfair to others. Ignorance of biases isn't bliss, as they do exist in *all* of us and, unchecked, can lead to stereotyping and bigotry.

Biologically, we're all naturally biased toward the things we like, the things we grew up with, the things familiar to us. Our brains readily identify with things that reflect situations in our own lives because those are typically the things that also mean safety, security, and ease. From an evolutionary standpoint, this affinity bias, or the desire to be around people like us, arose because people in our tribe or group or clan or cave tended to look like us. People who didn't could be dangerous marauders. Again, like many of our inherent systems for sorting the world around us, identifying someone we recognized as safe was automatic and done without thought. In today's multicultural, almost borderless world, the same safety parameters do not apply, and we must overcome our natural affinity bias to avoid excluding valuable "others."

Aside from being drawn to people like ourselves, another bias that alarms people — not being able to differentiate faces from an unfamiliar racial group, for example, "all Asian people look alike to me" — is also inborn. Scientists have documented what they call the "other-race effect" and have noted its presence from infancy. This effect is only one of a host of biases we harbor unwittingly.

UNCONSCIOUS BIAS

Since our brains are exposed to more information than we could ever process, mental shortcuts, many of which we've already studied, exist to help us automatically prioritize and filter. Unconscious biases are one of those shortcuts, and we all have them. They exist to quickly fill in the gaps for us so our bodies are engaged to fight or flee ahead of our slower, conscious thinking. If our ancestors didn't have them, they might have ended up someone's or something's prey before they even knew what was going on. Unconscious biases help us make decisions, whether we know it or not.

Our unconscious biases apply to situations, information, and things—it's why when you're on a diet you suddenly notice all of the delicious food commercials on TV, or when you or your partner is pregnant other pregnant women seem to be everywhere—but it's when they're directed at people that we need to be cautious because our preferences can turn into prejudices.

José Zamora found out firsthand just how easily unconscious bias can lead to prejudice. He had been looking for a job for months, submitting fifty to one hundred résumés every day. Even though he had solid sales experience, he didn't get any feedback at all . . . until he was struck by a thought: he needed to change his résumés. So he did, leaving all his work history and education intact but deleting just one letter: the *s* in his first name. José became Joe. And the interviews came pouring in. Zamora wisely concluded, "Sometimes I don't even think people know or are conscious or aware that they're judging, even if it's by name, but I think we all do it all the time."

He's right, we do. Even in a blind hiring process, our brain still finds ways to seek out the comfortable and cross off that which makes us uncomfortable.

Suppose you were walking down the street in London and you suddenly saw this situation. What do you think is happening here?

Since we've just talked about prejudice, I'm sure you don't want to jump to the conclusion that the black man is a criminal being chased by the white policeman. But if you did, you aren't alone. I've worked with both white and black police officers who readily admitted that, yes, that is what they saw, and I've had white and black participants tell me the opposite. The important thing to note is that different people from different backgrounds will have different interpretations. Our culture and our personal experiences influence how we perceive what is happening.

However, as we've seen throughout the book, we cannot rely on interpretations or perceptions. We need facts. Let's objectively assess and analyze the photograph.

Who is in the picture? Law enforcement participants in my class have noted a white man in uniform on the far left, and a black man on the right not in uniform. The white man wears a custodian helmet, the traditional headgear worn by constables in England; he appears to be a police officer of some kind. The black man is wearing long pants and a long-sleeved coat over his shirt. Where are they? On a street corner next to a concrete building with a crumbling façade and graffiti, possibly in an urban area, although we can't tell exactly where. When is it? It appears to be daytime, and from the black man's coat, a cooler day. Their clothing suggests the end of the twentieth century. What are they doing? Many participants in my class are eager to tell me that the white man is chasing the black man. Why? We don't know.

Even though we see a police officer, we cannot assume a crime has been committed. Nor can we assume that the black man is guilty of anything. We can't even assume that one is chasing the other. In fact, they are *both* police officers. The man on the right is an undercover detective. They're both headed the same way, both chasing an unseen suspect.

The photo was part of an ad campaign by the London Metropolitan Police with the heading: "Another example of police prejudice? Or another example of yours?" The campaign wasn't to scold the public but to recruit new officers. The text continued: "Do you see a policeman chasing a criminal? Or a policeman harassing an innocent person? Wrong both times. It's two police officers, one in plain clothes, chasing a third party. And it's a good illustration of why we're looking for more recruits from ethnic minorities."

Another reason it's important to know our biases, especially those that might lead to prejudice, is because they can be transferred to others, consciously and unconsciously. Convergence in the workplace happens slowly and subtly when people who've worked together over time start to think the same way. Even drug- and bomb-sniffing dogs are susceptible to minute, unintentional cues from their handlers. Recognizing this can help us work through any prejudice or bias, negative or positive, that we might be automatically adding to a situation that is then picked up and spread by others.

As with our perceptual filters, to identify our biases we need to look inward. What are our prejudices? Do they help or hinder our observations? Are we selling the solution to a problem because it's the right answer or because it lines up with our biases and desires?

To illustrate this, I show my classes this photograph of a baby being held by an older woman:

What can we see? The woman is smiling. She has earrings on, her hair is up, her eyes are brown, her skin is darker than the child's. The baby is very fair-skinned and has blond hair. The baby appears to be a boy, but we can't confirm that. The baby wears a shirt with white and dark stripes, and his or her mouth is open.

What could their relationship be? I get all kinds of answers for this. She's the mother, the nanny, a neighbor, the godmother, a teacher, a healthcare worker . . . there are infinite possibilities. The only one I won't accept is a hostage situation because they look comfortable together.

Are they genetically related or not? Their skin color is different, their facial features are different, but genes can do funny things.

One woman in New Orleans told me, "That is definitely the biological mother! They have the same nose!" I told her that no, I knew that the woman in the photograph was not the baby's mother. She answered, "You're racist by saying she 'can't be' the baby's mother."

That is quite an assumption, and I can tell you it's quite untrue. I explained that I didn't say she "couldn't be" the baby's mother, I said I "knew" she wasn't. I knew not because I was assuming it couldn't be true but because I have twenty-seven hours of labor and a C-section scar proving that it's not true. This photo shows my son and the beloved babysitter we've had since he was three months old.

The woman apologized and explained that she'd had the opposite experience with a friend, a black woman with a light-skinned baby, who was constantly, and she believed unfairly, referred to as her own son's nanny. The woman's experiences informed her decision to confront me. The same thing happens to all of us, whether we realize it or not. Our brain fills in the information gaps to form our biases by grabbing similar data from things we've already experienced—for better or worse.

When I showed the same photo of my son and his babysitter during grand rounds at a large urban hospital, the chief of emergency medicine raised his hand and told me, "That baby has Down syndrome."

"And what evidence do you have to support that?" I asked him.

"None," he answered, "but I know it when I see it."

Another doctor told me the baby had a thyroid condition, and he could tell because the "neck was compressed from multiple surgeries." Sorry, but my son was just a fat baby with multiple chins. I've heard that my child is albino, obese, and has emphysema because of his "barrel chest." None of the above is true.

We don't want to completely divorce ourselves from our experiences because they can be valuable when we're seeking information, but we need to be careful not to let them radically skew what we see. Important decisions are underscored by accountability, and if we jump directly to the conclusion we want to reach without articulating the observations and perceptions that got us there, we can be accused of being misguided by our biases.

To appreciate the effect experience has on our biases, look at the image opposite. What do you see? Write down or say aloud everything you observe about the painting. Don't move on until you've really explored it.

What did you see? A bridge? Yes. A footbridge, to be specific. Trees, one definitely a willow dipping into a body of water. Is it a lake or a pond or an outlet to the sea? We can't tell. There are plants and rushes growing on the banks. Lily pads float on the water's surface; some hold flowers. The bridge appears to be made of wood and is curved upward. We can't see either end: the left side is covered by foliage; the right leads off the side of the painting. It is a painting, yes. Lots of greens and yellows and blues. In the water you can see a re-

Claude Monet, *The Japanese Footbridge*, 1899.

flection of the trees. There are no people or animals in the painting. It's a close view of nature, but we can't see the sky. And if you're an art lover or you've ever seen an umbrella or notebook with this particular image on it, you might know that it is a Monet.

But which one? Claude Monet painted 250 paintings of water lilies in his lifetime; one hangs in almost every museum in the Western world. Eighteen of them feature the Japanese wooden footbridge that spanned a pond near his house in Giverny, France. They all have pretty much the same name — *Water Lilies, Pond with Water Lilies, Bridge over a Pond of Water Lilies* — so that designation wouldn't do us any good even if we knew. At first glance, Monet's water lily paintings might look very similar, but there are definite differences among them.

Visual Intelligence

How astutely did you see? Without turning the page back, pick out which of the Monet paintings on the left is the same as the one you were previously studying.

I do this exercise in my classes, but I pair everyone up and have one person face the front of the room while the other turns her back to it. One partner has to describe the painting out loud, while the partner who can't see it draws a picture of it. Generally about half of the pairs choose the correct painting, and half don't. The ones who are successful say it's because they specified that the bridge was blue-green with flecks of pink, which differentiates it from the color of the bridge in the other two. Some credit describing the circle of space in the water in the foreground surrounded by lily pads. Fewer than ten have attributed it to mentioning the drop shadow on the right and bottom of the original painting, which instantly sets it apart from the others. How astutely did you see? The correct answer is the painting in the middle.

Did you see the shadow on the right side and bottom of the image? If you missed it, go back and look now. Is that part of the painting? Technically, no. But I asked you to note "everything you observe." The drop shadow is there. It exists. I'm not trying to trick anyone; I want to illustrate that we must look at everything, not just what's right in front of us. We have to look outside the box, in the corners, and off the page. Sometimes that's where the answers are.

When I did this exercise with one of the most prestigious groups of military intelligence officers in our country, one officer in particular was devastated that he'd missed the shadow. He slumped in his seat, put his hand to his head, and kept muttering, "Oh man, I can't believe I missed the shadow!" A shadow is not a big deal to most of us, but in his line of work, it was of critical significance. Missing the shadow could mean the difference between rescue and failure, life and death.

Later, as I mulled over his reaction, I realized that everyone in that room with him was in the military. Why was he the only one who was visibly upset? Possibly because he had an incident in his past or knew someone who did where a shadow or other small detail made a big difference. His experience likely colored his reaction. What we see because of our experiences can be beneficial or disastrous, *depending on how we handle it.* Will we let our experiences lead us blindly into action, like the woman who called me a racist at a public event? To prevent such errors in judgment, we should recognize the role that our experiences play and attempt to disengage from them in an attempt to search for facts as objectively as possible.

That we all come from different perspectives and bring different experiences and different eyes to each situation is what makes collaboration so important. Look at this painting by Caravaggio. What do you think is happening here?

Cops generally try to determine what kind of crime is going on; financial analysts think it's about the counting of money; and counselors see a family disagreement. Having different people bring their different experiences to the table helps us see new viewpoints we might never have considered on our own. But the first person in any of my classes to properly identify this scene was a clergyman. Having studied paintings of the saints, he knew that it depicted Christ calling Saint Matthew to be a disciple.

We won't always have a priest with the right answer on hand when we need him, but the experiences other people bring to a situation or problem can add a new level of understanding that can move us all toward a solution or success. Those experiences and perspectives can help us make better and more informed decisions.

Consider this image from White House photographer Pete Souza:

White House photograph of the Situation Room.

There's a lot going on in the scene. We can see the faces of thirteen people, eleven men and two women, along with the hair of another and the elbow of still another. Seven people are standing, while six are seated around a shiny, rectangular, brown wood-topped table that holds five open laptops, a note pad, at least four printouts, file folders, two disposable cups, and a pair of eyeglasses. Everyone is wearing business attire except for one of the men at the table, who is dressed in a navy blue, highly decorated military uniform. Everyone in the room is looking at something out of frame to the left except for the military man, who looks down at the computer keyboard in front of him.

When I asked a group from the US Army Asymmetric Warfare Group what they saw, one officer offered: "The only guy in the photograph doing any work is the guy in uniform." That's what someone in the military sees; that's his perspective. Is it true that only the military man is working? Possibly, possibly not. Is it an objective fact? Since we can't prove it either way, it's not; it's a bias based on his experience. But we have two choices: we can use his experience to make further assumptions — *military guys are always the only ones working* — or use it to dig deeper for facts as Lucy Agate did with the nursing home stripper saga — *why does it appear that the military man is the only one working?*

Looking at the photograph from this angle gives us a different perspective we might not have considered. The military man is just one of thirteen people in the room. Zeroing in on him and what he could be doing that others are watching helps us find out more about the situation. It is in fact the Situation Room in the basement of the White House. The current US administration and national security team were receiving updates on the mission to find Osama bin Laden on May 1, 2011, and watching a live feed from drones over bin Laden's location. It now makes sense that the officer is looking down, hands on the keyboard, and everyone else is watching; he was in charge of Operation Neptune's Spear, and he was presenting their progress.

Personal experience is a valid resource that we can and should use to mine visual data for more facts — as long as we adhere to three simple rules.

THREE RULES FOR WORKING WITH (AND AROUND) OUR BIASES

Rule 1: Become Aware of Our Biases and Boot the Bad Ones

Our biases exist because we're hardwired to make unconscious decisions about others based on what we instantly perceive as safe, same, or comfortable. The first step to overcoming them or using them to our benefit is to acknowledge them. Knowing that biases are normal, universal, and not inherently bad can help us deal with them wisely. There is power in acceptance. If we're honest with ourselves and mindful of how we see the world, we can recognize the biases we need to work with or work against. No one has to know what we're dealing with in our heads; it's a private self-revelation that can help us be better observers, communicators, and generally better people.

Once we've recognized the biases in ourselves, we can then look at them and determine if they can be used productively to gather more factual information. To do this, ask yourself: Are my prejudices or my way of viewing things limiting how I listen to and communicate with others? Are my biases helpful or harmful to me and my success? If you find that they are detrimental, divorce yourself from them before they do harm. If you can't cut them, extricate yourself from the situation.

Many military officers, the very people who secure our democracy, abstain from voting in presidential elections to avoid their own internal dissension. They recognize how it might affect their perceptions, attitudes, and behavior if their candidate should lose. Whoever is elected president will be their commander-in-chief. They choose to set aside their personal political preferences to be the best employees possible.

Rule 2: Don't Mistake Biases for Facts; Instead Use Them to Find Facts

Our biases are not verified facts. They are feelings and experiences that make us want to believe something, but they aren't enough to create a conclusion. Instead, use them as a starting point to look further.

As we did in the last chapter with uncomfortable communication, we can turn any questionable inferences our biases raise into actual questions and then use those to investigate further for facts. Turn "The elderly residents felt abused by the stripper" into "Did the elderly residents feel abused by the stripper?" Turn "The guy in uniform is the only one working" into "Why does it appear that the man in military attire is the only one working?"

Rule 3: Run Our Conclusions Past Others

Since we are so close to our biases, and many of them are unconscious, we need others to help us discern which of our conclusions are faulty and which are not. Retired FBI special agent Jean Harrison, with whom I've worked for many years, shared a story with me about how she did just that.

Harrison was called in to investigate a homicide in the tightly knit Vietnamese community of a large city. One of the women the FBI had interviewed on the scene was withdrawn and practically expressionless. Special Agent Harrison's colleagues were convinced that the woman's "aloof" behavior meant she was lying. Harrison felt differently. For some reason, she believed that the woman was telling the truth. She knew she couldn't jump to that conclusion without facts, so she examined what she was working with: both the visual data in front of her and her own personal experience.

First, Harrison looked harder at the woman. She could see why the woman's demeanor and body language seemed standoffish to her colleagues. Her body language training told her the woman was possibly being untruthful, but something inside her said no. What bias could she possibly hold about the Vietnamese woman? Then she realized it was from past experience. Growing up, Harrison was exposed to many different cultures, including Vietnam's. She recalled many personal interactions in which the shy, cautious, and reserved behavior of the Vietnamese women she knew as a child was misinterpreted by Americans as defensive or deceitful.

Harrison explained her bias and her past experience to her colleagues and asked if they thought it was possible that the woman was being misinterpreted. Her colleagues agreed that it was and encouraged her to approach the woman from a different perspective. Harrison did and discovered that the woman was telling the truth. In fact, the Vietnamese woman, once she felt comfortable enough to open up, went on to become the prosecution's star witness and helped solve the case.

Harrison didn't throw out her personal experience; instead she analyzed it, ran it past others, and made sure it was a valid source of input and not the sole reason for a conclusion. She used it to find a conclusion, and a good one that her organization needed.

* * *

We all have cognitive biases shaping our decisions and stoking our actions. Like our perception and perspective, our biases are unique and shaped by our own experiences, beliefs, and biology. We need to be open to the same input from others, both to learn their perspective and to help balance ours.

To effectively observe, perceive, and communicate factual truths, we must be able to account for our biases and, in many cases, overcome them. And thankfully, science shows that we can with simple awareness and conscious replacement. To define this concept, Nilanjana Dasgupta, a psychologist at the University of Massachusetts Amherst, has spent more than a decade documenting successful interventions over our implicit biases, and confirms, "These attitudes can form quickly, and they can change quickly, if we restructure our environments to crowd out stereotypical associations and replace them with egalitarian ones." Jennifer Raymond, associate professor of neurobiology and associate dean in the Office of Diversity and Leadership at the Stanford University School of Medicine, concurs; "Just as one can overcome physical habits such as biting one's fingernails or saying 'umm' when one speaks, one can suppress undesirable mental habits such as gender bias through deliberate, conscious strategies." Researchers at the University of Queensland have even discovered that perceptual training during infancy will prevent the emergence of the inborn other-race effect; babies who were regularly shown photographs of different faces were able to later perform a level of recognition and race differentiation that untrained babies were not.

The human brain is malleable. We can change our perceptions, make new neural connections, and train it to think differently. Now let's take the final step and see how we can use it to navigate uncertainties.

11

What to Do When You Run Out of Gurneys

How to Navigate Uncertainty

IN 2012 I was invited to do a session for the nurses at the University of Colorado Hospital in Aurora. Six weeks earlier the trauma and critical care units had endured the aftermath of a mass shooting inside a local movie theater, and they were still recovering from it. During the midnight screening of *The Dark Knight Rises,* a man dressed in tactical clothing had deployed tear gas grenades and fired into the audience with a pistol, a rifle, and a shotgun, killing twelve people and injuring seventy others.

They told me how they'd coped with the sudden influx of wounded even when they ran out of basic necessities such as gurneys. One of the nurses, a young woman who looked fairly fresh out of school, reminded me that while they were in the thick of the crisis, they knew less about what had happened than people at home watching news reports about it. The hospital staff, emergency workers, passersby, family, and friends didn't know if it was a lone gunman or part of a larger attack, if it was domestic or international terrorism, or if the killer or killers had been caught. This particular nurse, still shaking, recalled that she hadn't known what to do, that she hadn't had any information at the time, and that she'd just wanted to quit.

How could she avoid feeling that way next time? she asked me.

She didn't want to ever feel so unprepared, so lost and helpless, when things went wrong.

I wanted to tell her that things would never go wrong for her again. I want to tell my son and everyone I care about and everyone I work with the same thing. But things will go wrong for all of us. Life will present us with too many uncertainties and too few gurneys. I call this place the gray area. In the gray area, things aren't clear-cut. Instead, they are weird, messy, noisy, and chaotic. The lines between good and bad, guilty and innocent, rational and irrational, and intentional and accidental are blurred.

The gray area is dangerous because it lends itself to sensationalism and emotionalism. Make a mistake, and *TMZ* will make sure everyone knows about it. You can go from miscommunication to damage control to disaster in the blink of an eye. The headlines are full of stories about situations where it isn't clear who was right and who was wrong, and the subjective opinions of a crowd can cause real damage, from lengthy investigations and lost business to death threats for those involved. The longer we live and the higher we move up in our careers, the more often we'll find ourselves having to negotiate this nebulous place, to make tough calls in perplexing situations.

I train many first responders in medicine and law enforcement, but in reality, everyone is a first responder at some point. As we saw in chapter 4, flight attendants are. Parents are on a daily basis; so are teachers. The same can be said of employees, bosses, students, and anyone who is ever out in public, really. The first people at the scene of an emergency, crisis, or crime usually aren't the news crews or emergency workers. They are regular people like you and me.

I took off my microphone, went into the audience, and sat with the nurse and her colleagues. I told them my own first-responder story, how on 9/11 I was exactly where you didn't want to be. I was right there in New York City. I saw, I smelled, and I heard things I never want to experience again. Every week when I step on a plane, I ask myself, "Is this the one that's going to go down?" Every time I kiss my little boy good-bye, I think, "If something happens, how am I going to get him?" I've been there. We all have been or will be. But we must go on.

How do we do that? How do we move forward in life despite the things we can't un-see or undo? How can we be confident in all scenarios, even in the face of constraint and chaos? How do we make decisions in a gray area where nothing seems to make sense? With the same organized and methodical processes we used in previous chapters.

In any situation, but especially in one that's gray, we need to focus on what we do know and let go of what we don't. The nurse I met was stuck on the unknown "why." But as we've seen, we don't need to know the why to move forward. That's the last piece of the observational puzzle and sometimes the one that's never filled in. On our list of priorities, "why" falls somewhere near the bottom. Instead of standing around waiting for answers to the why, focus on and objectively deal with what you can see: the who, what, where, and when. That's what the leaders in a small town in the South did the year before Trayvon Martin was shot, and why you've never heard of Jasmine Thar.

In December 2011, two months before Trayvon Martin's shooting gripped the nation, sixteen-year-old Jasmine Thar was killed standing in her godmother's driveway two days before Christmas. She died in front of her mother, younger brother, and other family members and friends. The bullet that killed her also hit and injured two women. It came from a high-powered rifle across the street. When the police went to the shooter's home, they found a Confederate flag, a noose, and neo-Nazi materials.

How did the local police manage to keep the peace in their town and keep the situation from escalating into a national incident? By conscientiously choosing open, inclusive, and objective information gathering and communication.

Time was of the essence, even though the young woman had already died.

Tensions ran exceedingly high. Perceptions and prejudices abounded as the shooter, a twenty-three-year-old white man, maintained that the gun had malfunctioned, while Jasmine's black family believed the shooting was racially motivated. On the surface, the notion that a man who possessed neo-Nazi materials would accidentally shoot a young black teenager across the street did seem unlikely, but before making any assumptions or bringing any charges, the chief of police in Chadbourn, North Carolina, had the presence of mind to send the gun to ballistics experts at the FBI to test for malfunction.

When we're working in the gray area, we must be extra careful, because it is likely that others will be scrutinizing our actions very closely. To get out in front of the crisis, local law enforcement invited the spiritual leaders of the community to participate in every step of the investigation.

When the FBI reported that the gun had in fact accidentally discharged, the shooter was not indicted. Not everyone in the community was satisfied with the findings — they didn't bring Jasmine back to life — but the leaders in North Carolina had effectively confronted the difficult perceptions head on, articulated them, and kept all parties apprised of the investigation. They carefully sorted through objective facts and subjective inferences. They kept the big picture in focus — the community's grief and need for answers — while taking care of the small details, such as having the gun checked right away. Doing so kept them off the map in the best possible way.

Johnson & Johnson provides another example of successfully navigating the gray area. In 1982, when news broke that seven people had died after ingesting Tylenol Extra-Strength capsules, panic spread quickly. The victims died within minutes of consuming pain reliever laced with sixty-five milligrams of cyanide; just seven micrograms is fatal. Advertising mogul Jerry Della Femina told the *New York Times,* "I don't think they can ever sell another product under that name."

The situation had many unknowns. How did the medicine get tainted? Who did it? Was it chemical terrorism, a deliberate poisoning by someone outside Johnson & Johnson, or the fault of the manufacturer? (Cyanide was available at the product plants.)

Instead of waiting for answers or attempting to duck responsibility, Johnson & Johnson acted quickly and decisively. Chairman James Burke prioritized the two most important questions the company was facing — first, "How do we protect consumers?" and second, "How do we save this product?" — and proceeded to work on answering them.

The company immediately stopped production and advertising

and recalled all Tylenol capsules from the market — approximately 31 million bottles valued at more than $100 million. It also offered to exchange all of the millions of Tylenol capsules already in consumers' homes. Going further, it offered counseling and financial assistance to the victims' families. It put up a reward for any information about the poisoned pills and pledged not to put any Tylenol products back on the market until they were more securely protected. They spent more money and time developing new three-part tamper-resistant packaging that included stronger glue on the boxes and both printed plastic seals and foil stamps on the bottles. Johnson & Johnson did all this before it was ever determined if the company was at fault.

The company also opened lines of communication with all news media outlets to ensure that warnings were distributed to the public and established relationships with local police departments, the FBI, and the Food and Drug Administration.

Johnson & Johnson never got its "why." The case was never solved and spawned several copycat crimes across the country. But rather than letting the unknown paralyze them or obsessing over what they didn't know, the company set its priorities on taking care of what it could, and as a result produced a corporate miracle. Johnson & Johnson completely recovered its market share and reestablished Tylenol as one of the most trusted brands in America. How? By objectively handling the facts and not letting the subjective suck them under.

SUBJECTIVE PROBLEMS, OBJECTIVE ANSWERS

That some situations aren't straightforward and might never have definitive answers doesn't mean we can't address them. When the problem or scene or challenge we face is nebulous, morally ambiguous, or otherwise in the gray area, consider it a subjective problem, then deal with it objectively.

A problem is a problem. Handle the subjective ones the same way you have learned to handle the objective ones. Gather what facts you can by looking at both the big picture and the small details, step back, consider other perspectives, analyze, prioritize, ask questions, and communicate clearly and concisely.

In 1993, a Denny's restaurant outside of Washington, DC, was accused of racially discriminating against customers. Six black uniformed Secret Service agents claimed they weren't served as quickly as their white counterparts because of their race. The waitress claimed that the delay was caused by the large size of the Secret Service contingent — twenty-one people entered the restaurant together, with the six black agents sitting at one table — the complexity of their orders, and the black agents having ordered last. The proof of the alleged prejudice? The waitress was seen rolling her eyes after turning to leave the black agents' table. The result? A class action lawsuit. Discrimination is hard to prove. Did the waitress do it on purpose? Only she knows.

Denny's Corporation didn't waste time with the subjective — did the waitress discriminate or not? — but rather immediately handled it objectively, understanding that it must overcome public suspicion at once by showing a clear opposition to racism and a respect for its customers in general. Denny's took responsibility, apologized, made restitution, instituted new policies, and communicated directly with the public that whether the accusations were true or not, the company wouldn't accept even the appearance of racial bias at its restaurants.

Gray areas will differ in size, importance, and context, but they will arise in both our professional and personal experiences. In either situation, a subjective response can increase the risk of negative escalation and, even more dangerous, obscure the facts. We must respond objectively even when the situation itself is subjective. In doing so, we might not be able to eliminate hard-to-solve problems, but we can minimize our risks when things get messy.

BEING CREATIVE WHEN RESOURCES ARE STRETCHED

Adapting our skills for success in a less-than-perfect world means not only managing the gray, subjective areas around and within us, it also means doing the very best we can with what we have. In situations with shocking shortfalls — in information, time, materials, manpower, money — leaders cannot shut down or walk away. In a crisis we don't get to fill out an acquisition report or complain to our boss. We throw someone over our shoulder and do what needs to be done without the luxury of all of the information, and in a stressful time crunch. Nobody has enough money. No one has enough time or manpower. Everyone's resources are stretched. But that doesn't have to be a bad thing.

As necessity is the mother of invention, so can constraints bring out the best in us. Tightened circumstances force us to rethink, reframe, and do things differently, instead of conducting business as usual.

El Anatsui, *Skylines*, 2008.

In art, this is called "objet trouvé," making new art from found objects. Ghanaian artist El Anatsui is famous for it. As you can see, he creates magnificent, room-size pieces that look like glittering mosaics from afar and are assembled to resemble woven cloth. Up close, you see that they're made of countless tiny pieces of metal, pinched, twisted, and shaped, linked together with copper wire. Get even closer and you can read words on the metal: Dark Sailor, Top Squad, Chelsea.

One day on a routine scavenger hunt for free, local material to work with, El Anatsui discovered his medium. It was plentiful along the roadsides in West Africa, thrown away with the trash: metal caps from liquor bottles. Using it to make art, he in turn makes a statement. The layers of his work are many: it is repurposed beauty; it's a comment on world issues such as industrial waste; it's a communal endeavor made by teams of people; it's endlessly flexible, never hanging the exact same way twice; it's inexpensive, created from literal trash; it's large and powerful and yet portable enough to fold down and fit into a suitcase.

If the son of a fisherman born on the Gold Coast can do this with discarded bottle caps and wire, what can we do with our own finite resources? How creative can we get?

El Anatsui, *Oasis* (detail), 2008.

The need to be resourceful doesn't just come around with quarterly budgets. It's ever-present in our personal finances, in our parenting needs, in our education system, in our government, and especially in emergencies. We can have confidence in the face of chaos when we know we can be creative with our resources no matter what the situation. To prove that we can deal effectively with a deficit, we're going to use the observation, perception, and communication skills we've learned throughout the book to analyze works of art that are not finished.

The Metropolitan Museum of Art in New York alone has more than two dozen unfinished works on view — not hidden in the closets or tossed aside but up on the wall installed next to their finished treasures. Why? Because art historians believe that they afford us the opportunity to study the process and appreciate the hard work, skill, and inspired thought that precede an object's completion. Life, after all, is a work-in-progress, and everything isn't always finished off with a neat bow on top.

Not everyone enjoys looking at unfinished works, however. Blank spaces where faces should be, missing hands, and visible scribbles can make some visitors extremely nervous. They're uncomfortable not because they have obsessive-compulsive disorder but because they are human.

Humans crave completeness, so much so that some psychologists claim we have an "incomplete" complex. Whether it's unopened emails, loose ends at work, or undone home-remodeling projects, things that aren't finished hang over us like a weight and haunt the corners of our minds. The unfinished occupies our brains because humans, as evidenced by numerous studies around the world, have a need to finish a task once it's been started. The search for closure stems from the brain's preference for efficiency. A completed task is a closed loop. An incomplete one is an open loop that uses up cognitive energy searching for a solution or worrying that there isn't one yet.

The phenomenon of incomplete tasks dominating our thoughts is called "the Zeigarnik effect." It's named for Russian psychologist Bluma Zeigarnik, who was in a café in the 1930s when she noticed that the waiters had exceptional recall skills only for the orders they hadn't yet filled; the minute they set the food and drink down, they were relieved of the pressure of thinking about it. Many believe that the Zeigarnik effect is why television shows ending in "cliffhangers" convince us to tune in next time, and how quiz shows suck us in. Dr. Tom Stafford from the psychology and cognitive science departments at the University of Sheffield in the United Kingdom writes, "You might not care about the year the British Broadcasting Corporation was founded or the percentage of the world's countries that have at least one McDonald's restaurant, but once someone has asked the question it becomes strangely irritating not to know the answer (1927 and 61%, by the way)." Stafford, author of *Mind Hacks,* even credits the Zeigarnik effect for the enduring success of the game Tetris. Invented by a Russian scientist in 1984 and still going strong thirty years later, Tetris has been played by an estimated one billion people because "it takes advantage of the mind's basic pleasure in tidying up — and uses it against us."

Incomplete things cause us stress. In his book *Getting Things Done,* productivity consultant David Allen argues that the major cause of everyday anxiety is that we all feel we have too much to do and not enough time to get it done, which frustrates us because our brains subconsciously obsess over the incomplete. According to Allen, the obsession is relatively democratic for all tasks including "everything from really big to-do items like 'End world hunger' to the more modest 'Hire new assistant' to the tiniest task such as 'Replace electric pencil sharpener.'"

Incomplete things that threaten our productivity aren't limited to the tasks on a to-do list. They also include everything we've internally agreed to do, such as the implicit understanding that we're obligated to answer every email, return every phone call, and answer every question that's asked of us. The stress of the incomplete can affect corporate managers and news bureau editors as easily as students or stay-at-home parents. We don't have to keep a conscious tally of how many incomplete things are circling in our brains to know that they sap our energy and attention. Backlogs drive us crazy.

And so, as with other things that cause us discomfort, we avoid them. Which makes them worse.

Instead of evading the incomplete tasks, we're going to trick our brains into not being caught in that infinite open loop by dealing with them as if they were complete. And we'll do it — you guessed it — with art.

Famous artworks are left unfinished for the same reasons projects, promotions, and problems in the workplace remain undone, unfilled, and unsolved: politics, disasters, indecision, changes in direction from above, death or illness, lack of time, money, or resources. The ability to pick up where someone else left off is invaluable, especially now, when the national annual employee turnover rate across all industries is over 40 percent, and new workers are expected to successfully complete projects they didn't start. If we can separate our subjective emotion concerning an unfinished project — our disappointment or frustration at having to work with the less-than-perfect — from the objective facts, we'll find that in many ways, working with the incomplete is no different from working with the complete.

Take a look at this unfinished sketch by Gustav Klimt:

Can we objectively assess and analyze it? Yes. The important elements are all there.

Who is it? A woman with dark hair, a long face, light eyes, dark eyebrows, and a thin nose. We can see the slender fingers on her right hand resting on her lap; her left hand is not visible. She appears to be alone. She wears a choker of black ribbon and lace that suggests she's from the early twentieth century, or at least dressing in the fashion of that time.

What is she doing? Sitting, looking straight ahead as if posing for a portrait. Where is she? It appears that she is indoors, possibly in a studio or other nondescript location.

When is it? Probably daytime, judging by the lighting. We cannot tell the time of year.

What don't we know? Her name, her relationship to the painter, where she is posing, what the remainder of her dress or covering looks like, why she is there, why the painting wasn't finished.

What would we like to know the most if we could get more information? What would answer the most important questions? Who she is.

Even though the painting itself is unfinished, we can use the objective facts we know to find out more.

We know the work is by Klimt. Why is it only half completed? Investigating what Klimt was working on near the end of his life, we can discover that the sketch is the beginning of a portrait he painted in Vienna from 1917 to 1918. It was left unfinished when he died suddenly of a stroke at the age of fifty-six.

So we now have a time and a place. Following those leads, with a little historical research we can uncover that the portrait Klimt was working on in 1917 was of a woman named Amalie Zuckerkandl, and from that the story blossoms.

Amalie Zuckerkandl knew all the right people. She was the sister-in-law of Klimt's good friend Berta Zuckerkandl, an art critic, journalist, and literary salon hostess, and a friend of Therese Bloch-Bauer, sister-in-law of one of Klimt's biggest patrons, the Jewish sugar baron Ferdinand Bloch-Bauer. Ferdinand Bloch-Bauer commissioned the portrait of Amalie along with at least seven others, including two of his wife, Adele. The Nazis entered Vienna in 1938, spreading chaos for both Jewish citizens and resident artists. While her daughter Hermine was able to hide safely in Bavaria, Amalie was executed in a concentration camp.

The painting of her was at that time hanging with the other Klimts in Ferdinand Bloch-Bauer's Vienna palais. Although Bloch-Bauer managed to flee to his castle in Czechoslovakia, he hired a lawyer in Vienna to protect his property; that lawyer turned out to be a high-ranking SS officer who then helped liquidate his estate for the Nazis. Bloch-Bauer's Vienna palais eventually became a German railway center and is now the Austrian rail headquarters.

The painting of Amalie was lost for a few years but is believed to have come into the possession of Amalie's non-Jewish son-in-law, who sold it to an art dealer. The dealer kept the painting in her private collection and donated it to the Austrian Gallery in 2001 when she died at the age of 101. In 2006 an Austrian arbitration panel ruled that all stolen works including *Portrait of Amalie Zuckerkandl (unfinished)* be returned to the Bloch-Bauer heirs, but then changed its mind and decided that Amalie should stay in Austria.

We never would have unearthed this rich, riveting story if we had shied away from the Klimt because it was unfinished. Instead, we tackled it the same way we tackle any finished work: with a methodical plan and a process. Being prepared to use our skills in less-than-ideal circumstances where important things are missing will prepare us for the curveballs that can bench other people: layoffs, firings, sudden departures, bad hires, drastic changes in policy, rules, and regulations. We need to make a go of it even when we have only incomplete information or resources. I did just that late one night at a hotel in Washington, DC, and I was more than satisfied with the possibly life-saving result.

I'm often in the capital for business and stay at the same hotel downtown so often, they've given me birthday gifts. However, during one stay I was awoken at 2 a.m. by screaming outside my door.

"I'm not going to let you do this to me again! I'm calling 911, I swear I will!" a woman's voice rang down the hallway.

I got out of bed and looked out my peephole; I saw nothing. As an experienced solo traveler, I knew better than to open the door and possibly put myself in harm's way. The screaming continued.

I had a very incomplete picture of what was going on. I didn't know who was involved, how they knew each other, or the context of their communication. But I could hear the tone in the woman's voice, and it told me she might be in trouble.

I called the front desk and reported what I had heard. I was very careful to articulate only what I knew: what I had heard being said, where, and when. The front desk summoned the police.

An hour later I got a call from the hotel asking if I would give my statement to the officers now on the scene. I was the only "ear witness" to the argument, the only person in the hotel who had called to report the incident. I'm sure I'm not the only person who heard the screaming. It was very loud and lasted a good while. I believe that other guests didn't call in because they were put off by the incompleteness of their information. They didn't know what was going on, so they ignored it. I didn't know either, but my entire professional career from attorney to education director to The Art of Perception president has taught me not to ignore anything.

During my interview, I was forthright about what I knew and didn't know. What I'd heard was incomplete, therefore both my observations and my perceptions were incomplete. But that lack of information didn't preclude me from cooperating. I relayed the facts I knew, leaving out the subjective, my opinions, and my assumptions: At approximately 2:15 a.m. I woke to screaming in the hallway outside my room, 226; I went to the door, looked out the peephole, and saw nothing; I heard a woman's voice scream and relayed exactly what I had heard, as I remembered it; I also heard a male voice with her but could not make out what he said; the screaming and arguing continued for at least fifteen minutes.

The police found the woman from the hallway hiding in the lobby behind some furniture. She had been unwillingly employed as a sex worker and was fighting with her pimp. Instead of this being a he said, she said situation, however, the police had an impartial third party on record confirming that the woman said what she did, that it wasn't a lover's quarrel as the man was claiming. As a result, the police were able to intercept a prostitution ring that had been operating out of the hotel.

We can employ the same techniques with other incomplete things in our lives. For instance, say it's the long list of bold, unread emails in your in-box that's currently clogging your brain. Instead of letting the subjective take over — *I'll never get to all of them! There are too many!* — look for the objective facts the same way you would with a finished piece of art. Start with numbers. Count how many you receive a day, and figure out how many you can reasonably answer. Determine when they come in, then schedule a time each day when you can focus on nothing else but email.

Ask yourself, what are the differences between the incomplete and the complete in this case? Incomplete emails are both read and unread but still unanswered. Complete emails are read and replied to. Can you do something to treat the incomplete as if it were complete? Perhaps you could read the emails all at once without answering them but with an eye toward sorting and prioritizing them. Don't have time to answer every one as quickly as you'd like? Remove that stress by doing what you would do for completion: answer them but with an autoresponse. *Inc.* columnist Kevin Daum suggests, "Thanks, I got this. I'm a little busy but I will respond within a day or two."

Amazingly, just planning to put this new email protocol in place, planning to attack the incomplete as if it were complete, alleviates much of the stress that causes us to avoid it in the first place, whether we're successful at implementing it or not. In a series of studies in 2011, psychologists at Florida State University found that the mere act of planning not only eliminated the mental interference caused by unfulfilled goals, it freed cognitive resources, which ultimately facilitated the attainment of that goal. Or as Dr. Stafford puts it, "[Our] mind loves it when a plan comes together — the mere act of planning how to do something frees us from the burden of unfinished tasks."

As we've seen throughout this book, the ability to see clearly, process, and communicate in any situation brings with it big benefits both professionally and personally, including job security, personal safety, financial gain, and universal respect — huge rewards for an easy and almost automatic process that anyone, with a bit of practice, can master.

Conclusion: Master Work

WHEN FUTURE CNN Hero Derreck Kayongo stepped out of his hotel shower with questions about a tiny bar of soap, he never dreamed that one small observation could have such a large, international impact. In the five years since he was inspired to found Global Soap Project, Kayongo has seen his initial idea for reusing refuse multiply many times over. What started as simply taking discarded bars of soap from American hotels, disinfecting them, and distributing them to people in his native Uganda who had no way to even wash their hands quickly turned into a hygiene revolution. His charity has since evolved to help curb the spread of Ebola in Sierra Leone and work with midwives to stop preventable puerperal sepsis, also known as "childbed fever," which regularly kills newly delivered mothers in developing countries. And in an initiative that brings his entrepreneurial and humanitarian journey full circle, Kayongo now provides micro-loans to local soap makers, like his father, so they can contribute to making their own communities healthier.

Most surprising, though, are the transformations Kayongo has personally witnessed. During his very first delivery of five thousand newly recycled bars of soap to a village in Kisumu, Kenya, things didn't go according to plan.

He recalls, "The mamas lined up with their children, smiling and laughing, as I piled the bars on little tables. I told them the story of the soap. I said, this is no ordinary bar of soap. It has been made lovingly by American volunteers just for you. This is the soap of hope."

When he returned the next morning to see how the women liked the soap, he learned that most of them had been afraid to use it.

"You said it was the soap of hope," they told him. "That it was made lovingly just for us. We could not use something so precious!"

"Oh no!" he remembers saying. "I told them, you must use it! You must go bathe!"

Then one of the villagers, a thin woman with large, dancing eyes, came up to him and confessed that she had used her bar but not in the way he imagined.

She said, "I took the bar of soap, it smelled so beautiful, and I put a little bit of water on it and I applied it all over my whole body."

"All over?" Kayongo asked.

"Yes, all over," she said, smiling. "And I did not rinse it off."

"Why?" he asked.

She answered, "Because I have never smelled like a girl before."

Kayongo was overwhelmed with the realization that when we recognize and act upon even the smallest of things, we have the power to change lives.

This is the true lesson of seeing what matters — that noticing the overlooked, the ordinary, or the seemingly unimportant can not only help solve our initial problem or cement our success, it can also produce unexpected, paradigm-shifting, and beautiful by-products. Side effects that impact us and the world around us more than we ever thought possible. The unwrapped bar of soap saves lives. A grainy photograph of a cow evolved from a lesson on visual acuity to a military training program that accurately detected enemy aircraft during World War II. A zipperless zipper inspired by burrs in nature changed the fashion industry but also made living and working in space possible.

What I teach is not rocket science. With all due respect to the rocket scientists of the world, I think it's better. Because when you reawaken your senses and re-engage your sense of inquiry, the possibilities for transformative change are endless.

While I've gotten thousands of testimonials through the years from past participants of The Art of Perception, I was surprised and delighted to receive the first one for this book before it was even published. It came from the only person who could have given it, since no one else had been able to read the book yet: my editor, Eamon Dolan, a first-rate professional communicator who I didn't think needed additional lessons in perception.

After months of being immersed in my world (and my manuscript), he was on the subway headed to work when he noticed a woman across the aisle who seemed uncomfortable. She was searching through her purse frantically, and she appeared to be sobbing. When she started coughing and gasping, a couple of people asked her what was wrong, but she couldn't talk. As the train pulled into a station, a few passengers just looked at one another as if wondering what to do, and one tried to comfort the woman.

Eamon ran out of the car and down the platform to the middle of the train, where he found the conductor with her window open.

"You need to take this train out of service now and call for medical assistance," Eamon said. "There's a woman in the second car — I think she's having an asthma attack, and she can't find her inhaler."

The train stayed in the station, cops and EMTs arrived, and they took care of the woman. As they helped her off the train, she was still breathing heavily, but she'd stopped coughing and could talk. She confirmed that she was having an asthma emergency and couldn't locate her rescue inhaler. Since 80 percent of asthma deaths can be prevented with normal medical treatment but often occur when adults forget to carry an inhaler, Eamon may have saved this woman's life.

"Before I edited your book," he told me afterward, "I wouldn't have done that. Not because I didn't give a damn but because I wouldn't have observed as closely as I did, acted as quickly as I did, or communicated as well as I did. Working on your book gave me the habit of observing my surroundings better — so I knew that the woman and I were in the second car from the front of the train, I noticed the woman behaving oddly, and I remembered that conductors sit in the middle of trains and usually open their windows in stations, unlike the motormen, who sit at the front."

Visual Intelligence hadn't just sharpened his observation skills; it also helped him establish a new pattern of thinking. As he went on to list the processes he had instantly engaged in, he might as well have been walking me through the chapters of the book. He recognized that other passengers saw the situation differently, and he didn't let that alter his own perceptions (chapter 3). He noted the who, what, when, and where of the scene (chapter 4). He perceived details such as the specific number car he'd boarded (chapter 5), he analyzed the scene from different angles (chapter 6), and he guessed what was missing: an asthma inhaler (chapter 7). He also told me that chapter 7's lesson on how to prioritize information on the fly had stuck with him, so he knew to tell the conductor the most urgent thing first: to stop the train rather than pulling out of the station. And he packaged his observations with a message tailored specifically for his listener (chapter 8).

"You made me more alert to word choice than I would have been otherwise," he said. "So I used the MTA's language — 'out of service,' 'medical assistance' — so the conductor might take in my message more easily and quickly."

He concluded that *Visual Intelligence* had given him the courage to act fast and make an educated guess about what was ailing the woman despite having incomplete information (chapter 11). I understood this last bit the best — and the rush of happiness that comes with it — because it's how I felt after the police told me I'd helped bust a prostitution ring in the hotel. When you tap into your visual intelligence, you are transformed — into a super sleuth, a case cracker, and a guardian angel all in one. You feel like you've uncovered a secret world that's been right there all along.

Every day I'm fortunate enough to watch as people from around the world — high school teachers, intelligence operatives, Fortune 500 CEOs, students, civil servants, and stay-at-home parents — uncover a power they didn't know they had. The same power you have. It's why I can't stop teaching The Art of Perception, and why I am so thrilled to share the same "secrets" with you. I cannot wait to hear about how you change your own life and the lives of those around you by using the faculties and fantastic abilities you were born with.

Remember in your quest for the big picture not to lose sight of the small details.

Don't be afraid of complexity, and don't rush to judgment. Step back and take things apart one layer at a time the way you would a complicated work of art. Start at ground zero. Prioritize by importance. Make sure you've considered all of the data possible. Did you miss a mahogany table?

Always ask questions, especially of yourself. No matter how "obvious" it seems to you, state what you see, because it's possible that no one else will see it. Don't forget the basics; say that one scene is a photo and one is a painting. To crystallize your communication, assume that the person you are communicating with can't see what you're seeing at all. Ask yourself, "Was I as clear as possible? Did I ask the right questions to elicit the answers I need?"

Make sure you are only dealing in objective facts. Describe what you see without letting your emotions and assumptions block your perception. Don't divorce yourself from your experience, but be conscious of it and how it might affect you so it doesn't lead you toward faulty assumptions.

When we choose to see the world differently, with a critical eye, we are choosing to be exceptional. To help you realize how far you've come and how exceptional you now are, I invite you to go back and look at one of our very first paintings, *The Portrait* by René Magritte on page 23. What was first a simple, if odd, still life — or perhaps a picture skimmed over without thought — is now ripe with possibility. Note the relationships and juxtapositions, the smudges and the sharp reflections, the textures, the smells, the realistic, and the fantastic. What do you see now that you didn't before? The painting itself did not change. You did. Now you're seeing what matters.

Acknowledgments

THERE ARE SO many people to whom I owe a debt of immeasurable gratitude for making this book possible. First and foremost are my father and sister, Robert Herman and Jane E. Herman, without whom The Art of Perception never would have happened. They, along with my mother, Diana S. Herman, who died in 2010, have been teaching me to see what matters since I was a young child. Their ideas, insights, edits, willingness to embrace new perspectives, and stalwart support in every aspect of my work have been invaluable to me and are appreciated beyond measure.

I am deeply indebted to Heather Maclean, without whom *Visual Intelligence* would not exist. Her vision, insight, creativity, intellect, collaborative spirit, and most especially her good humor are unparalleled. Simply put, it is an absolute delight to work with her. My gratitude to Heather must encompass an acknowledgment of her husband, Calum Maclean, for his cooperation, encouragement, and willingness to brainstorm with us throughout this project.

My agent at Writers House, Susan Ginsburg, has been a voice of reason and support, and a morale booster since the day we met. It was she who saw the potential for this project long before I did, and I am eternally grateful to her. Before I met Susan, however, fate conspired for me to cross paths with her Writers House colleague Robin Rue. Our chance encounter and delightful conversation set this whole initiative in motion, and I am indebted to Robin for her incredible foresight. I offer my heartfelt thanks, too, to Stacy Testa, also at Writers House, for her kind assistance with every aspect of this book.

My thanks to my editor, Eamon Dolan, at Houghton Mifflin Harcourt for his scrupulous eye, fierce intellect, and willingness to embrace The Art of Perception for the new and different perspectives it offers. I am grateful, too, to Courtney Young, who saw the potential for this book in its nascent stages and provided the momentum to initiate its journey. I am deeply appreciative of the delightful help of Rosemary McGuinness, editorial assistant at Houghton Mifflin Harcourt, whose attention to detail and calm demeanor sustained this project, and of Naomi Gibbs for all her assistance. I want to express my gratitude to the whole wonderful team at Houghton Mifflin Harcourt, including Taryn Roeder, Ayesha Mizra, and Debbie Engel. My thanks also go to Margaret Wimberger for her nimble and precise copyediting of this book and to Lisa Glover for her discerning eye and patience.

The Art of Perception began at The Frick Collection in New York. My colleagues there were unfailingly generous in their support of the program, both during my years as Head of Education and beyond. I am indebted to Peggy Iacono, Susan Galassi, Colin B. Bailey, Elaine Koss, Rebecca Brooke, Martha Hackley, Kate Gerlough, and Penelope Currier. My heartfelt thanks to the late Charles Ryskamp, director emeritus of The Frick Collection, whose encouragement to pursue museum education provided fertile ground for the development of The Art of Perception, and to Samuel Sachs II, former director of The Frick Collection, whose support of my endeavors in the Education Department was formative. Two additional individuals from The Frick Collection whose knowledge and insights have contributed so much to The Art of Perception and whose wonderful friendship have supported my work on the manuscript are Chari LeMasters and Serena Rattazzi.

Many sessions of The Art of Perception have been conducted at the Metropolitan Museum of Art in New York. My thanks to former associate director of education Kent Lydecker and former Chairman of Education Peggy Fogelman, and to Marlene Graham, senior manager of the Ruth and Harold D. Uris Center for Education, for their generosity in accommodating the program for the New York City Police Department.

The Art of Perception also has been conducted at the National Gallery of Art in Washington, DC, and my sincere thanks to Lynn Russell, head of education, and Kimberly Hodges for their generosity in making the National Gallery's collections accessible to the intelligence community. Thanks also to former director of education at the Smithsonian American Art Museum in Washington, DC, Susan Nichols, for her willingness to host the program there on so many occasions.

I believe that The Art of Perception would never have been created if it were not for my formative experience as a docent at the Princeton University Art Museum. The docents' generosity in sharing and imparting their knowledge of museum education has been instrumental in connecting me with audiences in museums around the world, and I am enormously grateful to them.

On a personal and professional note, I owe a debt of gratitude to Linda Friedlander, curator of education at the Yale Center for British Art, who, along with Dr. Irwin Braverman, professor of dermatology at Yale Medical School, initially designed a program for medical students to enhance their observation skills as part of that school's Humanities in Medicine program, and who so graciously shared her knowledge and insights with me.

My thanks to New York City police commissioner William Bratton and former police commissioner Raymond Kelly and the New York City Police Department for launching The Art of Perception in the law enforcement community, in New York and in communities across the country. The NYPD's imprimatur and support of this training initiative, in so many divisions, have been inspirational. Specifically, I would like to thank Captain Daniel Sosnowik, retired inspector Timothy Hardiman, Lieutenant Mark Albarano, Detective Ahmed Mahmoud, Officer Heather Totoro, and Officer Anita Carter.

My colleagues at the Federal Bureau of Investigation — and there are too many to name — have my gratitude for their willingness to embrace The Art of Perception, in so many facets, as part of the FBI's ongoing training programs. I have learned so much from each of them.

There are so many friends and colleagues I have met through The Art of Perception or who have given their unwavering support to my efforts to extend the reach of this program that I can't name them all, but I would like to cite a few: Dr. Charles Bardes, Sarah Miller Beebe, Christine Butler, Ellen Byron, Monica Chandler, Jacob Eastham, Beth Farcht, Peter Forest, Elise Geltzer, Bobbi Goodman,

Wayne Groh, Ed Hobson, Rachele Khadjehturian, Audrey Koota, Dr. Lyuba Konopasek, Richard Korn, Marilyn Kushner, the Lehrer family, Melissa Malhame, Bob Mattison, Robin McCabe, John and Carla Murray, Sheri Mecklenberg, Anne Radice, Donna Cohen Ross, and Allegra Stanek.

My son, Ian, to whom this book is dedicated, has been absolutely central to every aspect of The Art of Perception and this book. He has looked at countless works of art with me and engaged me in an ongoing dialogue that has been the light of my days. His willingness to share his view of the world with me and his untiring support have helped me to see what matters every single day.

Notes

Introduction

page

xv *It was very:* Christine DiGrazia, "Yale's Life-or-Death Course in Art Criticism," *New York Times,* May 19, 2002.

xvi *The* Wall Street: Ellen Byron, "To Master the Art of Solving Crimes, Cops Study Vermeer," *Wall Street Journal,* July 27, 2005.

After taking The: Neal Hirschfeld, "Teaching Cops to See," *Smithsonian,* October 2009.

"I felt like I had": Quoted in Mike Newall, "A Course Uses Art to Sharpen Police Officer's Observation," *Philadelphia Inquirer,* May 18, 2013.

xvii *"put a human face":* Elizabeth Day, "The Street Art of JR," *Guardian,* March 6, 2010.

1. Leonardo da Vinci and Losing Your Mind

3 *"I want to make sure":* Kayongo quotations from interview with author, September 2014. To find out how you can get involved, visit Global Soap Project at www.globalsoap.org.

4 *"I'm not a":* According to Global Soap Project, hotels in the United States alone discard an estimated 2.6 million bars of soap every day.

In 2011, Kayongo: Ebonne Ruffins, "Recycling Hotel Soap to Save Lives," CNN, June 16, 2011.

5 *"a major disaster":* Joel Greenberg, "Coat, Backpack, Sweat: Close Call in Israeli Cafe," *New York Times,* March 8, 2002, http://www.nytimes.com/2002/03/08/world/coat-backpack-sweat-close-call-in-israeli-cafe.html.

What made him see: Velcro Industries BV, "Velcro Industries History and George de Mestral," http://www.velcro.com/About-Us/History.aspx.

6 *Her invention, Eggies:* Lori Weiss, "One Woman's Egg-Cellent Idea Is Turning Her into a Millionaire," *Huffington Post,* January 9, 2013, http://www.huffingtonpost.com/2013/01/04/one-womans-egg-cellent-id-marlo-thomas-it-aint-over_n_2412204.html.

"When you ask": Leander Kahney, "John Sculley on Steve Jobs, the Full Interview Transcript," *Cult of Mac,* October 14, 2010, http://www.cultofmac.com/63295/john-sculley-on-steve-jobs-the-full-interview-transcript/.

"knowing how to see": Michael J. Gelb, *How to Think Like Leonardo da Vinci: Seven Steps to Genius Every Day* (New York: Delacorte Press, 1998).

7 *Not only does:* Society for Neuroscience, *Brain Facts: A Primer on the Brain and Nervous System,* 7th ed., www.brainfacts.org.

"It's definitely not": Dr. Sebastian Seung, interviews with author, September 2014. A huge thank-you to Dr. Seung. For a fantastic book about brain science, be sure to read his *Connectome: How the Brain's Wiring Makes Us Who We Are* (New York: First Mariner Books, 2013).

The retina isn't: The *Encyclopedia of Neuroscience* officially classifies the retina as "a true part of the brain displaced into the eye during development." *Encyclopedia of Neuroscience,* ed. Larry R. Squire (Philadelphia: Academic Press, 2009), s.v. "retina."

8 *I have seen:* I joined the EyeWire community at www.eyewire.org in August 2014; Joe Palca, "Eyewire: A Computer Game to Map the Eye," *Joe's Big Idea,* NPR, May 5, 2014.

With 100 million: Michael Land, *Encyclopedia Britannica Online,* accessed August 11, 2015, http://www.britannica.com/science/photoreception, s.v. "photoreception; biology," and s.v. "Sensory Reception: Human Vision: Structure and Function of the Human Eye."

9 *"Some of the":* Palca, "Eyewire."

Scientists have discovered: Lauran Neergaard, "At Age 40, Both Brain and Body Start to Slow," *NBC News,* Associated Press, November 3, 2008; Karlene K. Ball, Daniel L. Roenker, and John R. Bruni, "Developmental Changes in Attention and Visual Search Through Adulthood," *The Development of Attention: Research and Theory,* ed. James T. Enns (New York: North-Holland, 1990), 489–92; Meghomala Das, David M. Bennett, and Gordon N. Dutton, "Visual Attention as an Important Visual Function: An Outline of Manifestations, Diagnosis and Management of Impaired Visual Attention," *British Journal of Ophthalmology* vol. 92, no. 11 (November 2007): 1556–60.

Fortunately for all: Marian Cleeves Diamond, "The Brain . . . Use It or Lose It," *Mindshift Connection* vol. 1, no. 1, reprinted in Johns Hopkins School of Education website, http://education.jhu.edu/PD/newhorizons/Neurosciences/articles/The%20Brain...Use%20it%20or%20Lose%20It/.

11 *"exorbitant stockpiles":* Jennifer L. Roberts, "The Power of Patience," *Harvard Magazine,* November–December 2013.

12 *In 1908:* Melinda Beck, "Anxiety Can Bring Out the Best," *Wall Street Journal,* June 18, 2012.

15 *"We are all":* Alexander Graham Bell, "Discovery and Invention," *National Geographic* vol. 25 (June 1914): 650.

16 *Today more people:* Yue Wang, "More People Have Cell Phones Than Toilets, U.N. Study Shows," *Time,* March 25, 2013; and Victoria Woollaston, "How Often Do You Check Your Phone?" *Daily Mail,* October 8, 2013.

A 2005 study: "E-mails 'Hurt IQ More Than Pot,'" CNN, April 22, 2005.

A fifteen-point deficiency: Travis Bradberry, "Multitasking Damages Your Brain and Career, New Studies Suggest," *Forbes,* October 8, 2014.

Our brain's prefrontal: ABC Science, "Impacts of Multi-Tasking," Australian Broadcasting Corporation Science in conjunction with the University of

Queensland's School of Psychology, Queensland Brain Institute, and Science of Learning Centre, National Science Week 2011, http://www.multitaskingtest. net.au/.

The Journal of: Steve Sisgold, "Is Too Much Juggling Causing You Brain Drain?" *Psychology Today,* February 26, 2014.

In the hospitality: Ragina Johnson, "The Battle at the Hilton and Beyond," *Socialist Worker,* October 20, 2010; "Creating Luxury, Enduring Pain: How Hotel Work Is Hurting Housekeepers," *Unite Here,* April 2006.

While the changes: Jane Levere, "America's Dirtiest Hotels," ABC News, July 27, 2011.

17 *In 2012, scientists:* Lawrence LeBlond, "Hotel Rooms Swarming with Nasty Bacteria," *Red Orbit,* June 18, 2012.

"*You have time*": Adam Savage, "Commencement Keynote Address" (Sarah Lawrence College, May 18, 2012, http://www.slc.edu/news-events/events/ commencement/adam-savage-commencement-keynote-address.html).

"*Rushing leads*": Adam Savage, "Get Noticed. Get Promoted" (speech, Maker Fair Bay Area, San Mateo, CA, May 19, 2013).

In 2013, researchers: Pam A. Mueller and Daniel M. Oppenheimer, "The Pen Is Mightier Than the Keyboard," *Psychological Science,* June 2014.

18 "*You can't even*": Justin Massoud, "Beyoncé Tells Fan 'Put That Damn Camera Down' During Show," K94.5 FM, July 18, 2013.

"*blocked by a throng*": Daphne Merkin, "All Those Phone Lights? A Don't," *Glamour,* September 2014.

19 *Dr. Sebastian Seung:* Arvind Suresh, "Citizen Powered Neuroscience with Project EyeWire — Using Your Neurons to Map the Brain!" *Discover,* May 20, 2014.

"*Students need to*": Meredith Raine-Middleton, "A Picture of Health," *University of Texas Houston Medicine,* May 30, 2003.

"*explicitly designed*": Roberts, "Power of Patience."

22 "*If I have ever*": Isaac Newton, *The Principia: Mathematical Principles of Natural Philosophy* (1687; repr., New York: Snowball Publishing, 2010).

We've already started: In *The Art of Scientific Investigation,* scientist William Ian Beardmore Beveridge writes that exceptional observation skills are more important than "large accumulations of academic learning," and defines observation as "not passively watching but an active mental process." W. I .B. Beveridge, *The Art of Scientific Investigation* (New York: W. W. Norton, 1957), 104.

2: Elementary Skills

24 *In 1877 an:* Katherine Ramsland, "Observe Carefully, Deduce Shrewdly: Dr. Joseph Bell," *Forensic Examiner,* August 18, 2009.

"*Where is your cutty pipe?*": Ibid.

"*I knew she had*": Ibid.

"*What is the matter*": Carolyn Wells. *The Technique of the Mystery Story* (Springfield, MA: Home Correspondence School, 1913).

"*Hip-joint disease, sir!*": Ibid.

"*Hip-nothing!*": Ibid.

25 "*Gentlemen, we have*": Joseph V. Klauder, "Sherlock Holmes as a Dermatologist, with Remarks on the Life of Dr. Joseph Bell and the Sherlockian Method of Teaching," *AMA Archives of Dermatology and Syphilology* vol. 68, no. 4 (October 1953): 368–77.

"*The gentleman has ears*": Wells, *Technique of the Mystery Story.*

"*Glance at a man*": Harold Emery Jones, "The Original of Sherlock Holmes," *Conan Doyle's Best Books in Three Volumes: A Study in Scarlet and Other Stories; The Sign of the Four and Other Stories; The White Company and Beyond the City* (New York: P. F. Collier & Son, 1904).

"*elementary" talents:* Ibid.

"*Use your eyes*": "Fiction Imitates Real Life in Case of True Inspiration," *Irish Examiner,* November 4, 2011.

"*Most people see but*": Wells, *Technique of the Mystery Story.*

26 "*You see, but you*": Sir Arthur Conan Doyle, *The Adventures of Sherlock Holmes* (Vancouver: Engage Books, 2010), 6.

27 *It helps establish:* Daniel B. Schneider, "F.Y.I.," *New York Times,* June 28, 1998.

28 *To watch the performance:* You can watch an excerpt of his lecture online at the *Princeton Alumni Weekly* website: Michael Graziano, "Video: Consciousness and the Social Brain (Excerpt)," http://paw.princeton.edu/issues/2014/04/23/pages/0973/index.xml.

29 "*attention schema theory*": Graziano's groundbreaking attention schema theory posits a completely different approach to explaining consciousness by arguing that awareness is a physical essence. For more information, I highly recommend reading his book *Consciousness and the Social Brain* (New York: Oxford University Press, 2013), or the following articles: Anil Ananthaswamy, "How I Conjure a Social Illusion with Ventriloquism," *New Scientist,* June 9, 2014; and Y. T. Kelly et al., "Attributing Awareness to Oneself and to Others," *Proceedings of the National Academy of Sciences USA* vol. 111, no. 13 (2014): 5012–17.

"*We don't magically*": Dr. Michael Graziano, interviews with author, September 2014. A huge thank-you to Dr. Graziano for his patient explanations and wonderful hospitality. For more about Dr. Graziano's attention schema theory and the neuroscience of a consciousness, check out his highly readable book *Consciousness and the Social Brain.*

They re-created: Daniel J. Simons and Christopher F. Chabris, "Gorillas in Our Midst: Sustained Inattentional Blindness for Dynamic Events," *Perception* vol. 28 (May 9, 1999): 1059–74.

30 *Eighty-three percent:* Alix Spiegel, "Why Even Radiologists Can Miss a Gorilla Hiding in Plain Sight," *Morning Edition,* NPR, February 11, 2013.

Investigators did not: After ten years of appeals, during which time he was allowed to remain free, Kenneth Conley's conviction was overturned and he was exonerated and allowed to return to the police force with back pay. His charges were not dismissed because of the court's sudden belief in inattentional blindness, however, but because it was discovered that the prosecutor at the time had failed to turn in all evidence. Conley continues to serve with the Boston Police

Department and was involved in the capture of Boston Marathon attack suspect Dzohkar Tsarnaev in 2013. "Kenneth Conley," *National Registry of Exonerations,* A Joint Project of Michigan Law and Northwestern Law, http://www.law.umich.edu/special/exoneration/Pages/casedetail.aspx?caseid=3120; and Kathy Curran, "New Details Uncovered About Suspect's Arrest," WCVB5, ABC News, April 26, 2013.

31 *"You Do Not Talk":* Christopher F. Chabris et al., "You Do Not Talk About Fight Club if You Do Not Notice Fight Club: Inattentional Blindness for a Simulated Real-World Assault," *Iperception,* June 9, 2011; and Alix Spiegel, "Why Seeing (the Unexpected) Is Often Not Believing," *Morning Edition,* NPR, June 20, 2011.

"proper seeing": Henry Oakley, "Other Colleges Say —," *The Technique,* student newspaper of Georgia Institute of Technology, December 9, 1949, https://smartech.gatech.edu/bitstream/handle/1853/19396/1949-12-09_33_43.pdf.

Likewise, multiple studies: Todd W. Thompson et al., "Expanding Attentional Capacity with Adaptive Training on Multiple Object Tracking Task," *Journal of Vision* vol. 11, no. 11 (September 23, 2011): 292; Hoon Choic and Takeo Watanabe, "Changes Induced by Attentional Training: Capacity Increase Vs. Allocation Changes," *Journal of Vision* vol. 10, no. 7 (August 2, 2010): 1099; and Jennifer O'Brien et al., "Effects of Cognitive Training on Attention Allocation and Speed of Processing in Older Adults: An ERP Study," *Journal of Vision* vol. 11, no. 11 (September 23, 2011): 203.

The success of: Karen N. Peart, "Artwork Can Sharpen Medical Diagnostic Skills, Yale Researchers Report," *Yale News,* September 4, 2001.

A two-year study: The study found that medical students who attended the visual training session in the art museum increased their diagnostic skills related to dermatological lesions by 56 percent. See Jacqueline C. Dolev, Linda K. Friedlander, and Irwin M. Braverman, "Use of Fine Art to Enhance Visual Diagnostic Skills," *Journal of the American Medical Association* vol. 286, no. 9 (September 2001): 1019–21.

"statistically significant": Peart, "Artwork Can Sharpen."

32 *"I had no idea":* Dr. Allison West, interview with author, June 28, 2014. I am indebted to Dr. West not just for sharing her experiences with me but for working tirelessly to make sure that the Art of Perception program would continue at NYU Medical School.

33 *She is now:* "The Graduates," Best Doctors, *New York,* June 3, 2012, http://nymag.com/health/bestdoctors/2012/medical-school-graduates/.

"Powers of observation": W. I .B. Beveridge, *The Art of Scientific Investigation* (New York: W. W. Norton, 1957), 105.

35 *"man who sees":* "Read Any Good Records Lately?" *Time,* January 4, 1982.

3: The Platypus and the Gentleman Thief

38 *After picking the:* Adam Green, "A Pickpocket's Tale," *New Yorker,* January 7, 2013.

39 *"Almost every single"*: Ruth Oosterman, interview with author, April 2015. You can read more about Ruth at her website, www.ruthoosterman.com, and her blog, *The Mischievous Mommy,* http://themischievousmommy.blogspot.ca, and purchase prints at her Etsy shop, Eve's Imagination: https://www.etsy.com/ca/shop/EvesImagination. Other references for this story: Ruth Oosterman, "Through a Child's Eyes," *The Mischievous Mommy,* September 8, 2014, http://themischievousmommy.blogspot.ca/2014/09/through-childs-eyes.html; and Rachel Zarrell, "This Artist Turns Her 2-Year-Old's Doodles into Gorgeous Paintings," *BuzzFeed,* September 7, 2014.

41 *It can color:* Daniel L. Schacter, Daniel T. Gilbert, and Daniel M. Wegner, *Psychology* (New York: Worth, 2011): 125–71.

42 *"reflections on terror"*: Don DeLillo, "In the Ruins of the Future: Reflections on Terror and Loss in the Shadow of September," *Harper's Magazine,* December 2001.

44 *"wonderful"*: Holland Cotter, "The Beast in the Human, and Vice Versa," *New York Times,* April 25, 2013.
    "subversive": Allison Meier, "Apartheid Subversion in the Cathedral of St. John the Divine," *Hyperallergic,* May 1, 2013.
    "disturbing": Marion Dreyfus, "St. John and the 'Divine' Art of Jane Alexander," *American Thinker,* June 2, 2013; and Sarah Roth, "New Installation Brings South Africa to St. John the Divine," *Columbia Daily Spectator,* April 22, 2013.
    "off-putting considering": Alex and Ben, "St. John the Divine," *Snap It. Taste It. Blog It.,* snaptasteblogit.com/st-john-the-divine.html.

46 *Tony Matelli's February:* Jess Bidgood, "At Wellesley, Debate over a Statue in Briefs," *New York Times,* February 6, 2014; and Keerthi Mohan, "Near Nude Statue of Sleepwalking Man 'Freaks Out' Students; Should the Statue Be Removed?" *International Business Times India,* February 8, 2014.
    "Each person comes": David A. Fahrenthold, "Sculpture of Near-Naked Man at Wellesley Has Its Critics," *Washington Post,* February 5, 2014; Jaclyn Reiss, "Realistic Statue of Man in His Underwear at Wellesley College Sparks Controversy," *Boston Globe,* February 5, 2014.

47 *Experimenters at the:* Vinoth K. Ranganathan et al., "From Mental Power to Muscle Power: Gaining Strength by Using the Mind," *Neuropsychologia* vol. 42, no. 7 (June 2004): 944–56.
    Scientists at the: Tori Rodriguez, "Mental Rehearsals Strengthen Neural Circuits," *Scientific American,* August 14, 2014, accessed August 10, 2015, http://www.scientificamerican.com/article/mental-rehearsals-strengthen-neural-circuits/.

48 *The moment we become:* John F. Kihlstrom, "The Cognitive Unconscious," *Science* vol. 237 (September 18, 1987): 1445–52.

52 *confirmation bias:* Daniel Reisberg, *Cognition,* 3rd ed. (New York: W. W. Norton, 2005): 469–71.

53 *That wishful seeing:* Pacific Standard Staff, "There's a Name for That: The Baader-Meinhof Phenomenon," *Pacific Standard,* July 22, 2013.
    it is less well known: David Dunning and Emily Balcetis, "Wishful Seeing: How

Preferences Shape Visual Perception," *Current Directions in Psychological Science* vol. 22, no. 1 (February 2013): 33–37.

In the Netherlands: Guido M. van Koningsbruggen, Wolfgang Stroebe, and Henk Aarts, "Through the Eyes of Dieters: Biased Size Perception of Food Following Tempting Food Primes," *Journal of Experimental Social Psychology* vol. 47, issue 2 (March 2011): 293–99.

In New York: Emily Balcetis and David Dunning, "Wishful Seeing: More Desired Objects Are Seen as Closer," *Psychological Science,* December 2009; Kohske Takahashi et al., "Psychological Influences on Distance Estimation in a Virtual Reality Environment," *Frontiers in Human Neuroscience* vol. 7 (September 18, 2013): 580.

56 *One reporter investigating:* David G. Wittels, "You're Not as Smart as You Could Be," *Saturday Evening Post,* three-part series, April 17, April 24, and May 1, 1948.

57 *Daniel Simons and:* Graham Davies and Sarah Hine, "Change Blindness and Eyewitness Testimony," *Journal of Psychology,* July 2007.

Apollo Robbins: Brain Games, season 2, episode 11, National Geographic Channel, braingames.nationalgeographic.com.

Considering that: Natalie Angier, "Blind to Change, Even as It Stares Us in the Face," *New York Times,* April 1, 2008.

58 *He was so:* You can follow Mark Hirsch's photo journal *That Tree* online and purchase prints or his book about the lonely bur oak at: http://thattree.net; Huffington Post Staff, "'That Tree': Photographer Mark Hirsch Becomes One with an Oak Tree in Lovely Documentary Project," *Huffington Post,* May 29, 2013, http://www.huffingtonpost.com/2013/05/29/that-tree-photographer-mark-hirsch-becomes-one-with-an-oak_n_3347786.html.

"foreign land": Mark Hirsch, "How a Tree Helped Heal Me," *CBS Sunday Morning,* September 16, 2013.

59 *"the knowledge that":* Bill Weir, "Apollo Robbins: King of Thieves," *Nightline,* July 12, 2013, ABC.

4. Delta Employees Do It on the Fly

61 *For four days:* Faith Karimi, Steve Almasy, and Lillian Leposo, "Kenya Mall Attack: Military Says Most Hostages Freed, Death Toll at 68," CNN, September 23, 2013.

62 *The deadly confusion:* Michael Pearson and Zain Verjee, "Questions Linger After Kenya Mall Attack," CNN, September 25, 2013, and "Source: Store in Besieged Kenyan Mall Run by Attackers or Associates," CNN, September 27, 2013; and Dashiell Bennett, "Tragic and Heroic Stories from Survivors of the Kenyan Mall Attack," *Atlantic Monthly,* September 27, 2013.

From 2005 to: KGW Staff, "History of Shootings at Malls Worldwide," *KGW-NBC Portland,* December 12, 2012; and John Swaine, "Al-Shabaab Mall Threat 'All the More Reason' to Avoid Shutdown, Says Homeland Security Chief," *Guardian,* February 22, 2015.

In our current: Knowing the Risks, Protecting Your Business: A Global Study, Freshfields Bruckhaus Deringer, 2012, www.freshfields.com.

64 *Those who did:* Hannah McNeish, "Hero Helped American Family Survive Kenya Mall Terror," *USA Today,* September 27, 2013.

73 *Many others:* Dana Ford, "Kenya Mall Attack Survivor Plays Dead to Live," CNN, October 10, 2013.

74 *The BBC reported:* Karen Allen, "Kenya's Westgate Siege: 'Militants Hired Shop to Hide Arms,'" BBC News, September 27, 2013.

75 *"their eyes focused":* Vivian Ho, "Absorbed Device Users Oblivious to Danger," *San Francisco Chronicle,* October 7, 2013.
    And since bruises: Tomika S. Harris, "Bruises in Children: Normal or Child Abuse?" *Journal of Pediatric Health Care* vol. 24, no. 4 (July 2010): 216–21.
    If just one: Calculated using the Specialty Coffee Association of America's 2011 survey of the cost of the components of a 16-ounce cup of coffee equaling $1.17; Specialty Coffee Association of America, "SCAA Quarterly Growth and Trends Survey (April–June 2011)," *Specialty Coffee Chronicle,* July 7, 2011.

78 *For instance, location:* Jaclyn Reiss, "Realistic Statue of Man in His Underwear at Wellesley College Sparks Controversy," *Boston Globe,* February 5, 2014.
    "a schlumpy guy": Ibid.
    "prominent": Sebastian Smee, "Threshold States and Dark Wit in Standout Show by Tony Matelli," *Boston Globe,* February 15, 2014.

79 *Yet citing that:* Maggie Lange, "Statue of Undressed Man Terrorizes Wellesley College," *New York,* February 5, 2014.
    "connect the exhibition": Reiss, "Realistic Statue."
    Assumptions are dangerous: Lemony Snicket, *The Austere Academy* (New York: HarperCollins, 2000).

80 *Tomasevic explained :* Bennett, "Tragic and Heroic Stories."

81 *"Its principal causes":* Commission on the Intelligence Capabilities of the United States Regarding Weapons of Mass Destruction, *Report to the President of the United States,* March 31, 2005, www.fas.org/irp/offdocs/wmd_report .pdf.

5: What's Hiding in Plain Sight?

83 *You can visit her: Mrs. John Winthrop,* by John Singleton Copley (American, Boston, Massachusetts 1738–1815 London), 1773, is currently on view in Gallery 748 at the Metropolitan Museum of Art in New York City. You can also view the painting online in the museum's collection at http://www.metmuseum.org/ collection/the-collection-online/search/10531.

84 *"refrigerator blindness:* Andrew J. Macnab and Mary Bennett, "Refrigerator Blindness: Selective Loss of Visual Acuity in Association with a Common Foraging Behaviour," *Canadian Medical Association Journal* vol. 173, no. 12 (December 6, 2005): 1494–95.

85 *On October 30:* Bruce Lambert, "Real Estate Agent Found Slain in 5th Ave. Home," *New York Times,* November 1, 2007; Max Abelson, "Remembering

Linda Stein," *New York Observer,* November 1, 2007; Robert Kolker, "Death of a Broker," *New York,* November 18, 2007; and Laura Kusisto, "Linda Stein Murder Trial: The Photos," *New York Observer,* February 17, 2010.

86 *Lowery had entered:* John Eligon, "Trial Begins for Woman Accused of Killing Linda Stein," *New York Times,* January 25, 2010.

Lowery admitted that: Associated Press, "Seymour Stein, Sire Records Founder, Testifies at Linda Stein's Murder Trial," *Huffington Post,* February 4, 2010, http://www.huffingtonpost.com/2010/02/05/seymour-stein-sire -record_n_450475.html; and Kolker, "Death of a Broker."

Detectives discovered that: Patrick O'Shaughnessy, "How Personal Assistant Natavia Lowery Killed Celebrity Realtor Linda Stein, Who Wouldn't Back Down," *Daily News* (New York), February 28, 2010.

87 *In its place:* Melissa Grace, "Linda Stein Murder Trial: Suspect Natavia Low-ery Sent Odd Text Messages on Day of Realtor's Slaying," *Daily News* (New York), February 19, 2010.

"The pants were": Melissa Grace and Bill Hutchinson, "Jury Finds Natavia Lowery Guilty of Celebrity Realtor Linda Stein's Murder After Short Delibera-tion," *Daily News* (New York), February 23, 2010; Lowery was sentenced to twenty-five years to life for the second-degree murder of Linda Stein, and re-ceived an additional two years for larceny. See Beth Karas, "Personal Assistant Gets 27 to Life in Celebrity Realtor's Murder," CNN, May 3, 2010.

For no physiological: Steven B. Most et al., "What You See Is What You Set: Sustained Inattentional Blindness and the Capture of Awareness," *Psychologi-cal Review* vol. 112 (January 2005): 217–42; and Ethan A. Newby and Irvin Rock, "Inattentional Blindness as a Function of Proximity to the Focus of At-tention," *Perception* vol. 27, no. 9 (1998): 1025–40.

However, our cognitive: John Gosbee, "Handoffs and Communication: The Un-derappreciated Roles of Situational Awareness and Inattentional Blindness," *Clinical Obstetrics & Gynecology* vol. 53, no. 3 (September 2010): 545–58.

88 *If our eyes:* David Owen, "The Psychology of Space," *New Yorker,* January 21, 2013.

"The world is terribly": Sheila M. Eldred, "How Our Brains Miss the Obvi-ous," *Discovery News,* May 22, 2013.

89 *Without it, we:* Arne Öhman, "Has Evolution Primed Humans to 'Beware the Beast'?" *Proceedings of the National Academy of Sciences of the United States of America* vol. 104, no. 42 (October 16, 2007): 16396–97; and Gervais Tompkin, "Survival of the Focused," *GenslerOnWork,* November 11, 2013, http://www. gensleron.com/work/2013/11/11/survival-of-the-focused.html.

"We need to": I am indebted to Dr. Tversky for her patient explanations of how the brain uses memory, categorization, and spatial cognition. Interview with author, June 27, 2014.

This instant organization: Ming Meng, David A. Remus, and Frank Tong, "Filling-in of Visual Phantoms in the Human Brain," *Nature Neuroscience* vol. 8, no. 9 (August 7, 2005): 1248–54; Melanie Moran, "The Brain Doesn't Like

Visual Gaps and Fills Them In," *Exploration: Vanderbilt's Online Research Magazine,* Vanderbilt University, August 19, 2007.

This skill accounts: Marguerite Reardon, "Americans Text More Than They Talk," CNET, September 22, 2008; and Sherna Noah, "Texting Overtakes Talking as Most Popular Form of Communication in UK," *Independent,* July 18, 2012.

91 *The company consciously:* Yoni Heisler, "Inside Apple's Secret Packaging Room," *Network World,* January 24, 2012.

"People can feel": Bruce Jones, "Success Is in the Details: How Disney Over-manages the Customer Experience," *Talking Point: The Disney Institute Blog,* January 9, 2014.

It's not a: "Virgin Atlantic Wins Top Customer Service Award," Virgin Atlantic press release, January 19, 2009.

"We get all": The tagline appeared on the Virgin Atlantic company website under "Virgin experience" when accessed June 22, 2014, http://www.virgin -atlantic.com/gb/en/the-virgin-experience.html.

Marcus Sloan wasn't: This and following quotations from "Marcus Sloan" interview with author, June 29, 2014. I am deeply indebted to him for speak-ing with me about his experiences as a high school math teacher and for his exemplary dedication to his students. Sloan taught at a public high school in the Bronx, New York, from 2004 to 2007.

Passing the mathematics: John Hildebrand, "Regents Rule Change Aids Special Education," *Newsday,* October 9, 2012. The graduation rate at Sloan's school was 75.5 percent in 2005, and 53.6 percent in 2006. "2006 Graduation Rates in New York High Schools," *New York Times,* April 25, 2007.

92 *"economically disadvantaged":* High School State Rankings, *U.S. News & World Report,* 2014 Academic Indicators.

The school suffered: Ibid.

He cites an: University of the State of New York Regents High School Examina-tion, Mathematics A, given on Thursday, June 15, 2006 from 1:15 to 4:15 p.m., "Question 39: A person measures the angle of depression from the top of a wall to a point on the ground. The point is located on level ground 62 feet from the base of the wall and the angle of depression is 52°. How high is the wall, to the nearest tenth of a foot?"

94 *Even better: the:* Percentage of students who met standard for Mathematics A portion of Regents Exam for 2006–2009 per New York City Department of Education via http://www.schooldigger.com/go/NY/schools/0008705181/ school.aspx.

Was the increase in the Regents scores directly related to Sloan's students' art training and new appreciation for seeking out details? It can't be proven, but it's worth noting that the year after Sloan left the school, taking his unique style of teaching with him, the school's percentage of students who met the Regents mathematics standard fell back to 44 percent and sank even lower, to 36 per-cent, the following year.

"Most people falsely": Marc Green, "Inattentional Blindness & Conspicuity," *Human Factors,* January 4, 2011, and "Do Mobile Phones Pose an Unacceptable Risk? A Complete Look at the Adequacy of the Evidence," *Risk Management,* November 1, 2001.

95 *The State Farm insurance:* State Farm Mutual Automobile Insurance Company, "Managing Blind Spots," April 8, 2013.

Perception requires attention: Michael A. Cohen, George A. Alvarez, and Ken Nakayama, "Natural-Scene Perception Requires Attention," *Psychological Science* vol. 22, no. 9 (September 2011): 1165–72; and L. Pessoa et al., "Neural Processing of Emotional Faces Requires Attention," *Proceedings of the National Academy of Sciences of the United States of America* vol. 99, no. 17 (August 20, 2002): 11458–63.

96 *If we did:* Papers of John and Hannah Winthrop, 1728–1789, Harvard University Archives.

99 *In our multitasking:* Jessica Keiman, "How Multitasking Hurts Your Brain (and Your Effectiveness at Work)," *Forbes,* January 15, 2013.

A new study: Clara Moskowitz, "Mind's Limit Found: 4 Things at Once," *Live Science,* April 27, 2008.

"multitaskers are terrible": Leo Widrich, "What Multitasking Does to Our Brains," *Buffer,* June 26, 2012.

"terrible at ignoring": "Interview with Clifford Nass," *Frontline,* February 2, 2010, PBS.

"Any time you": Camille Noe Pagán, "Quit Multitasking (and Start Getting More Done)," *Forbes,* January 21, 2010.

When the brain: Christopher D. Wickens, "Multiple Resources and Mental Workload," *Human Factors: The Journal of the Human Factors and Ergonomics Society* vol. 50, no. 3 (June 2008): 449–55.

100 *"focus is a mental"*: Jenna Goudreau, "12 Ways to Eliminate Stress at Work," *Forbes,* March 20, 2013; and Sandra Bond, "Why Single-Tasking Makes You Smarter," *Forbes,* May 8, 2013.

The human brain: Jon Hamilton, "Think You're Multitasking? Think Again," *Morning Edition,* NPR, October 2, 2008.

Second, relax for: Geil Browning, "10 Ways to Rejuvenate Your Brain While You Work," *Inc.,* September 10, 2012.

Excessive noise and: Carol F. Baker, "Sensory Overload and Noise in the ICU: Sources of Environmental Stress," *Critical Care Quarterly* vol. 6 (March 1984): 66–80.

Many famous people: David Biello, "Fact or Fiction? Archimedes Coined the Term 'Eureka!' in the Bath," *Scientific American,* December 8, 2006.

Sir Isaac Newton: Steve Connor, "The Core of Truth Behind Sir Isaac Newton's Apple," *Independent,* January 18, 2010.

101 *"Often when one works"*: Henri Poincaré, "Mathematical Creation," *The Monist,* July 1901.

"heavily laden": John Eligon, "Trial Begins for Woman Accused of Killing Linda Stein," *New York Times,* January 25, 2010.

104 *At 11:32 p.m.*: "File No. 1-0016, Aircraft Accident Report, Eastern Air Lines, Inc., L-1011, N310EA, Miami, Florida, December 29, 1972," National Transportation Safety Board, Washington, DC, June 14, 1973.
"It looks like": CVR transcript Eastern Air Lines Flight 401, December 29, 1972, Aviation Safety Network.
105 *After examining the:* "File No. 1-0016."
The pilots could: Cockpit recordings show that the captain repeatedly told the second officer to go down and physically look at the landing gear beneath the cockpit, but his instructions were initially ignored. The second officer did leave and return complaining of the darkness and his inability to see. After the crash, investigators determined that the both the visual indicator light for the nose gear and the nose wheel well service light were in place and operational. See ibid.
Instead, 101 of: Ibid.
Educators believe that: "Visual/Spatial Learning," *Study Guides and Strategies* website, www.studygs.net/visual.htm, accessed June 30, 2014.
107 *When caseworker Joanna:* Interview with author, 2014. Joanna Longley is a pseudonym for a real practicing caseworker.

6: Keep Your Head on a Swivel

115 *In June 2008:* "Troops Held Over Rio Gang Deaths," BBC News, June 17, 2008.
116 *The eyes were:* A huge thank-you to JR for allowing me to use his work. For more information on his worldwide exhibitions, to buy prints, or to find out how to get involved in his latest project, visit his website at http://www.jr-art.net/.
117 *"The favela is"*: Raffi Khatchadourian, "In the Picture," *New Yorker,* November 28, 2011.
He notes how: Inside Out: The People's Art Project, directed by Alastair Siddons (New York: A Social Animals production in association with Notting Hills Films, Tribeca Film Festival/HBO, 2013).
"I left Brazil": Lina Soualem, "JR: The Power of Paper and Glue," *Argentina Independent,* March 5, 2013.
"For once, the media": Ibid.
With his project: JR's goal with Women Are Heroes was to highlight the role of women and show how they are pillars of support in a violent community. For more information, visit his website at www.jr-art.net/projects/women-are -heroes-brazil.
118 *The mayor of:* Ibid.
Perspective: Merriam-Webster's Collegiate Dictionary, 11th ed., s.v. "perspective."
119 *Dr. Wayne W.:* Thomas Boswell, "To Bryce Harper and Davey Johnson, 'Play Me or Trade Me' Is Just a Healthy Joke," *Washington Post,* July 7, 2013; and Wayne W. Dyer, "Success Secrets," *DrWayneDyer.com,* Hay House, www. drwaynedyer.com.
120 *Instead of a:* While the picture might look like something clever you've seen

on the Internet, it's actually by a sixteenth-century Italian painter, Giuseppe Arcimboldo. Arcimboldo was famous for his visual double entendres, creating portraits of people out of fruit, vegetables, books, and even other people.

122 *"Nor has there ever"*: Giorgio Vasari, *Lives of the Most Eminent Painters, Sculptors and Architects* (London: Macmillan, 1912): 352-53.

Art critics have: "Michelangelo's David," Accademia Gallery, Florence, Italy, http://www.accademia.org/explore-museum/artworks/michelangelos-david; and Fiachra Gibbons, "The Perfect Man's Chiseled Squint," *Guardian,* June 7, 2000, accessed August 11, 2015.

"transmits exceptional": "Michelangelo's David," accessed August 11, 2015. http://www.accademia.org/explore-museum/artworks/michelangelos-david/.

"the perfect man": Gibbons, "Perfect Man's Chiseled Squint."

"the standard by which": Ibid.

123 *"is consistent with"*: John Hooper, "How David Shrank as He Faced Goliath," *Guardian,* January 22, 2005.

Close scrutiny also: Gibbons, "Perfect Man's Chiseled Squint."

His head seems: Rossella Lorenzi, "Michelangelo's David is Missing a Muscle," *ABC Science,* Australian Broadcasting Corporation, October 18, 2004.

124 *"malevolent stare"*: Saul Levine, "The Location of Michelangelo's David: The Meeting of January 25, 1504," *Art Bulletin* vol. 56, no. 1 (March 1974): 31-49.

Stanford University's Digital: Digital Michelangelo Project, directed by Marc Levoy, can be viewed online at http://graphics.stanford.edu/projects/mich/.

125 *While David's eyes:* Graham Lawton, "Michelangelo Cheated," *New Scientist,* June 10, 2000.

127 *It's the key:* Tim Hindle, *The Economist Guide to Management Ideas and Gurus* (London: Profile Books, 2008): 89-90.

In gemba *walks:* Bill Wilder, "Gemba Walk," *IndustryWeek,* January 9, 2014.

128 *"Unless you go"*: Bob Herman, "9 Ingenious Ways to Cut Costs at Your Hospital," *Becker's Hospital CFO,* February 26, 2013.

Just as the: Professor Yianis A. Pikoulas, "Cart-wheel Road Communication," *Kathimerini,* January 4, 1998; Martijn P. van den Heuvel et al., "Efficiency of Functional Brain Networks and Intellectual Performance," *Journal of Neuroscience* vol. 29, issue 23 (June 10, 2009): 7619-24.

"I limit myself": Jess McCann, interview with author, March 18, 2015. Jess McCann is the author of *Was It Something I Said?* and *You Lost Him at Hello.* For more information, visit www.jessmccann.com.

"The very act": Roderick Gilkey and Clint Kilts, "Cognitive Fitness," *Harvard Business Review,* November 2007.

129 *"Experience gained through"*: Ibid.

"functional fixedness": Drew Boyd, "Fixedness: A Barrier to Creative Output," *Psychology Today,* June 26, 2013.

"Our appreciation": Corey S. Powell, "Unlocking the Other Senses of Space," *Discover,* October 23, 2014.

134 *"You never really"*: Harper Lee, *To Kill a Mockingbird* (New York: Grand Central, 1960): 33.

"the force that moves": Jayson M. Boyers, "Why Empathy Is the Force That Moves Business Forward," *Forbes,* May 30, 2013.

"The reality is": Ibid.

"the key to having": Leana Greene, "Empathy: The Key to Unlocking Successful Relationships," *Kids in the House,* March 4, 2015.

135 *"The circumstances"*: Dan Fastenberg, "'Undercover Boss' CEOs Tell What Really Happened After the Show," *AOL Jobs,* June 10, 2013.

"Dickensian struggles": Dan Fastenberg, "Fast Food CEO Shuts Down Struggling Branch During 'Undercover Boss' Episode," *AOL Jobs,* February 20, 2012.

"They wouldn't be": Ibid.

"I call [my]": Fastenberg, "'Undercover Boss' CEOs."

"I learned how": Jennifer Miller, "The Halloween Trading Places Challenge," *Confident Parents Confident Kids,* October 29, 2014, www.confidentpar entsconfidentkids.org.

136 *Putting ourselves in:* "Hall of Fame: Shakespeare in Your Kitchen," *Five Whys,* February 10, 2012, https://fivewhys.wordpress.com/2012/02/10/shakespeare-in -your-kitchen/.

When Marlene Mollan's: Marlene Mollan, interview with author, November 3, 2014.

139 *And in July:* "Providência Gondola Finally Opens in Rio," *Rio Times,* July 8, 2014.

Matisse spent countless: Hilary Spurling, *Matisse the Master: A Life of Henri Matisse, the Conquest of Colour, 1909–1954.* (New York: Alfred A. Knopf, 2005): 161–63.

141 *In fact, according:* "Great Figures of Modern Art: Henri Matisse," Centre Pompidou, Paris, http://mediation.centrepompidou.fr.

142 *Elizabeth A. Phelps:* Tali Sharot, Mauricio R. Delgado, and Elizabeth A. Phelps, "How Emotion Enhances the Feeling of Remembering," *Nature Neuroscience,* December 7, 2004.

However, while emotional: Ulrike Rimmele et al., "Emotion Enhances the Subjective Feeling of Remembering, Despite Lower Accuracy for Contextual Details," *Emotion* vol. 11, no. 3 (June 2011): 553–62; Elizabeth A. Kensinger, "Remembering the Details: Effects of Emotion," *Emotion Review* vol. 1, no. 2 (April 2009): 99–113; Elizabeth A. Kensinger and Daniel L. Schacter, "Retrieving Accurate and Distorted Memories: Neuroimaging Evidence for Effects of Emotion," *NeuroImage* vol. 27, no. 1 (August 1, 2005): 166–77.

143 *The final definition: Merriam-Webster's Collegiate Dictionary,* 11th ed., s.v. "perspective."

7. Seeing What's Missing

149 *"We started hearing":* "Doctor Cleared in Katrina Deaths Recounts Scene," Associated Press, July 20, 2008.

"help [them] through": Sheri Fink, "The Deadly Choices at Memorial," *New York Times,* August 25, 2009.

The case was: Julie Scelfo, "Vindicated Katrina Doc Tells Her Story," *Newsweek,* August 24, 2007.

Following deadly accidents: Janelle Burrell, "Riders Upset After Panel Finds Metro-North Didn't Prioritize Safety," *CBS New York,* August 28, 2014.

Also in 2013: Associated Press, "Report Blames Arizona Forestry Division for Firefighter Deaths," Fox News, December 5, 2013.

150 *"one crucial, overarching":* Julianne Pepitone, "Where BlackBerry's Ousted CEO Went Wrong," CNN, November 5, 2013.

While $10 million: Manny Fernandez, "In Texas, Another Skirmish Brews at the Alamo," *New York Times,* November 30, 2012.

The furor resulted: Scott Huddleston, "Land Office Cancels DRT Contract to Run Alamo," *San Antonio Express-News,* March 12, 2015.

153 *"Interviewing the Victim":* "Interviewing the Victim," Baltimore Police Department, viewable at National Center for Victims of Crime website, https://www.victimsofcrime.org/docs/dna-protocol/baltimore-interviewing-the-victim.pdf?sfvrsn=0.

And it is: "Improving Police Response to Sexual Assault," *Human Rights Watch,* January 2013.

The one I've: Richard J. Heuer, *The Psychology of Intelligence Analysis* (Washington, DC: Center for the Study of Intelligence, Central Intelligence Agency, 1999).

154 *Let's practice with: Time Transfixed* by René Magritte gives us yet another reason not to go straight for the label: the artist doesn't always agree with it, in this case for reasons of perspective and perception. Magritte, a Belgian artist, had originally titled the piece *La Durée Poignardé,* which translates into English as *Ongoing Time Stabbed by a Dagger.* At first glance, this doesn't make much sense — there is no dagger — but Magritte, who was commissioned to create it for the London home of a wealthy art collector, intended that the painting would be installed at the bottom of the patron's staircase so the train would look as if it were "stabbing" guests as they walked up past it. This perspective was lost entirely when the collector instead hung it in the most ironic position: over his fireplace. When the painting was later exhibited in galleries and museums — it's currently in the collection of the Art Institute of Chicago nowhere near a stairwell — officials unofficially renamed it *Time Transfixed,* and much to the displeasure of the artist, it stuck. See James N. Wood, *The Art Institute of Chicago: The Essential Guide* (Chicago: Art Institute of Chicago, 2013): 267.

158 *"into space":* Information from an interview with a former Disney web development specialist, June 14, 2014.

159 *"pertinent negative":* "Pertinent Negative," *Medical Terminology, Emory*

University Emergency Medical Services, http://www.emory.edu/EEMS/Medi
calTerms.html.

"That was the": Arthur Conan Doyle, "Silver Blaze," *The Memoirs of Sherlock
Holmes* (London: Oxford University Press, 2009): 22.

162 *"missing perspective":* Terry Prince, "The Importance of What's Missing,"
Terry's Thinking!, May 22, 2009, https://terrysthinking.wordpress.com/author/
terrysthinking/page/22/.

Her charity, Warm Detroit: For more information on Warm Detroit, to donate,
or start a collection in your area, go to www.warmdetroit.org.

163 *"Perhaps most troubling":* Commission on the Intelligence Capabilities of the
United States Regarding Weapons of Mass Destruction, *Report to the President
of the United States,* March 31, 2005.

167 *"Urgent tasks":* Brett McKay and Kate McKay, "The Eisenhower Decision Matrix: How to Distinguish Between Urgent and Important Tasks and Make Real
Progress in Your Life," *The Art of Manliness* website, October 23, 2013, http://
www.artofmanliness.com/2013/10/23/eisenhower-decision-matrix/.

168 *The title of:* Jonathon Keats, "Do Not Trust This Joel Sternfeld Photograph,"
Forbes, September 6, 2012.

169 *Sternfeld confirmed only:* Alex Selwyn-Holmes, "Joel Sternfeld; McLean, Virginia; December 1978," *Iconic Photos,* October 25, 2012, https://iconicphotos.
wordpress.com/2012/10/.

Aviation enthusiasts who: Civil Aviation Forum, "Only NW for Smooth Flights?"
Airliners.net, www.airliners.net; and Forums, "Fly Northwest Operated Flights
for Smooth Rides," *Turbulence Forecast,* www.turbulenceforecast.com.

8. Making Your Unknown Known

175 *In the absence:* Daniel Kurtzman, "Gary Condit & Chandra Levy Scandal:
Quips, Quotes & Late-Night Jokes," Political Humor, About.com, http://politi
calhumor.about.com/library/blconditlevy.htm; "How can one Chandra be so
Levy?" (a play on the pronunciation of Levy's last name sounding like "leave-
y") was a lyric featured on the song "Business" on *The Eminem Show* album
by Eminem, released by Aftermath in 2002, six days after Levy's body was
discovered.

Her body wasn't: Sari Horwitz, Scott Higham, and Sylvia Moreno, "Who Killed
Chandra Levy?" *Washington Post,* July 13, 2008.

177 *In 2008, the global:* IDC, "$37 Billion — US and UK Businesses Count the Cost
of Employee Misunderstanding," Cognisco, June 18, 2008, http://www.mar
ketwired.com/press-release/37-billion-us-and-uk-businesses-count-the-cost-of
-employee-misunderstanding-870000.htm.

178 *Whole Foods CEO:* Brad Stone and Matt Richtel, "The Hand That Controls the
Sock Puppet Could Get Slapped," *New York Times,* July 16, 2007.

"Among [Mackey's] many: Peter Sagal, "Not My Job: Richard Price (AKA Harry
Brandt) Gets Quizzed on Pseudonyms," *Wait Wait . . . Don't Tell Me!* NPR,
March 21, 2015.

People fired for: Stacy Conradt, "16 People Who Tweeted Themselves into Unemployment," *Mental Floss,* December 21, 2013.

Firefighters, actors, teachers: Kim Bhasin, "13 Epic Twitter Fails by Big Brands," *Business Insider,* February 6, 2012.

In March 2015: Mike Foss, "Yankees Fire Employee Over Vulgar Tweet About Curt Schilling's Daughter," *USA Today,* March 3, 2015.

179 YANKEES FIRE: Craig Bennett, "Sean MacDonald & Adam Nagel: 5 Fast Facts You Need to Know," *Heavy.com,* March 3, 2015, http://heavy.com/sports/2015/03/sean-macdonald-adam-nagel-curt-schilling-daughter-twitter-trolls-college-yankees-bio-gabby/.

Throughout their lives: Carlo Angerer, "Adolf Hitler Watercolor Set to Be Auctioned in Germany," NBC News, November 19, 2014; and Ron Cynewulf Robbins, "Churchill as Artist—Half Passion, Half Philosophy," *Finest Hour,* Churchill Center (Autumn 1998): 32.

180 *"making your unknown":* Roxana Robinson, *Georgia O'Keeffe: A Life* (Hanover, NH: University Press of New England, 1989): 256.

"Being an artist": Maria Popova, "What It Really Takes to Be an Artist: MacArthur Genius Teresita Fernández's Magnificent Commencement Address," *BrainPickings.org,* December 29, 2014. http://www.brainpickings.org/2014/12/29/teresita-fernandez-commencement-address/.

181 *"I can control":* "Jackson Pollock: Autumn Rhythm (Number 30)" (57.92), *Heilbrunn Timeline of Art History,* New York: Metropolitan Museum of Art, 2000–. http://www.metmuseum.org/toah/works-of-art/57.92 (June 2007).

182 *One of my:* Anne Charlevoix, interview with author, January 21, 2014.

184 *A lack of:* Janette Williams, "Miscommunication May Have Led to Painting Over $2,500 Mural at Pasadena Business," *Pasadena Star-News,* November 29, 2009.

"spectacular": Ibid.

185 *"She pointed to":* Karin Price Mueller, "Bamboozled: What Happens When a 'Thirty-Seven-Fifty' Bottle of Wine Really Costs $3,750," *NJ.com,* November 3, 2014, http://www.nj.com/business/index.ssf/2014/11/bamboozled_what_happens_when_a_3750_bottle_of_wine_really_costs_3750.html.

"Joe had asked": Ibid.

186 *"Borgata is confident":* Lee Moran, "Borgata Casino Diner Hit with $3,750 Bill After Server Recommended Wine for 'Thirty-Seven Fifty,'" *Daily News* (New York), November 6, 2014.

187 *"We weren't at the table":* Ibid.

"Instead of telling": Neal Hirschfeld, "Teaching Cops to See," *Smithsonian Magazine,* October 2009.

188 *"Publishers need to know":* Susan Ginsburg, interview with author.

In 2001, when: Sara Blakely, interview with author.

190 *"We have gotten":* Elise Reuter, "Colorado Distributes Cold Case Cards to Raise Clues to Unsolved Crimes," *Summit Daily* (Summit County, CO), April 1, 2015.

"Think of a ballet": Dani Shapiro, *Still Writing: The Perils and Pleasures of a Creative Life* (New York: Atlantic Monthly Press, 2014).

191 *"I've seen supremely"*: Bill Connor, "Fear Not, Introverts," *Oratorio,* March 5, 2013.

"Practice it": Susan Cain, "10 Public Speaking Tips for Introverts," *Psychology Today,* July 25, 2011, https://www.psychologytoday.com/blog/quiet-the-power -introverts/201107/10-public-speaking-tips-introverts.

She warned me: Margaret Snowling, D. V. M. Bishop, and Susan E. Stothard, "Is Preschool Language Impairment a Risk Factor for Dyslexia in Adolescence?" *Journal of Child Psychology and Psychiatry* vol. 41, no. 5 (July 2000): 587–600; Bruce A. Bracken, ed., *The Psychoeducational Assessment of Preschool Children* (Mahwah, NJ: Lawrence Erlbaum, 2004): 181–84; and M. Perkins, "Preschool Children with Inadequate Communication: Developmental Language Disorder, Autism, Mental Deficiency," *Archives of Disease in Childhood* vol. 75, no. 5 (May 1997): 480.

192 *"everyday objects shriek"*: "Magritte: The Mystery of the Ordinary, 1926–1938," Art Institute of Chicago, http://www.artic.edu/exhibition/magritte-mystery -ordinary-1926–1938.

193 *"an ennobling moral"*: Popova, "What It Really Takes."

"as little to the surface": Nicholas Forrest, "The Next Cy Twombly? First, Jan Frank Paints for Australia and Tim Olsen Gallery," *Blouin Artinfo,* October 3, 2012.

194 *The work, Ralph Steiner's:* Ralph Steiner, *American Rural Baroque,* Collection, Museum of Modern Art, New York City.

"verbal vomit": McCann quotes from interview with author, April 29, 2015; Jess McCann, *Was It Something I Said?: The Answer to All Your Dating Dilemmas* (Guilford, CT: Skirt!, 2013): 19.

198 *"On Nov. 4, 2008"*: Learning Network, "Nov. 4, 2008: Obama Is Elected President," *New York Times,* November 4, 2011.

199 *a hat is:* In 2014, a conservator for the Fitzwilliam Museum discovered that a beached whale had been carefully painted over on artist Hendrick van Anthonissen's original seventeenth-century *View of Scheveningen Sands.* The retouching is believed to have been done to suit new owners who possibly wanted to display the piece in their house but found the whale carcass "unsavory." See "Whale Tale: A Dutch Seascape and Its Lost Leviathan," University of Cambridge, June 4, 2014, http://www.cam.ac.uk/research/news/ whale-tale-a-dutch-seascape-and-its-lost-leviathan; and Emma del Valle, "Undercover Art: 6 Paintings That Were Hiding Something," *Mental Floss,* August 21, 2014.

200 *"unpaintable beauty"*: Carter Ratcliff, "The Scandalous Madame X," *Chicago Tribune,* February 1, 1987.

"My daughter is lost!": Ibid.

He fled to: Jason Farago, "Who Was the Mysterious Madame X in Sargent's Portrait?" BBC, January 2, 2015; and Trevor Fairbrother, "The Shock of John Singer Sargent's 'Madame Gautreau,'" *Arts Magazine* (January 1981): 90–97.

"We were told": Tamara Jones and Ann Scott Tyson, "After 44 Hours, Hope Showed Its Cruel Side," *Washington Post,* January 5, 2006.

202 *"We waited and waited":* James Dao, "False Report of 12 Survivors Was Result of Miscommunications," *New York Times,* January 4, 2006.

"In the process": Ibid.

"crisis upon a crisis": Scott Baradell, "Crisis Upon a Crisis: International Coal Group's 'Miscommunication' Is a Disaster in Itself," *Idea Grove,* January 4, 2006, http://www.ideagrove.com/blog/2006/01/crisis-upon-a-crisis-internation al-coal-groups-miscommunication-is-a-disaster-in-itself.html/.

The company's stock: Mario Parker and Aaron Clark, "Arch to Acquire International Coal for Steelmaking Assets," *Bloomberg Business,* May 2, 2011.

"Hatfield should have": Ibid.

203 *He designed special:* Collections, "Georges Seurat: *A Sunday on La Grande Jatte,*" *Art Institute of Chicago,* http://www.artic.edu/aic/collections/art work/27992.

Van Gogh, too: Phil Daoust, "Edge Trimming," *Guardian,* January 2, 2013.

"the most important": Ibid.

"the total impact": Barbara Pease and Alan Pease, *The Definitive Book of Body Language* (New York: Bantam, 2006): 9–10.

Joe Navarro, body: Joe Navarro, "The Art of Handshaking," *Psychology Today,* July 13, 2013.

206 *"Do not ask":* Dr. David G. Javitch, "Preventing Miscommunication in Your Business," *Entrepreneur,* March 1, 2004.

"Ask the receiver": Ibid.

As the work: John Richardson, *A Life of Picasso: The Cubist Rebel, 1907–1916* (New York: Alfred A. Knopf, 1991): 325.

The work itself: Ibid.

207 *"Sometimes you can":* Harvey Mackay, *Pushing the Envelope All the Way to the Top* (New York: Ballantine Books, 2000): 107.

"A rose by any": William Shakespeare, *Romeo and Juliet* (1597, repr. New York: Simon & Schuster, 2004).

The frame was: "From Wood to Canvas: Attached Frames and Artists' Choices," *National Gallery of Art,* http://www.nga.gov/feature/frames/canvas .shtm.

9: Big (Naked, Obese) Sue and the High School Principal

211 *"avoid uncomfortable truths":* Wayne Waxman and David Hume, *Hume's Theory of Consciousness* (Cambridge: Cambridge University Press, 1994): 278.

212 *"There have been many":* Brent Gleeson, "These 7 Motivational Navy SEAL Sayings Will Kick Your Butt into Gear," *Inc.,* April 2015.

215 *"raising questions":* Raffi Khatchadourian, "In the Picture," *New Yorker,* November 28, 2011.

219 *The 1850 painting:* Dante Alighieri, *Inferno* (1317; repr. New York: Random House, 1996).

"willful blindness": Margaret Heffernan, "The Wilful Blindness of Rupert

Murdoch," *Huffington Post,* July 14, 2011, http://www.huffingtonpost.com/margaret-heffernan-/wilful-blindness-rupert-murdoch_b_898157.html.

220 *In March 2012:* Martin Robinson, "Everyone to Blame but No One Punished: Teachers, Doctors, the Police and Social Workers Escape Justice After Missing 27 Chances to Save Tragic Daniel Pelka," *Daily Mail,* September 17, 2013.
"four dot-shaped": Ibid.
His stepfather claimed: Ibid.
an "obsession": Ibid.
"The practitioners involved": Ibid.

223 *"Over time":* Ron L. Deal, "Parenting Troubling Emotions," *Smart Stepfamilies,* http://www.smartstepfamilies.com/view/troubling-emotions.

224 *"They have to":* Paul Ekman, "Outsmart Evolution and Master Your Emotions," video, *Big Think,* August 1, 2013, http://bigthink.com/big-think-tv/paul-ekman-outsmart-evolution-and-master-your-emotions.

225 *"You might not even":* Ibid.
Trying to suppress them: Tori Rodriguez, "Negative Emotions Are Key to Well-Being," *Scientific American,* April 11, 2013.

226 *A 2012 experiment:* Ibid.

228 *"you should attempt":* Daniel C. Dennett, *Intuition Pumps and Other Tools for Thinking* (New York: W. W. Norton, 2013): 33–34.

10. Nothing Is Black-and-White

239 *Even though she:* Lucy Agate, interview with author, July 15, 2014.
"The elderly residents": Selim Algar, "Nursing Home Hired Strippers for Patients: Suit," *New York Post,* April 8, 2014.
"The outrage!": Agate interview.

240 *"a traditional Baptist":* Ibid.
"nursing home employees": Ibid.
"In any case": Associated Press, "Lawsuit: Male Stripper Did Show at NY Nursing Home," *Daily Mail,* April 8, 2014.

241 *"A committee of residents":* Agate interview.
"They have the right": Ibid.
"They all said": Ibid.
"Everyone was so": Ibid.

243 *Our brains readily:* Saundra Hybels and Richard L. Weaver II, "Self, Perception, and Communication," *Communicating Effectively,* 7th ed. (New York: McGraw-Hill, 2004): 25–47.
"other-race effect": David J. Kelly et al., "The Other-Race Effect Develops During Infancy," *Psychological Science,* December 2007.

244 *"Sometimes I don't":* Quoted in Cate Matthews, "He Dropped One Letter in His Name While Applying for Jobs, and the Responses Rolled In," *Huffington Post,* September 2, 2014. http://www.huffingtonpost.com/2014/09/02/jose-joe-job-discrimination_n_5753880.html.

245 *"Another example":* John Silvester, "Sambo Unchained in Life's Skin Game," *The Age,* Victoria, Australia, March 2, 2013.

246 *Even drug- and:* M. K., "Clever Hounds," *Economist,* February 15, 2011.

249 *Eighteen of them:* Claude Monet, "Bridge Over a Pond of Water Lilies," *Collection Online,* Metropolitan Museum of Art, New York.

255 *Retired FBI special:* Interview with author; Jean Harrison is a pseudonym.

257 *"These attitudes can":* Siri Carpenter, "Buried Prejudice: The Bigot in Your Brain," *Scientific American,* April/May 2008.
"Just as one can": Jennifer Raymond, "Most of Us Are Biased," *Nature,* March 7, 2013.
Researchers at the: Michelle Heron-Delaney et al., "Perceptual Training Prevents the Emergence of the Other Race Effect During Infancy," *PLoS One,* May 18, 2011.

11: What to Do When You Run Out of Gurneys

258 *During the midnight:* Clayton Sandell, Kevin Dolak, and Colleen Curry, "Colorado Movie Theater Shooting: 70 Victims the Largest Mass Shooting," *Good Morning America,* July 20, 2012, ABC.

260 *When the police:* Ryan Sullivan, "Family Says Race a Factor in Charlotte Girl's Shooting Death," Fox 8 WGHP, April 19, 2012.
Perceptions and prejudices: Ibid.

261 *When the FBI reported:* "Columbus Co. District Attorney Statement on Jasmine Thar's Death," WSOCTV, April 22, 2013.
"I don't think they": Rick Atkinson, "The Tylenol Nightmare: How a Corporate Giant Fought Back," *Kansas City Times,* November 12, 1982.
Chairman James Burke: Department of Defense, "Case Study: The Johnson & Johnson Tylenol Crisis," *Crisis Communications Strategies,* Department of Defense and University of Oklahoma Joint Course in Communication.

262 *The company also:* Lawrence G. Foster, "The Johnson & Johnson Credo and the Tylenol Crisis," *New Jersey Bell Journal* vol. 6, no. 1 (1983): 57–64.

263 *A class action:* Lynne Duke, "Secret Service Agents Allege Racial Bias at Denny's: Six Blacks to File Lawsuit Saying They Were Denied Service at Annapolis Restaurant," *Washington Post,* May 24, 1993.
Denny's took responsibility: Department of Defense, "Case Study: Denny's Class Action Lawsuit," *Crisis Communications Strategies.*

265 *The layers of:* Holland Cotter, "A Million Pieces of Home," *New York Times,* February 8, 2013.

266 *The Metropolitan Museum:* Roberta Smith, "The Fascination of the Unfinished," *New York Times,* January 9, 2014.
The unfinished occupies: Noah Schiffman and Suzanne Greist-Bousquet, "The Effect of Task Interruption and Closure on Perceived Duration," *Bulletin of the Psychonomic Society* vol. 30, no. 1 (January 1992): 9–11; Colleen M. Seifert and Andrea L. Patalano, "Memory for Incomplete Tasks: A Re-examination of

the Zeigarnik Effect," *Proceedings of the Thirteenth Annual Conference of the Cognitive Science Society,* January 1991; and A. D. Baddeley, "A Zeigarnik-like Effect in the Recall of Anagram Solutions," *Quarterly Journal of Experimental Psychology* vol. 15, no. 1 (1963): 63–64.

It's named for: Roy F. Baumeister and Brad Bushman, "Choices and Actions: The Self in Control," *Social Psychology and Human Nature* (Belmont, CA: Cengage Learning, 2007): 131–35.

267 *"You might not care":* Tom Stafford, "The Psychology of the To-Do List," BBC, January 29, 2013.

"it takes advantage": Tom Stafford, "The Psychology of Tetris," BBC, October 23, 2012; and Tom Stafford and Matt Webb, *Mind Hacks* (Sebastopol, CA: O'Reilly Media, 2005): 144.

"everything from really": David Allen, *Getting Things Done* (New York: Penguin, 2002): 12.

268 *The ability to:* "2013 Turnover Trends: Part 1 — National Statistics and Top Separation Reasons," *Unemployment Services Trust (UST),* www.chooseust. org/2014/blog/2013-turnover-trends-part-1-national-statistics-and-top-separation-reasons/.

270 *In 2006 an:* E. Randol Schoenberg, "London's National Gallery Hosts Klimt Portrait Seized by Nazis," *Aljazeera America,* October 20, 2013; and Anne-Marie O'Connor, "Fighting for Her Past," *Los Angeles Times,* March 20, 2001.

272 *"Thanks, I got":* Kevin Daum, "Want to Be Truly Productive? End Each Day Like This," *Inc.,* January 27, 2014.

In a series: E. J. Masicampo and Roy F. Baumeister, "Consider It Done! Plan Making Can Eliminate the Cognitive Effects of Unfulfilled Goals," *Journal of Personality and Social Psychology,* June 20, 2011.

"[Our] mind loves": Stafford, "Psychology of the To-Do List."

Illustration Credits

page 63, top right: Edward Hopper, American (1862–1967). *Hotel Room,* 1931. Oil on canvas, 152.4 x 165.7 cm. Museo Thyssen-Bornemisza, Madrid, 2015./© Photo SCALA, Florence.

page 63, bottom left: Fernand Léger, French (1881–1955), *Maud Dale,* 1935. Oil on canvas, overall: 100.4 x 79.7 cm (39½ x 31⅜ inches), framed: 136.8 x 112.1 cm (53⅞ x 44⅛ inches). National Gallery of Art, Chester Dale Collection, 1963.10.36./© 2015 Artists Rights Society (ARS), New York/ADAGP, Paris.

page 63, bottom right: George Bellows (1882–1925). *Maud Dale,* 1919. National Gallery of Art, Chester Dale Collection, 1944.15.1./Bellows Trust.

page 69: Jan Steen (1626–1679). *As the Old Sing, So Pipe the Young* (1668–1670). Mauritshuis, The Hague.

page 83: John Singleton Copley (1738–1815). *Mrs. John Winthrop,* 1773. Oil on canvas, 35½ x 28¾ inches (90.2 x 73 cm). Image copyright: © The Metropolitan Museum of Art, Morris K. Jesup Fund, 1931 (31.109)./Image source: Art Resource, NY.

page 108, left: Gilbert Stuart (1755–1828). *George Washington (Lansdowne Portrait),* 1796. Oil on canvas. Place of execution: Germantown. Stretcher: 247.6 x 158.7 cm (97½ x 62½ inches); Frame: 283.5 x 194.3 x 17.8 cm (111⅝ x 76½ x 7 inches); Acquisition date: 2001-07-16. National Portrait Gallery, Smithsonian Institution. Acquired as a gift to the nation through the generosity of the Donald W. Reynolds Foundation, NPG.2001.13./Art Resource, NY.

page 108, right: Alexander Gardner (1821–1882). *Abraham Lincoln,* 1865. Library of Congress, Prints and Photographs Division, Washington, DC, no. LC-B812-9773-X.

page 116: JR (b. 1983). Women Are Heroes, Brazil. *Action in the slums Morro da Providência, tree, moon, horizontal, Rio de Janeiro,* 2008. L'Agence VU, Paris, France.

page 119: Giuseppe Arcimboldo (c. 1526–1593). *L'Ortolano (The Vegetable Gardener),* c. 1590. Sistema Museale della Città di Cremona.

page 120: Giuseppe Arcimboldo (c. 1526–1593). *L'Ortolano (The Vegetable Gardener),* c. 1590. Sistema Museale della Città di Cremona.

page 121: Michelangelo (1475–1564). *David,* 1501–1504. Photograph by Jörg Bittner Unna (https://commons.wikimedia.org/wiki/File:Michelangelo-David_JB01.JPG).

page 123: Michelangelo (1475–1564). *David* (detail), 1501–1504. Rachel Sanderoff/Shutterstock.

page 124: Michelangelo (1475–1564). *David,* 1501–1504. Digital Michelangelo Project, Stanford University.

page 125, top: Michelangelo (1475–1564). *David* (detail), 1501–1504. Photograph by Jörg Bittner Unna (https://commons.wikimedia.org/wiki/File:%27David%27_by_Michelangelo_JBU16.JPG).

page 125, bottom: Michelangelo (1475–1564). *David* (detail), 1501–1504. Photograph by Jörg Bittner Unna (https://commons.wikimedia.org/wiki/File:%27David%27_by_Michelangelo_JBU08.JPG).

page 126: Michelangelo (1475–1564). *David* (detail), 1501–1504. Photograph by Jörg Bittner Unna (https://commons.wikimedia.org/wiki/File:Michelangelo-David_JB01.JPG).

page 131: Édouard Manet (1832–1883), *A Bar at the Folies-Bergère,* 1882. Oil on canvas, 96 x 130 cm. P.1934.SC.234. The Samuel Courtauld Trust, The Courtauld Gallery, London.

page 140, top: Henri Matisse, French (1869–1954), *Open Window, Collioure,* 1905. Oil on canvas, overall: 55.3 x 46 cm (21¾ x 18⅛ inches), framed: 71.1 x 62.4 x 5.1 cm (28 x 24½ x 2 inches). National Gallery of Art, Collection of Mr. and Mrs. John Hay Whitney 1998.74.7./© 2015 Succession H. Matisse/Artists Rights Society (ARS), New York.

page 140, bottom: Henri Matisse, French (1869–1954), *French Window at Collioure,* 1914. Oil on canvas, 116.5 x 89 cm. Photo by Philippe Migeat; CNAC/MNAM/Dist. RMN: Grand Palais, Art Resource, NY./© 2015 Succession H. Matisse/Artists Rights Society (ARS), New York.

page 151: Joel Sternfeld (b. 1944). *McLean, Virginia, December 1978;* n:1978 p:2003; Digital C-print; Edition of 10 and 2 artist's proofs; image size: 42 x 52½ inches; paper size: 48 x 58½ inches. © Joel Sternfeld. Courtesy of the artist and Luhring Augustine, New York.

page 154: René Magritte, Belgian (1898–1967). *Time Transfixed,* 1938. Oil on canvas, 57⅞ x 38⅞ inches (147 x 98.7 cm). Joseph Winterbotham Collection, 1970.426. Photography © The Art Institute of Chicago./© 2015 C. Herscovici/Artists Rights Society (ARS), New York.

page 158: Sarah Grant, *The Furniture City Sets the Table for the World of Art,* 2009. Installation © Sticks/photo by Adam Bird.

page 165: Fundamentalist Church members. AP Photo/Tony Gutierrez.

page 170: Philip Evergood (1901–1973), © Copyright. *Dowager in a Wheelchair,* 1952. Oil on fiberboard, 47⅞ x 36 inches (121.5 x 91.4 cm). Courtesy ACA Galleries, New York. Photo credit: Smithsonian American Art Museum, Washington, DC, Gift of the Sara Roby Foundation, 1986.6.90/Art Resource, NY.

page 192: René Magritte (1898–1967). *The Key to Dreams,* 1927. Oil on canvas, 38 x 53 cm. Inv. L 1953. bpk, Berlin/Art Resource, NY./© 2015 Artists Rights Society (ARS), New York.

page 193: Ralph Steiner (1899–1986). *American Rural Baroque,* 1930. Gelatin-silver print, 7⁹⁄₁₆ x 9½ inches. Ralph Steiner photograph, courtesy estate./Digital image © The Museum of Modern Art, Gift of the photographer (892.1965)./Licensed by SCALA/Art Resource, NY.

page 195: First Corinthian Baptist Church. Redux Pictures/*The New York Times*/photo by David Goldman.

page 198: Teens on a stoop. Redux Pictures/*The New York Times*/photo by Hiroko Masuike.

page 201, top: John Singer Sargent (1856–1925). Scrapbook of photographic reproductions of paintings by Sargent. Published/Created [S.I.: s.n., 1893?] p. 49, Madame X, 1884, albumen print (shows an earlier state of the painting: John Singer Sargent, Madame X (Madame Pierre Gautreau), (16.53) in the collection of the Metropolitan Museum of Art). The Thomas J. Watson Library, Gift of Mrs. Francis Ormond, 1950 (192Sa7 Sa78 Q). Image copyright © The Metropolitan Museum of Art./Image source: Art Resource, NY.

page 201, bottom: John Singer Sargent (1856–1925). *Madame X (Madame Pierre Gautreau),* 1883–1884. Oil on canvas, 82⅛ x 43¼ inches (208.6 x 109.9 cm). Arthur Hoppock Hearn Fund, 1916 (16.53). Image copyright © The Metropolitan Museum of Art./Image source: Art Resource, NY.

page 209, top: Pieter Brueghel the Elder (c. 1525–1569). *The Painter and the Buyer,* c. 1565. Heritage Images/Getty Images.

page 209, bottom: Richard Diebenkorn, *Studio Wall,* 1963. Oil on canvas, 45⅜ x 42½ inches (115.3 x 108 cm). Estate #1395. © The Richard Diebenkorn Foundation.

page 212: Francisco de Goya y Lucientes (1746–1828). *The Naked Maja,* circa 1795–1800. © Madrid, Museo Nacional del Prado.

page 213: Lucian Freud, *Benefits Supervisor Sleeping,* 1995. Oil on canvas. Lucian Freud (1922–2011). © The Lucian Freud Archive/Private Collection/The Bridgeman Art Library.

page 217, top: Hieronymus Bosch (c. 1450–1516). *The Garden of Earthly Delights,* c. 1500–1505. Universal History Archive/Getty Images.

page 217, bottom: Hieronymus Bosch (c. 1450–1516). *The Garden of Earthly Delights* (detail), c. 1500–1505. Universal History Archive/Getty Images.

page 218: William-Adolphe Bouguereau (1825–1905). *Dante and Virgil in Hell,* 1850. Universal History Archive/Getty Images.

page 221: Hieronymus Bosch (c. 1450–1516). *The Garden of Earthly Delights* (detail), c. 1500–1505. Universal History Archive/Getty Images.

page 226: Jacques-Louis David (1748–1825). *Comtesse Daru,* 1810. Copyright The Frick Collection.

page 244: Photograph of two running police officers, 1993. Don McCullin/Contact Press Images.

page 246: Nanny and child. Courtesy of the author.

page 249: Claude Monet (1840–1926). *Bridge Over a Pond of Water Lilies,* 1899. ACME Imagery/Superstock.

page 250, top: Claude Monet (1840–1926). *The Japanese Footbridge,* 1899. The National Gallery of Art, Washington, DC, Marco Brivio, age fotostock/Superstock.

page 250, middle: Claude Monet (1840–1926). *Bridge Over a Pond of Water Lilies,* 1899. ACME Imagery/Superstock.

page 250, bottom: Claude Monet (1840–1926). *The Japanese Footbridge and the Water Lily Pool, Giverny,* 1899. Philadelphia Museum of Art, Philadelphia, PA, Mr. and Mrs. Carroll S. Tyson, Jr., Collection, 1963./Bridgeman Images.

page 252: Caravaggio (1571–1610). *The Calling of Saint Matthew,* 1599–1600. Pii Stabilimenti della Francia a Roma e Loreto, San Luigi dei Francesi, photo by Mauro Coen.

page 253: The Situation Room. White House Press Office, photo by Pete Souza, 2011.

page 264: El Anatsui (b. 1944). *Skylines,* 2008. Aluminium and copper wire, 118.1 x 324.8 inches (300 x 825 cm). Courtesy of October Gallery Trust, photo Scope Basel 2013 and © Georgios Kefalas/epa/Corbis.

page 265: El Anatsui (b. 1944). *Oasis* (detail), 2008. Aluminium and copper wire, 106 x 90 inches (269.24 x 228.6 cm). Private collection. Courtesy of October Gallery Trust and Bill Greene, *The Boston Globe*/Getty Images.

page 268: Gustav Klimt (1862–1918). *Amalie Zuckerkandl,* 1917–1918, Canvas, 128 x 128 cm, unfinished. Oesterreichische Galerie im Belvedere. Erich Lessing/Art Resource, NY.

Index

Page references in italics refer to illustrations.

Abraham Lincoln (Gardner), *108,* 108-10
accountability, 136, 248
action, objective assessment of, 69-71
Action in the Slums Morro da Providência, tree, moon, horizontal, Rio de Janeiro (JR), *116,* 116-18
adaptation, 14, 87-89
   biases and, 239-57
   uncertainty and, 258-72
affinity bias, 243
Afghanistan war, 176
Agate, Lucy, 239-42
aircraft recognition, 31, 56
air traffic controllers, 206
Alamo (Texas), 150
Alderete, Christian, 184-85
Alexander, Jane, 44-45
Allen, David, 267
al-Shabaab, 62
American Rural Baroque (Steiner), *193,* 193-94
analyzing, 14, 115-43
Android, 150
appearances, deceptive, 65
Apple, 6, 150
Arcimboldo, Giuseppe, 119-20
Arizona Division of Occupational Safety and Health, 149-50
art. *See also individual artworks*
   in attention development, 31-36
   as communication, 179-81
   discomfort caused by, 215-19
   framing of, 203, 207
   in observation skill development, xiv-xv, 10-14
   physical perspective and, 119-27
   taking time to observe, 19-22
   unfinished, 266-72
articulation, 14. *See also* communication
Art of Manliness (McKay and McKay), 167
The Art of Perception program, xv-xvii, 14
The Art of Scientific Investigation (Beveridge), 33

assessment
   art for practicing, 11-14, 19-22
   autopilot vs. focus in, 14-16
   distraction and, 16-18
   exercising the brain in, 9-10
   in prioritization, 153-59
   seeing what matters and, 3-22
   trusting your senses for, 18-22
assumptions vs. facts, 62-65, 79-82, 187
As the Old Sing, So Pipe the Young (Steen), *10, 69,* 69-70
attention
   blind spots and, 29-31, 88-89
   to detail, 90-97
   developing/training, 31-36
   emotions and, 224
   as finite resource, 15-16, 29-31
   multitasking and, 16-17
   one thing at a time and, 99-100
   schema theory, 29
attentional blindness, 87
audience, in communication, 187-90, 205
Audio-Animatronics, 91
The Austere Academy (Snicket), 79-80
Automat (Hopper), *60, 63, 63,* 66-69, 71-72, 73, 74, 77, 78, 80, 163-64
autopilot, 14-16, 58-59
awareness, 35. *See also* attention
   of bias, 242-43, 246-47, 254-55
   of details, 91-97
   of emotions, 225
   of perspective, 137
   of prioritization systems, 150-52

Bach, Oscar, 80
Baltimore Police Department, 153
Baradell, Scott, 202
A Bar at the Folies-Bergère (Manet), *131,* 131-33
Barnes, Latrice, *195,* 195-98
Beaumont Health System, 127-28
behavior, 11, 66-68
Bell, Alexander Graham, 14-15
Bell, Joseph, 24-25, 35, 159

Bellows, George, 63–64
Benefits Supervisor Sleeping (Freud), *213,*
    213–14, 215
Beveridge, William Ian Beardmore, 33
bias, 239–57
    awareness of, 242–43, 246–47, 254–55
    definition of, 242
    experience, 248–54
    perceptual filters and, 41–47, 52–59
    prejudice and, 244–47
    rules for working with, 254–57
    seeing what we want to see, 52–54
    transferring, 246
    unconscious, 243–47
big picture, seeing, 104–5
Big Sue. See *Benefits Supervisor Sleeping*
    (Freud)
bin Laden, Osama, 254
BlackBerry, Ltd., 150
Blakely, Sara, 188–89
blanks, automatically filling in, 89–90
blindness
    inattentional, 29–31
    neuroscience of, 87–89
    strategies for overcoming, 97–104
    unawareness of, 94–95
    to what's in plain sight, 83–111
    willful, 219–23
blind spots, 22, 95
    neuroscience of, 28–31, 87–89
    self-assessment of, 26–28
    what's in plain sight and, 83–111
Bliss, Dave, 102–3
Bloch-Bauer, Ferdinand, 268–70
Bloom: A Site-specific Installation (Haber),
    xviii–xx, *xix*
Bobby Flay Steak, 185–87, 206
body language, 65, 68, 96–97, 107, 203–5,
    225
Borgata Hotel Casino, 185–87
Bosch, Hieronymus, 216–18, 221
Bouguereau, William-Adolphe, 218–19
Boyers, Jayson, 134
brain
    attention delegation by, 15–16, 29–31
    blind spots and, 28–31, 87–89
    effects of movement on, 128–29
    effects of practice on, 33
    exercising, 9–10
    filling in the blanks by, 89–90
    illusion confusion and, 37–39
    malleability of, 9–10, 47, 257

memory and, 142
    multitasking and, 99
    novelty and, 12
    observation training for, 31–36
    perception skills and, xiv–xv
    perceptual filters and, 47–52
    in sight, 6–9
Brain Games television show, 57
Brainwave program, 37–39
Braverman, Irwin, 31
breaks, taking, 100–101, 128–29
Bright, Josh, 188
Brueghel, Pieter the Elder, 208–9
bruises, 75
Burke, James, 261

Cain, Susan, 191
camouflaged things, noticing, 98–99
Canadian Medical Association Journal, 84
Caravaggio, 252–53
Carrasco, Marisa, 37–39
CARVER matrix, 152
Cathedral Church of Saint John the Divine,
    44–45
Chabris, Christopher, 29–31
change, 56–59, 87, 273–77
change blindness, 56–59, 87
Charlevoix, Anne, 182
charting by exception, 54–55
child abuse/neglect, 75, 106–8, 220
Chin, Don, 185
Churchill, Winston, 179–80
CIA, 153
Cleveland Clinic, 47
clothing, objective assessment of, 66–68
COBRA strategy, 97–104, 110
cognitive bias, 52–54
cold-case investigations, 189–90
collaboration, 134
Collioure, France, 139–41
Colorado Bureau of Investigation, 189–90
Columbia University photo, 26–27
communication, xiv
    art as, 179–81
    audience in, 187–90
    avoiding breakdowns in, 175–210
    believing what you see and, 219–23
    with children, 222–23
    correcting poor, 199–202
    cost of poor, 177–78
    editing, 193–99
    emotions and, 223–31

communication (*cont.*)
    expectations set by, 179
    of facts vs. opinions, 214–19
    framing, 203
    of hard truths, 210–36
    heated, moving on from, 227–31
    as invitation, 208–10
    nonverbal, 96–97
    painting a picture in, 105–10
    perception differences and, 47
    practicing, 190–93
    receiving, 232–36
    renaming, 229–31
    under stress, 210–36
    subjective vs. objective, 77–79
    three Rs in, 205–8
    word choice in, 77–78, 181–87
completion, desire for, 266–72
complexity, 11–12, 277
Comtesse Daru (David), *226,* 226–27
Conan Doyle, Arthur. *See* Doyle, Arthur
    Conan
Condit, Gary, 175
confirmation bias, 52–54
conflict management, 134
Conley, Kenneth, 30–31
Connor, Bill, 191
Consciousness and the Social Brain
    (Graziano), 28
Copley, John Singleton, 83–84, 95–96
cow photo, 37–39, 55, 56
C photograph, 26–27, 27
creativity, 134, 263–65
crises, 60–62, 148–53
cultural differences, 16–17, 162–63, 188–89,
    203–5, 255–56
customer service, 91

Dang, Elaine, 72–73
danger
    of assumptions, 64–65, 79–81
    from being on autopilot, 14–15
    of filters, 59
    location assessment and, 72–73
    from miscommunication, 177–78
    objective observation and, 60–62, 74–75
    perspective and, 136–37
    prioritization plans and, 150–53
Dante and Virgil in Hell (Bouguereau), *218,*
    218–19
Darby, John, 153
Dasgupta, Nilanjana, 257

Daughters of the Republic of Texas, 150
Daum, Kevin, 272
David (Michelangelo), *121,* 121–26, *123, 124,*
    125, 126
David, Jacques-Louis, 226–27
da Vinci, Leonardo, 6, 22
Deal, Ron L., 223
deception, body language and, 96–97
Della Femina, Jerry, 261
Les Demoiselles d'Avignon (Picasso), 206
Dennett, Daniel C., 228
Denny's restaurant, 263
Department of Defense, xvi
Department of the Army, 11
desires, in perceptual filters, 53–54
details
    big picture and, 104–5
    communicating, 105–10
    importance of, 90–94, 110–11
    in nonverbal communication, 96–97
    orientation to, developing, 94–96
    strategies for seeing, 97–104
Diebenkorn, Richard, 209–10
Digital Michelangelo Project, 124–25
discomfort, 12
Discover magazine, 129
Disney, Walt, 91, 204
distractions, 16–19, 99–100
Dolan, Eamon, 232, 275–76
Dowager in a Wheelchair (Evergood), *170,*
    170–71
Doyle, Arthur Conan, 24–25, 35, 159
Dyer, Wayne W., 119

Eastern Air Lines crash, 104–5
East Neck Nursing Center, 239–42
Ebola, 273
editing, 193–99
Eggies, 6
Eisenhower, Dwight D., 167
Eisenhower Decision Matrix, 167
Ekman, Paul, 224, 225
El Anatsui, 264–65
email, 158–59, 272
Eminem, 175
emotions
    discomfort, 215–19
    memory and, 142
    moving on from in communication,
        227–36
    outsmarting, 223–27
    from the unfinished, 266–72

empathy, 134–36
engagement, 35, 93–94
errors, 17, 199–202. *See also* filters, perceptual
Evergood, Philip, 170–71
everyday situations, 11–12, 35
exclusive language, 184
exercise, 47, 100
expectations, 52–56, 101–2, 179
experience, 12, 41–47, 129, 248–54
eye contact, 96–97, 203, 204
EyeWire, 6–9

Fabritius, Carel, 10
facts, 65, 277
  about location, 72–73
  assumptions vs., 62–65
  biases vs., 255
  in emotional communication, 233–36
  omitting because of uncertainty, 158–59
  opinions vs., 51–52, 77–78, 214–19
  perceptual filters and, 51–52
  seeing what we want to see and, 52–54
  system for gathering, 65–73
  verification of, 64
  willful blindness toward, 219–23
familiarity blindness, 87
family protective services, 106–8
FBI, xvi, 126–27, 130
Fernández, Teresita, 180, 193
filling in the blanks, 89–90
filters, perceptual, 41–47. *See also* perspective
  bias, 239–57
  blind spots and, 87–89
  in children, 56
  common, 52–59
  developing awareness of, 47–52, 48–52
  expectations and, 101–2
  facts vs. opinions and, 51–52, 62–65
  filling in the blanks with, 89–90
  not seeing change, 56–59
  in prioritization, 153
  seeing through our subconscious, 47–52
  seeing what we're told to see, 54–56
  seeing what we want to see, 52–54
firearm training simulator (FATS), 144–48, 164–65
Fischman, Lisa, 79
flight attendants, 76–77, 205
Florida State University, 226, 272
focus, 16–17, 29–31, 99–100, 100–101

Folk, Charles, 99
Forbes, 100, 134
found objects, 264–65
framing, 203, 207–8, 231
Frank, Jan, 193
Freaky Friday challenges, 135–36
French Window at Collioure (Matisse), 139–41, *140*
frequency illusion, 53
Freshfields Bruckhaus Deringer, 62
Freud, Lucian, 208, 213–14, 215
The Frick Collection, xiv–xv, 226–27
Fundamentalist Church of Jesus Christ of Latter-Day Saints, *165*, 165–67
fund-raisers, 134
The Furniture City Sets the Table for the World of Art (Grant), 158, *158*

Galvan, Judy, 142–43
The Garden of Earthly Delights (Bosch), 216–18, *217*, 221, *221*
Gardner, Alexander, 108–10
Gautreau, Virginie Amélie Avegno, 200, *201*
gemba walks, 127
genchi genbutsu, 127
George Washington (Lansdowne Portrait) (Stuart), *108*, 108–10
Getting Things Done (Allen), 267
Gilkey, Roderick, 128–29
Ginsburg, Susan, 188
Gleeson, Brent, 212
Global Soap Project, 3–6, 22, 273–74
"go and see," 127–29
The Goldfinch (Fabritius), 10
Goldman, David, 195–98
González, Wellington, 118
Goya, Francisco de, 212–14, 215
Grant, Sarah, 158
Graziano, Michael, *28,* 28–29
Green, Marc, 94–95

Haber, Anna Schuleit, xviii–xx
Harrigian, Jeffrey, 176
Harrison, Jean, 255–56
Hatfield, Bennett K., 202
healthcare
  art in enhancing observation skills in, 31–33
  charting by exception in, 54–55
  communication in, 188
  diagnostic skills in, xv
  hospice care, 142–43

healthcare (*cont.*)
    managed, quality vs. quantity in, 17
    mental, xviii–xx
    perspective changes in, 127–28
    power of observation in, 24–25
    prioritization in, 148–49, 150, 152
    seeing what's in plain sight in, 84–85
    uncertainty and, 258–60
    what is not known in, 159–63
Heins, Thorstein, 150
help, asking for, 102
Heuer, Richard J., 153
Hirsch, Mark, 57–58
Hitler, Adolf, 179–80
Holmes, Sherlock, 24–25, 159
Holt, Tom, 187
Homer, Winslow, 207
Honthorst, Gerrit van, 13–14
Hopper, Edward, 60, 63, 66–69, 71–72, 73, 74, 77, 78, 80, 163–64
Horn & Hardart, 73
hospice care, 142–43
hotels, 3–6, 16–17, 22, 72, 273–74
Hound and Hunter (Homer), 207
Hume, David, 211
Hurricane Katrina, 148–49, 150, 152

IDC, 177
illusion confusion, 37–39
illusions, 59
impatience, 17
important vs. urgent, 167–69
inattentional blindness, 29–31, 87–89, 94–95
inclusive language, 184
Industrial Cottage (Rosenquist), 176–77
Industry Week, 127
Infantry with beast (Alexander), *44,* 44–45
information-gathering model, 65–73
innovation, 5–6, 100–101, 127–29, 263–65
Institute of Customer Service, 91
Integrity and Accuracy Conference, 144–48
International Civil Aviation Organization, 76–77
International Coal Group, 200, 202
In the Studio exhibition, 208–10
intuition, 12
IQ, effect of distraction on, 16
Iraq Intelligence Commission, 81, 163

The Japanese Footbridge (Monet), 248–52, *249, 250*
Javitch, David G., 206

Jeffs, Warren, 165–67
Jobs, Steve, 6, 22
Johnson & Johnson, 261–62
Joselit, David, 11
Journal of Experimental Psychology, 16
Journal of Vision, 31
JR (artist), xvii–xviii, 116–18, 139, 215

kaizen, 127–28
Kaufman, Betsy Ravreby, 6, 22
Kayongo, Derreck, 3–6, 22, 273–74
Kentridge, William, 216
The Key to Dreams (Magritte), *192,* 192–93
Kilts, Clint, 128–29
KISS principle, 194–95
Klimt, Gustav, 268–70
Krznaric, Roman, 134

labels, 55–56
law enforcement, xv–xvi
    body language of, 96
    communication in, 175–76, 187, 189–90
    cultural differences and, 255–56
    focus and perspective of, 101
    inattentional blindness and, 30–31
    painting a picture and, 106–10
    perspective changes in, 126–27
    pertinent negative in, 160–61
    prioritization in, 144–48, 150–52, 153, 164–65
    sexual assault and, 138–39, 141
    Stein homicide, 85–87
    use of all senses in, 129–30
Le, Annie, 130, 137
Léger, Fernand, 63–64
Lehman Brothers, 220–21
Lentini, Joe, 185–87
Leonardo da Vinci, 6, 22
Levy, Chandra, 175–76
Lintgen, Arthur, 35–36
London Metropolitan Police, *244,* 244–46
London University, 16
Longley, Joanna, 107–8
Lowery, Natavia, 86–87, 98, 101
Lupo, Joseph, 186

MacDonald, Sean, 178–79
Mackay, Harvey, 207
Mackey, John, 178
Maclean, Hunter, 162
Madame X (Madame Pierre Gautreau) (Sargent), 200, *201*

Magritte, René, 23, 33–35, 154–57, 192–93, 277
MakerBot, 8
Manet, Édouard, 131–33
Marshall, Kerry James, 43
Martin, Trayvon, 260
mass shootings, 258–60
Matelli, Tony, 46–47, 48–52, 78–79
Matisse, Henri, 139–41, 203
Maud Dale (Bellows), *63,* 63–64
Maud Dale (Léger), *63,* 63–64
McCann, Jess, 128, 194–95
McDonald, Glenn, 19
McKay, Brett, 167
McKay, Kay, 167
McLean, Virginia (Sternfeld), *151,* 151–52, 168–69
Mehrabian, Albert, 203
memory, rewriting of, 141–42
mental blocks, breaking, 128–29
mental health care, xviii–xx
Merkin, Daphne, 18
Mestral, George de, 5–6, 22
Metro-North Railroad, 149–50
Metropolitan Museum of Art, 266
Michelangelo, 121–26
Miller, Jennifer, 135–36
Mind Hacks (Stafford), 267
Mistress and Maid (Vermeer), *20,* 20–22
Monet, Claude, 248–52
mono-tasking, 99–100
Morro da Providência, Brazil, 115–18, 139
motivation, 138–39
Mrs. John Winthrop (Copley), *83,* 83–84, 95–96
Mueller, Karin Price, 187
multitasking, 16–17, 99–100
Murrell, Jerry, 200, 202
myside bias, 52–54

Nagel, Adam, 178–79
Nairobi mall terrorist attack, 60–62, 64, 70–71, 72–73, 74, 80
Naish, Benjamin, xvi
The Naked Maja (Goya), *212,* 212–14
Nass, Clifford, 99
National Gallery of Art, 207
National Institutes of Health 3D Print Exchange, 8
National Transportation Safety Board, 105
Navarro, Joe, 203–4
neurons, 6–9, *8,* 9–10, 19. *See also* brain

Newton, Isaac, 22, 100–101
Newton, Kelly, 87
New York Metropolitan Transportation Authority, 149–50
New York Post, 239
New York State Regents Exam, 91–94
New York Times, 150, 158, 198–99
9/11 attacks, 42
nonverbal communication. *See* body language
Northwest Airlines, 169
note taking, 17
novelty, 12
nursing home stripper, 239–42

Oasis (El Anatsui), *264,* 264–65
Obama, Barack, election of, 195–98
objective language, 77–78, 181–87
objective surveillance, 60–62, 277
   assumptions vs., 79–82
   avoiding subjectivity in, 77–79
   cost of failure in, 60–62
   fact gathering in, 65–73
   facts vs. fiction in, 62–65
   in personal and professional life, 75–77
   senses in, 129–33
   uncertainty and, 262–63
   "what?" in, 69–71
   "when?" in, 71
   "where?" in, 72–73
   "who?" in, 65–68
objet trouvé, 264–65
observation
   accurate description and, 13–14
   autopilot vs., 14–16
   benefits of accurate, 5–6
   big picture in, 104–5
   danger of assumptions in, 81
   definition of, 41
   facts as basis of, 51–52
   importance of, xiv, xx
   multisensory, 129–33
   neuroscience on, xiv–xv
   objective surveillance in, 60–62
   retention and, 34–35
   seeing vs., 24–26
   seeing what matters and, 3–22
   senses vs. technology for, 18–19
   skill development in, xiv–xv, 23–36
   strategies for, 97–104
   taking time for, 19–22

observation (*cont.*)
    transformative change from, 273–77
    value of art in developing, 10–14
    of what's in plain sight, 83–111
O'Keeffe, Georgia, 180
one thing at a time, 99–100
Oosterman, Eve and Ruth, *39, 39*–41
Open Window, Collioure (Matisse), 139–41,
    140
Operation Neptune's Spear, 253–54
opinions, facts vs., 51–52, 77–78, 214–19
organization, 89–90. *See also* prioritization
L'Ortolano (The Vegetable Gardener)
    (Arcimboldo), *119,* 119–20, *120*
other-race effect, 243, 257

The Painter and the Buyer (Brueghel),
    208–9, *209*
painting a picture in communication, 105–10
Pasadena mural, 184–85
Paulo da Silva, Marcos, 118
Peace Corps, 138–39, 141
Pelka, Daniel, 220
pentimento, 199–200
perception. *See also* observation
    attention in, 29–31
    awareness of others', 44–47
    blind spots and, 28–31
    definition of, 41
    differences between individuals', 37–59
    errors in, neurology of, xiv
    filters in, 41–59
    importance of others', 43–47, 55–56
    labels and, 55–56
    not seeing change, 56–59
perceptual blindness, 87
perspective, 12. *See also* perception
    analyzing from multiple, 115–43
    asking someone else for, 102
    changeability of, 139–42
    changing to observe more, 98–99
    in communication, 233–35
    definition of, 118, 143
    mental, 134–37
    motivation and, 138–39
    movement and, 127–29
    physical, 119–27
    in prioritization, 153
    seeing from others', 133–42
    service-oriented, 142–43
    sharing your, 137
    using all senses for, 129–33

pertinent negative, 159–63
Phelps, Elizabeth A., 142
Philadelphia Police Department, xvi,
    153
phonographic records, reading, 35–36
Picasso, 206
planning, benefits of, 272
Poincaré, Henri, 101
pointing, 204–5
points of view. *See* perspective
police. *See* law enforcement
Pollard, Jon, 185
Pollock, Jackson, 181
Popova, Maria, 193
The Portrait (Magritte), *23, 33*–35, 277
Portrait of Amalie Zuckerkandl (Klimt), *268,*
    268–70
Pou, Anna, 148–49, 150, 152
Powell, Corey S., 129
practice, 33–36, 47–52, 131–33, 190–93
prejudice, 55–56, 244–47
Prince, Terry, 162
Princeton Neuroscience Institute, 6–7
Princeton University, 17
prioritization, 144–71, 277
    awareness of personal systems for,
        150–52
    blind spots and, 88–89
    importance of, 150
    influence of circumstances on, 156
    practicing, 164–67
    systems for, 152
    three-prong approach to, 153–67
    uncertainty and, 158–59, 261–62
    unconscious bias in, 243–47
    urgent vs. important in, 167–69
    "what do I know?" and, 153–59
    "what do I need to know?" and,
        163–64
    "what don't I know?" and, 159–63
problem solving, 91–94, 136
project planning, 162
The Psychology of Intelligence Analysis
    (Heuer), 153
public speaking, 191
puerperal sepsis, 273

quality vs. quantity, 17
quantification, in observation, 77–79
quantity vs. quality, 17
Queensland University of Technology,
    225–26

questions, 231, 255, 277
Quiet (Cain), 191

Raymond, Jennifer, 257
reactive mode, 167
The Red Boat (Oosterman and Oosterman), 40, *40*
Redd, Jasmine, 194–98
reframing, 207–8, 231
refrigerator blindness, 83–111
The Refusal of Time (Kentridge), 216
renaming, 206–7, 229–31
Renshaw, Samuel, 31, 37–39, 55, 56
Renshaw's Cow, 37–39, *37, 38,* 55, 56
repetition, 205–6, 227–29
resident advisors (RAs), 161
resource allocation, 15–17, 29–31, 167–68, 263–65
responsive mode, 167
retention, 34–35
retina mapping, 6–9, 19
Richards, Caroline, 228–29
Richards, Charles, 228–29
Right and Left (Homer), 207
Rio de Janeiro, Brazil, 115–18, 139
Robbins, Apollo, 37–39, 57, 59
Roberts, Jennifer L., 19
Rosenquist, James, 176–77
Rubin Museum of Art, 37–39

Sagal, Peter, 178
Sago, West Virginia, miners, 200, 202
Sarah Lawrence College, 17
Sargent, John Singer, 200, 201
SATs, 91
Savage, Adam, 17
"A Scandal in Bohemia" (Doyle), 24–25
schema theory, attention, 29
Schilling, Curt, 178–79
Schultz, Bonnie, 97
seeing what matters, 3–22
seeing what we're told to see, 54–56
seeing what we want to see, 52–54
Self-Portrait in a Woman's Eye (JR), *xvii,* xvii–xviii
senses, 10–14, 18–19, 129–33. *See also* sight
sensory overload, 100
Seung, Sebastian, 6–9, 19
Seurat, Georges, 203
sex trafficking, 5
sexual assault response teams, 138–39, 141, 153

Shapiro, Dani, 190
Sidwell Friends School, 14–15
sight, 6–9, 37–59, 129–33
Silva, Rick, 135
"Silver Blaze" (Doyle), 159
Simkins, Audrey, 190
Simons, Daniel, 29–31, 57
single-tasking, 99–100
Six Sigma, 152
skimming, 33
Skylines (El Anatsui), *264,* 264–65
Sleepwalker (Matelli), *46,* 46–47, 48–52, 78–79
Sloan, Marcus, 91–94
Smiling Girl, a Courtesan, Holding an Obscene Image (Honthorst), *13,* 13–14
Smithsonian American Art Museum, 43, 55, 170–71
Snicket, Lemony, 79–80
soap bars, recycling, 3–6, 22, 273–74
SOB, SOB (Marshall), 43
social media, 136–37, 178–79
Souza, Pete, 253–54
Spanx, 188–89
specificity, in language, 184–87, 213–14
Stafford, Tom, 266–67, 272
standardized tests, 91–94
Stanford University, 124–25
Starbucks, 75
State Farm insurance, 95
Steen, Jan, 10, 69–70
Stein, Linda, 85–87, 98, 101
Steiner, Ralph, 193–94
Sternfeld, Joel, 151–52, 168–69
stress, 12, 100, 210–36, 267
Stuart, Gilbert, 108–10
Studio Wall (Diebenkorn), *209,* 209–10
subjectivity, 44–45
    avoiding, 77–79
    communication and, 233–36
    emotions and, 223–27
    of memory, 141–42
    spotting, 81
    uncertainty and, 262–63
    word choice and, 77–78, 181–87
A Sunday on La Grande Jatte (Seurat), 203
Surveys (from the Cape of Good Hope) (Alexander), 44–45

technology, 16–17, 18–19, 178–79
"Teenage Summer, the Fasting Version," *198,* 198–99

terrorist attacks, 42, 60–62, 64, 70–74, 80
Tetris, 267
Texas General Land Office, 150
Thar, Jasmine, 260
That Tree (Hirsch), 57, 57–58, *58*
Thephakaysone, Nikhom, 74–75
Tilley, Sue, 215
Time Transfixed (Magritte), *154,* 154–57
Titanic, 220
To Kill a Mockingbird (Lee), 134
Tomasevic, Goran, 80
Toyota, 127
trading places, 135–36
transformative change, 273–77
Transportation Security Administration, 65
tunnel vision, 52–54
Tversky, Barbara, 88, 89
Two Japanese Wrestlers by a Sink (Freud),
  208
Tylenol poisonings, 261–62

uncertainty, 12, 158–59, 258–72
Undercover Boss television show, 135
unfinished, anxiety of the, 266–72
Unicore, 233–35
University of California, Los Angeles, 17
University of Colorado Hospital, 258–60
University of Oslo, 47
University of Queensland, 257
University of Virginia School of Nursing,
  54–55
unknown, in prioritization, 159–63
urgent vs. important, 167–69
US Army Asymmetric Warfare Group,
  253–54

Valdez, Justin, 74–75
Vasari, Giorgio, 122
Velcro, 5–6
Velcro parents, 161
Vermeer, Jan, 20–22
Villanova University, 99
Vincot, Bruce, 233–35
Virgin Atlantic, 91
vision, biology of, 6–9
visual intelligence, 6
visual learners, 105
visual-spatial intelligence, 105

Wall Street Journal, xvi
Warhol, Andy, 205–6
Warm Detroit, 162

Was It Something I Said? (McCann), 194
water lily paintings (Monet), 248–252, *249,*
  250
Wellesley College, 46–47
West, Allison, 31–33
Westgate Mall, Nairobi, Kenya, terrorist
  attack, 60–62, 64, 70–71, 72–73, 74,
  80
What Every Body Is Saying (Navarro),
  203–4
White House Situation Room, *253,* 253–54
"who, what, when, where" in fact gathering,
  65–73
Whole Foods, 178
"why?," understanding, 138–39, 260
Wilder, Bill, 127
willful blindness, 219–23
Wilson, David, 228
Winokur, Kay, 128
wish fulfillment, 53
wishful seeing, 52–54
Women Are Heroes (JR), *xvii,* xvii–xviii,
  116, 116–18
word choice, 77–78, 181–87
work and workers
  anxiety of the unfinished and, 265–72
  attention to detail and, 90–94
  bias in, 246
  communication and emotions, 223–27
  cost of poor communication in, 177–78
  distractions and, 16–17, 99–100
  email policies and, 158–59
  perspective changes and, 127–29
  prioritization in, 149–50
  service perspective in, 142–43
  what they don't know, 162–63
World Trade Center attacks, 42
World War II, 31, 56
Wright, Gerald, 160–61

Yarnell Hill, Arizona, fire, 149–50
Yearning for Zion Ranch, 165–67
"You Do Not Talk About Fight Club If You
  Do Not Notice Fight Club" (Simons
  and Chabris), 31
Youngblood, Franklin, 240–41

Zamora, José, 244
Zeigarnik, Bluma, 266
Zeigarnik effect, 266–67
zoning out, 14–15
Zuckerkandl, Amalie, *268,* 268–70